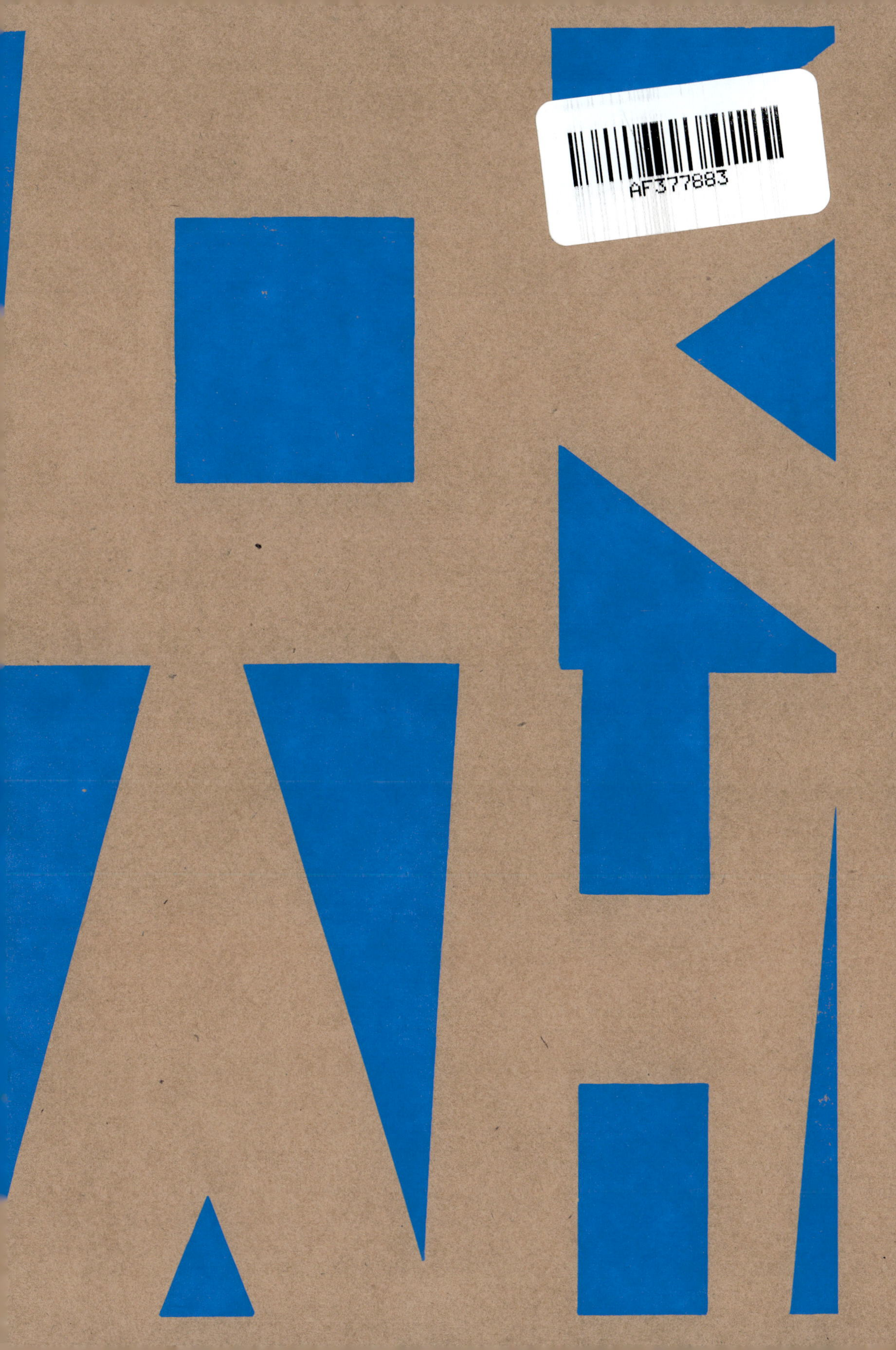

SPEECH PATTERNS

NADIA HERNÁNDEZ
AND
JON CAMPBELL

Art Gallery of
Western Australia

1

The Art Gallery of Western Australia acknowledges the traditional custodians of the lands on which we work: both the Whadjuk Noongar people in Boorloo, Perth, and the Traditional Owners from across Australia. We honour and pay respect to community Elders and to their ancestors who survived and cared for this Country. The Art Gallery recognises that sovereignty was never ceded.

Contents

I am very pleased to introduce this publication which accompanies the exhibition *Speech Patterns: Nadia Hernández and Jon Campbell*. The project includes material spanning each artist's career which has been selected, in large part, to demonstrate approaches to themes within their individual practices and to signal areas of mutual affinity. Embodying the spirit of the artists' visions, both catalogue and exhibition are full of life, poetry and feeling.

As the title implies, a key element that unites these two artists from different backgrounds and generations, is the way their work evolves in relation to the aural, physical and material aspects of language: they write in paint, print, paper cut and textile – staging words singly and in phrases, often in relation to other signs and motifs. Creating from personal experience and the vernacular, they make work that we feel personally addressed by; they gather in and voice responses to local and global concerns, questions of belonging, and the possibilities and constructions of various value systems. They include all of us as participants in their exuberant protest against specific political issues and everyday idiocies, and in their buoyant celebration of broader human expression and connection.

This book features three new texts that expand upon these qualities. In his introductory essay, exhibition curator Robert Cook examines individual works and the nuanced artistic strategies that shape Hernández's and Campbell's particular contributions to Australian cultural life. This is followed by two inventive and idiosyncratic responses by fellow artists and writers: Lisa Radford and Diego Ramírez. Radford's examination of Hernández's work is as expansive and evocative as her own creative practice. She writes in a conversational tone that reflects the growing friendship between the two artists, offering frameworks which intimately engage with the layers of Hernández's work. This includes a consideration of modes of longing and belonging as impacted by Venezuelan political history, and also makes space for readings and responses that travel in new directions. Ramírez's take on Campbell's work is equally generative, as he maintains the pitch and power of a highly performative writing style that he labels as para-fiction. In restlessly antsy first-person mode, he focuses on a single work of Campbell's from 2015. Amplifying its sentiments in a biting and funny performative

dialogue (almost at war with himself and those around him), Ramírez plays out the ramifications of Campbell's artwork in today's cultural moment.

I would like to express my considerable gratitude for the enthusiasm and professionalism with which the artists, Nadia Hernández and Jon Campbell, embraced the exhibition at AGWA. Thanks also to the gallery team who worked on various aspects of the project. They have been wonderfully supported by the artists' gallerists Samantha Barrow, Laura Couttie, and Philippa Griffin from STATION Gallery; and Darren Knight and Suzie Melhop from Darren Knight Gallery. We are also deeply grateful to the many generous lenders of works who have made this exhibition possible.

Colin Walker
Director, Art Gallery of Western Australia

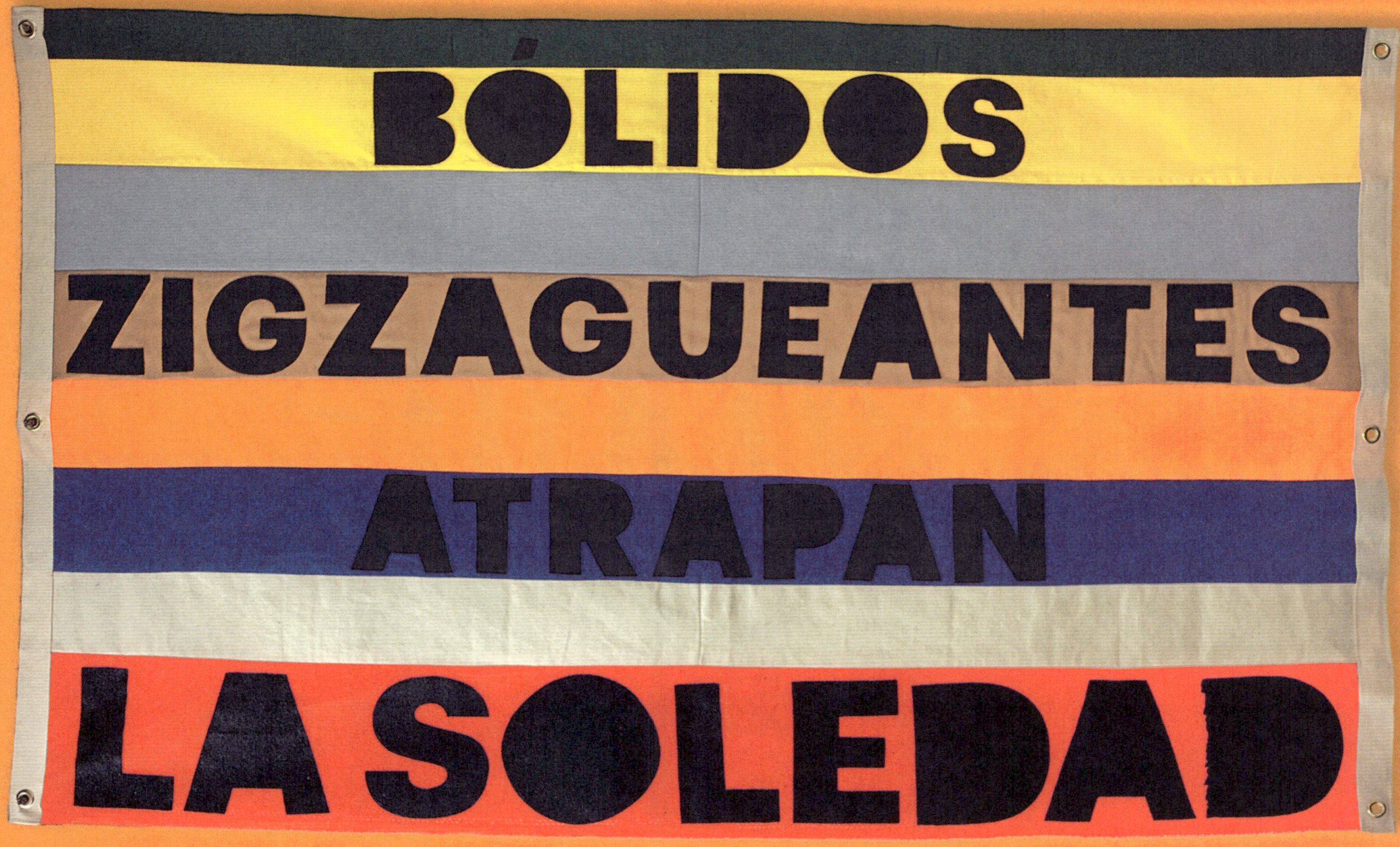

BÓLIDOS
ZIGZAGUEANTES
ATRAPAN
LA SOLEDAD

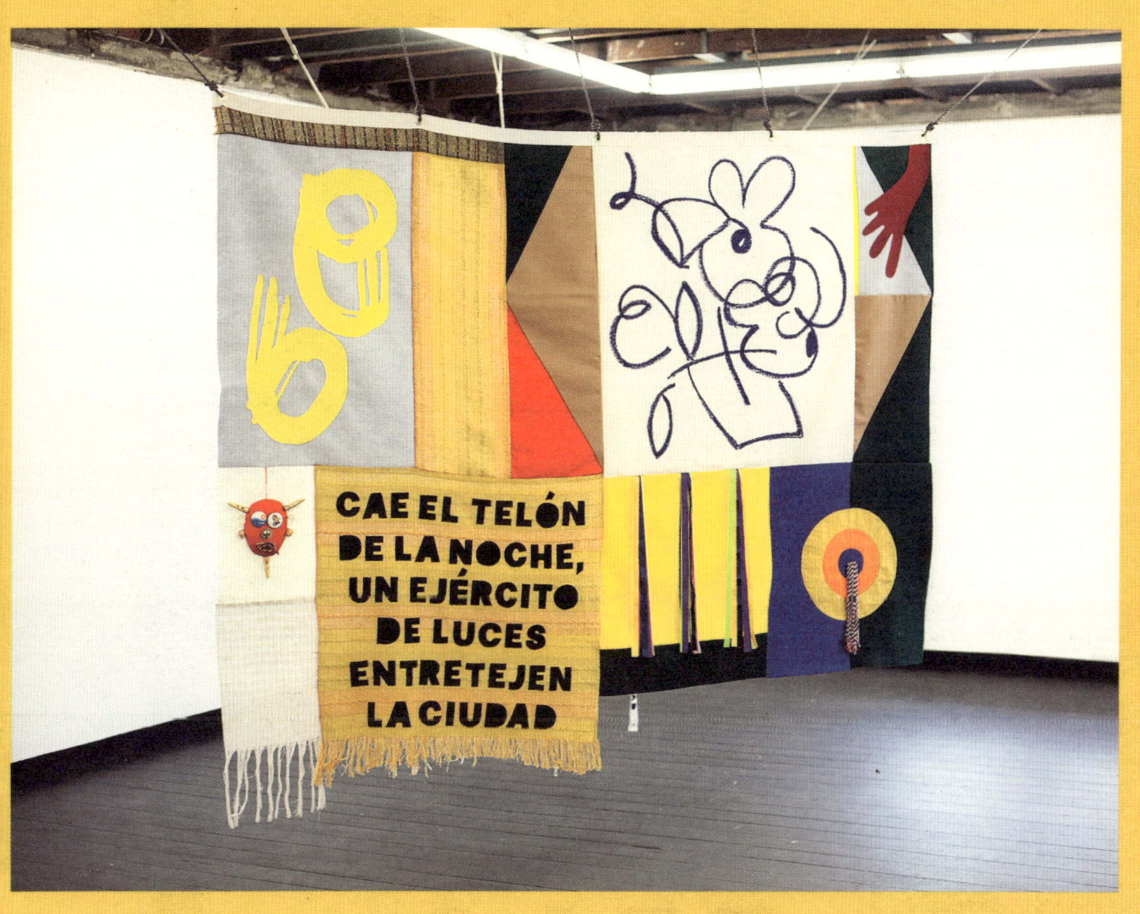

CAE EL TELÓN
DE LA NOCHE,
UN EJÉRCITO
DE LUCES
ENTRETEJEN
LA CIUDAD

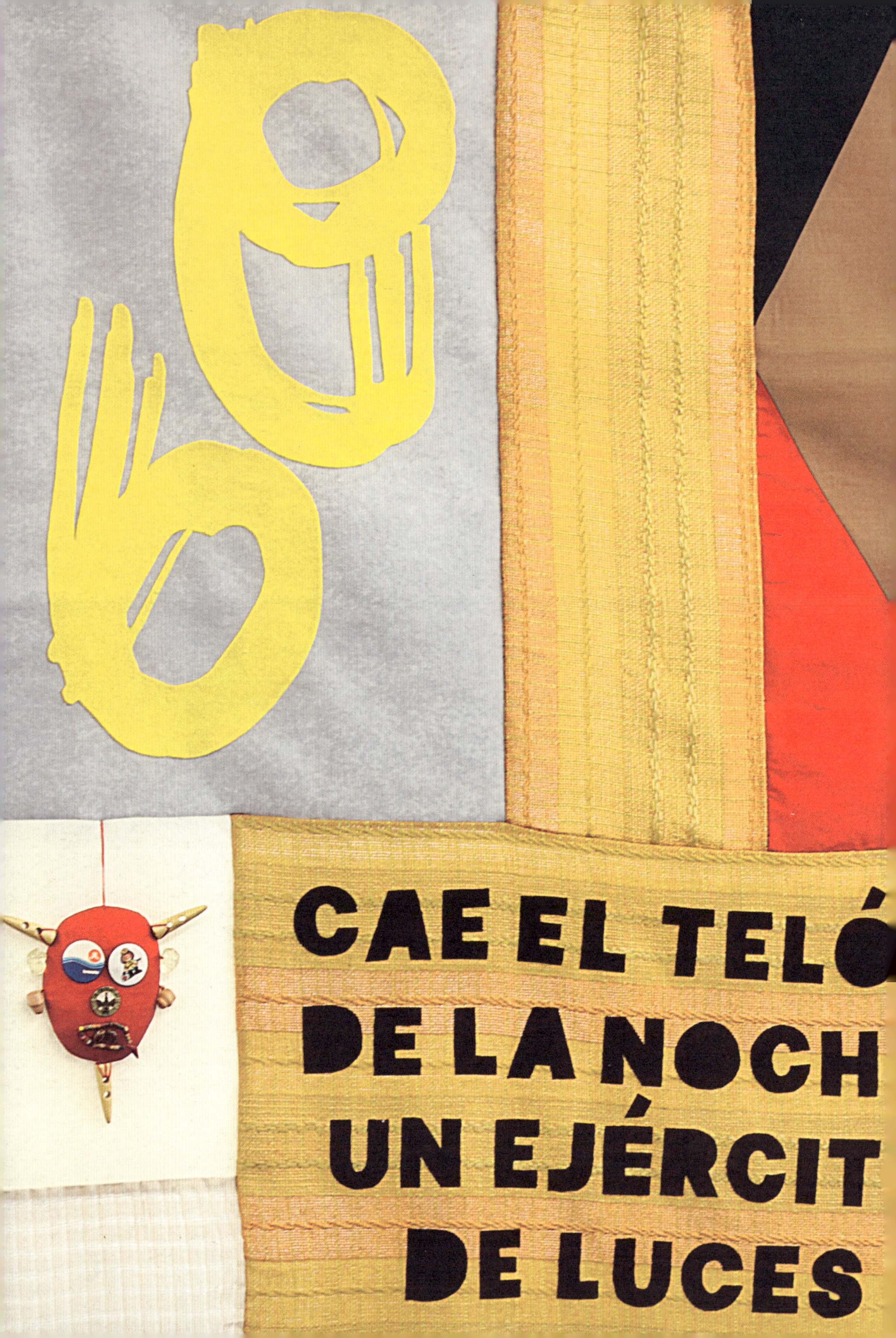
CAE EL TELÓ
DE LA NOCH
UN EJÉRCIT
DE LUCES

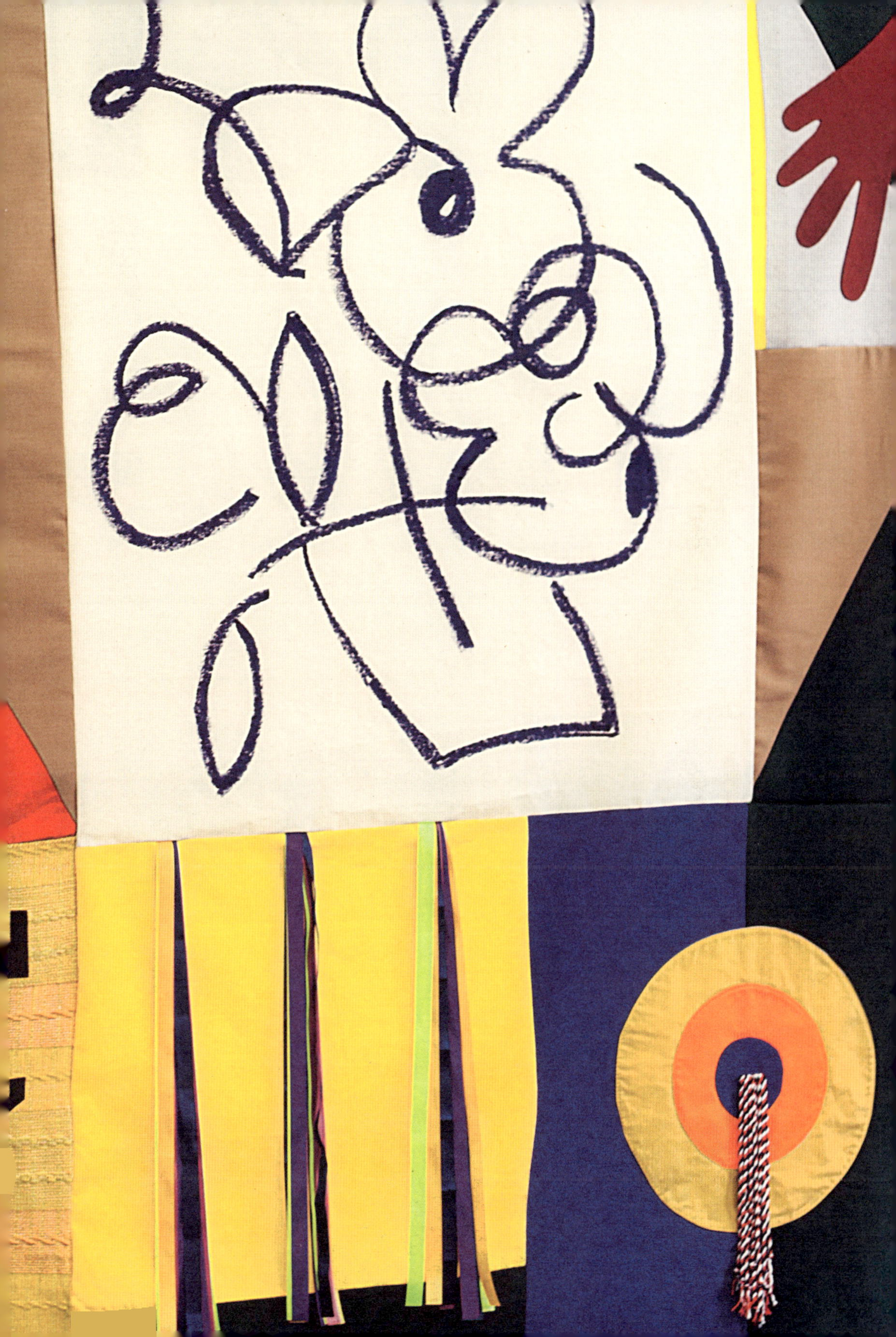

BOL

IGZAGU

ATRA

A SO

DOS

UEANTE

APAN

LEDA

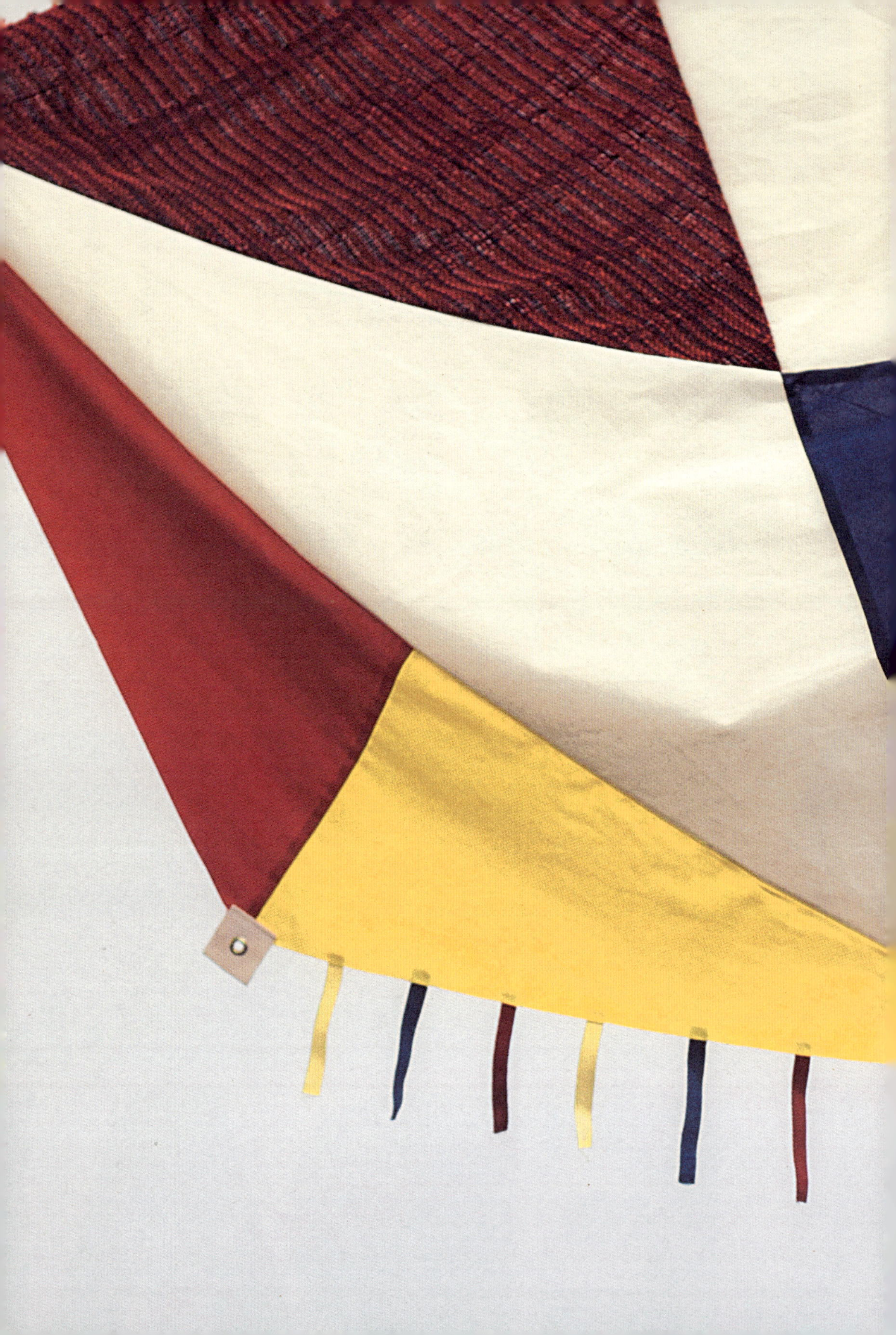

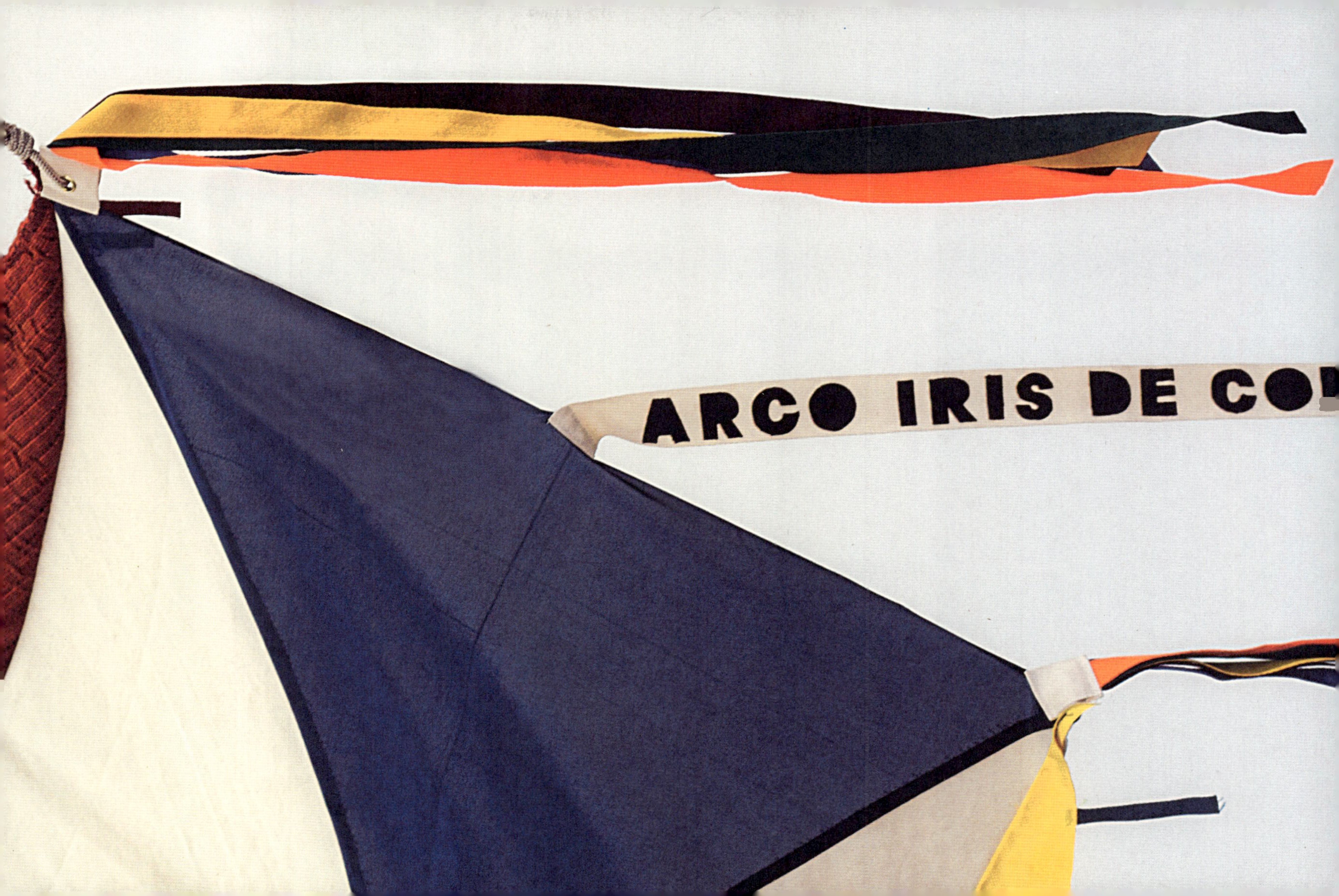

ARCO IRIS DE CO

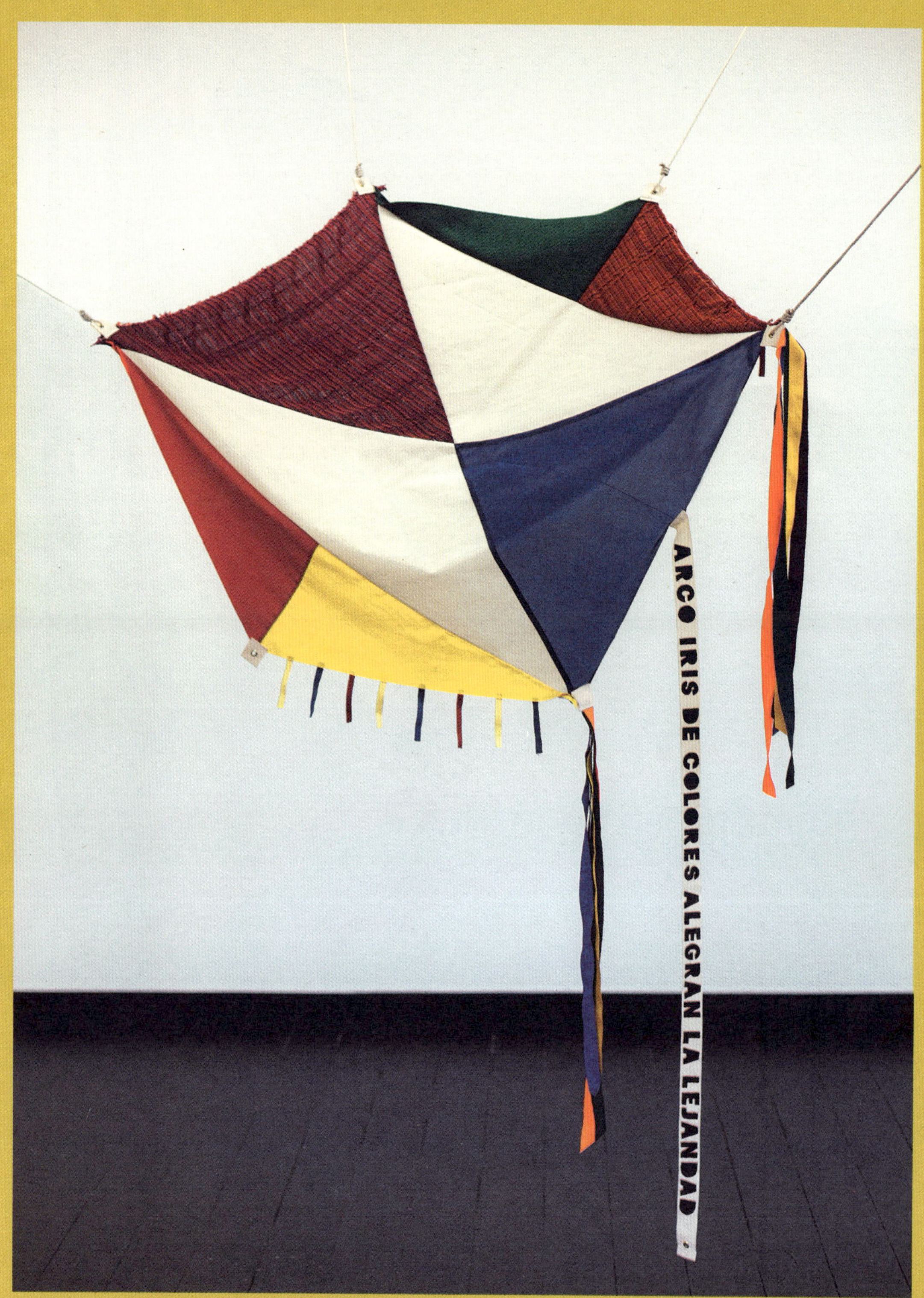

ARCO IRIS DE COLORES ALEGRAN LA LEJANDAD

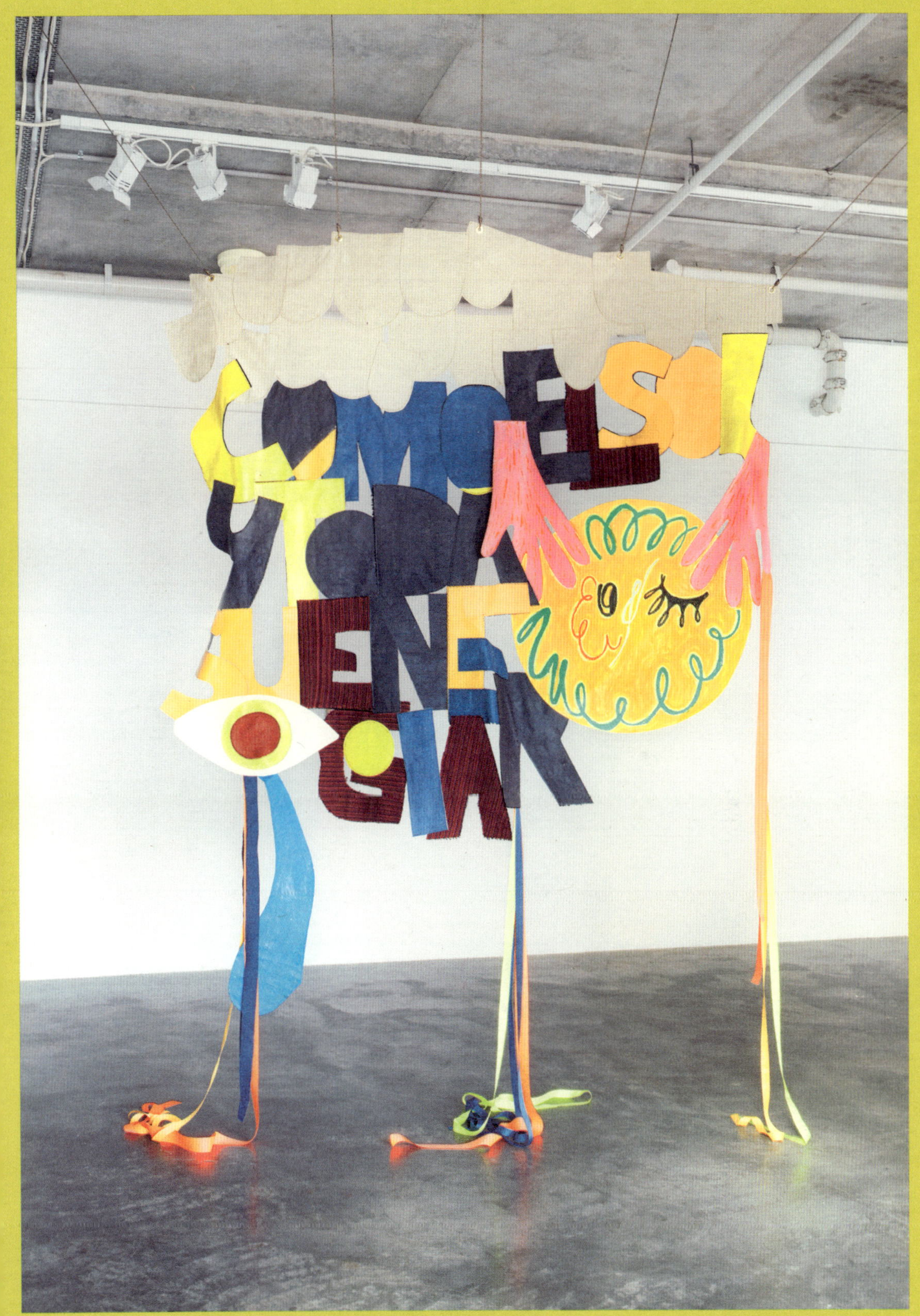
COMOELSOL
YTODALAENERGIA

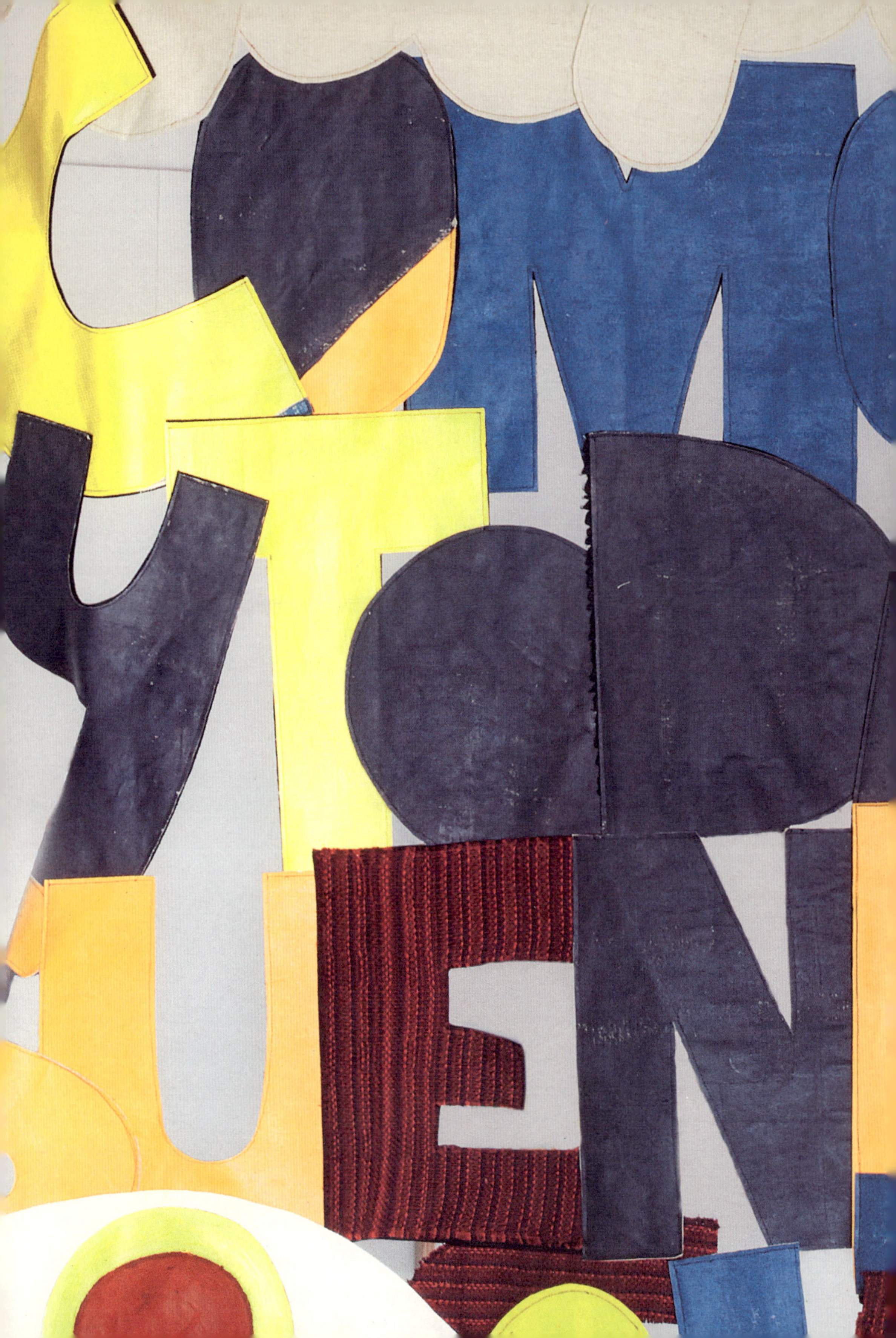

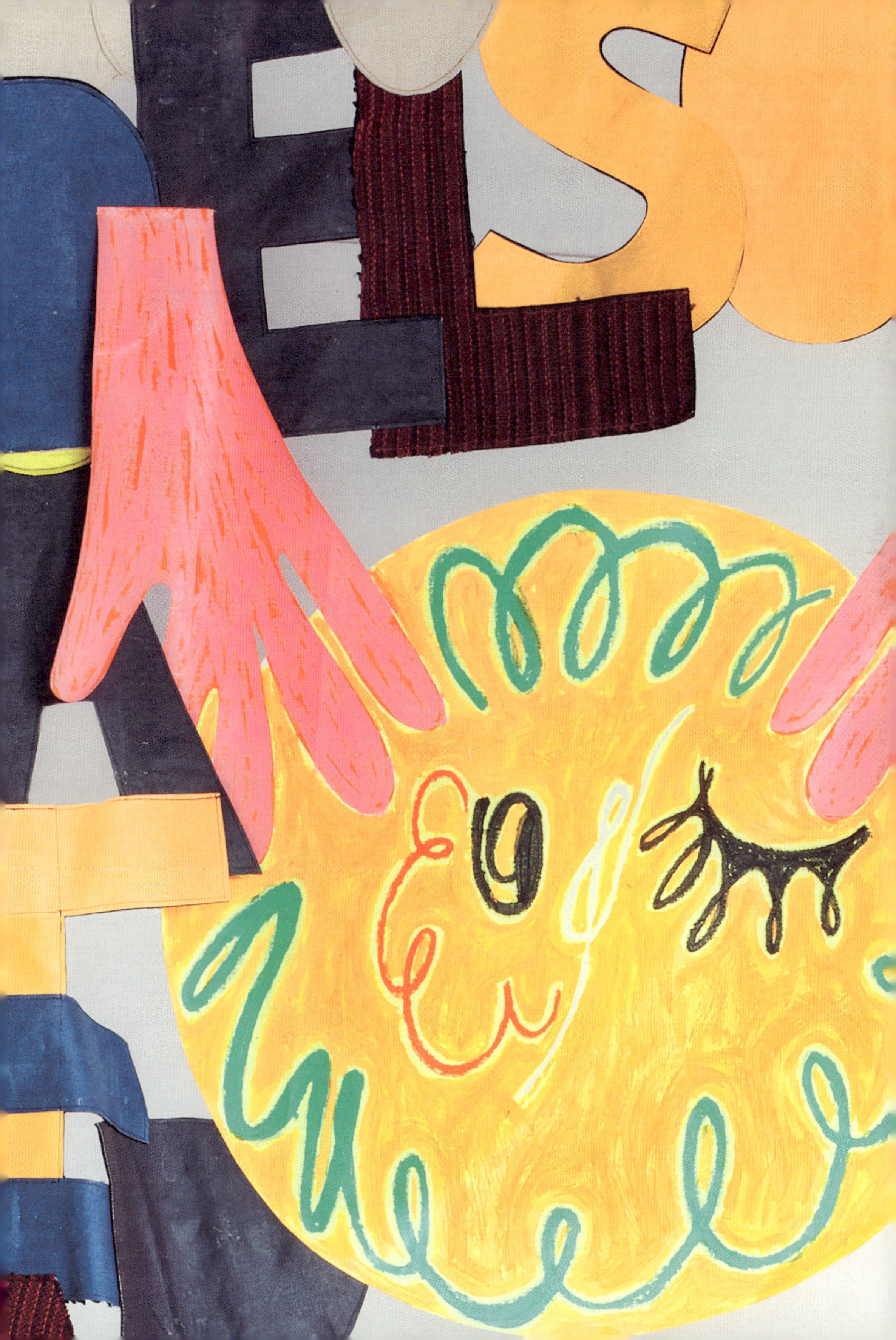

DE
MANTE
QUI
LA

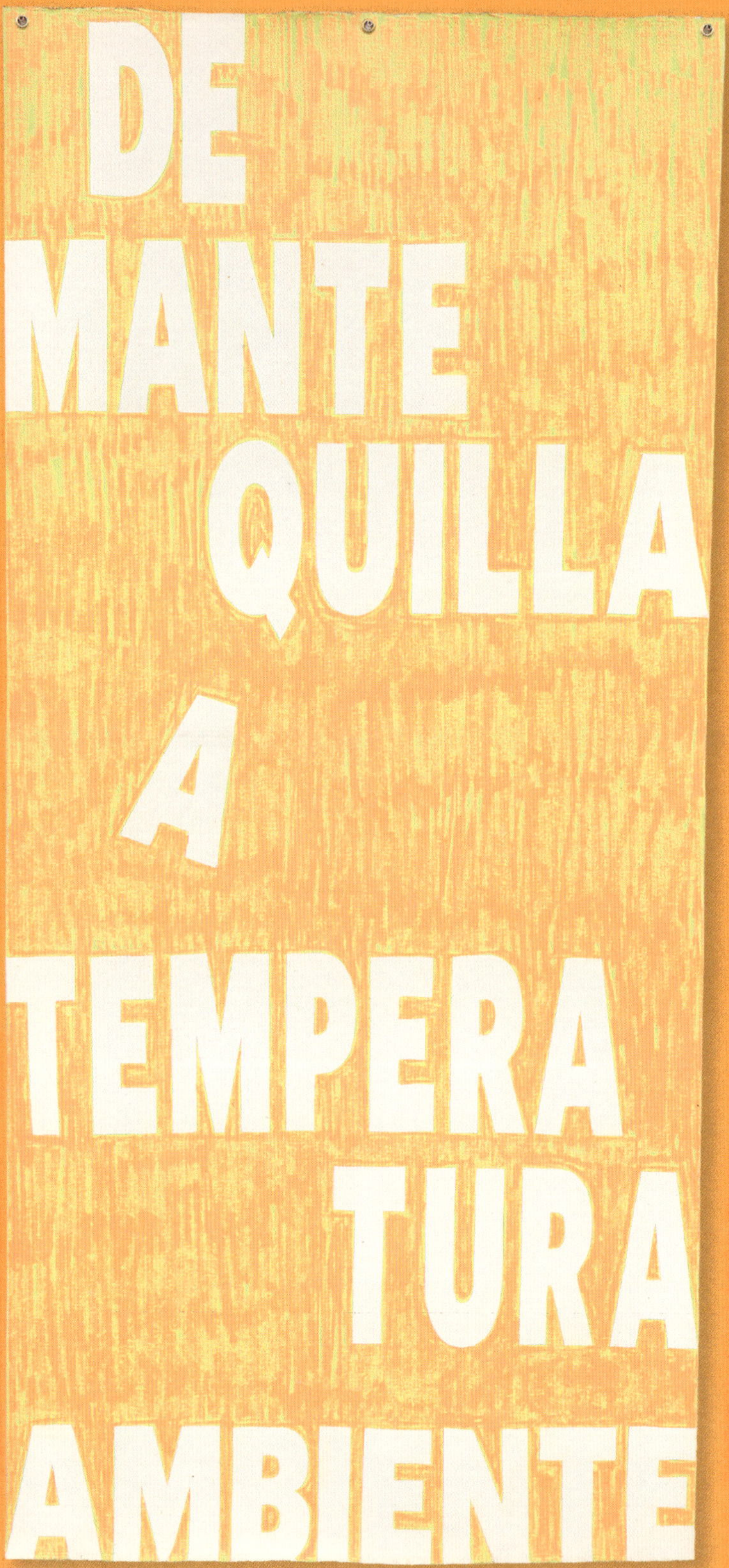

DE
MANTE
QUILLA
A
TEMPERA
TURA
AMBIENTE

No corras.

Que provocarás una estampida.

Tienes que relajarte

/

Don't run.

You'll cause a stampede.

You've got to chill.

–José Rubén Hernández [1]

COSAS ANTES Y DESPUÉS (Things Before and After)
is a body of work Nadia Hernández made following
her return to Australia after visiting Mérida, her
hometown in Venezuela.

♥

I've only met you recently. Our conversations are
long and full. As I read through the transcript made
by an anonymous A.I. in 48-hour delivery turn
around, I can see the beginnings of a friendship in
the 11pt Calibri font, kerning and spacing, pauses
and ellipses. We both have a habit of saying 'WOW',
using repetition as emphasis and of finishing the
other's sentences.

And put them all together,
*   ... and put them all together.*
*   Yeah.*
*   ... from across the world.*
*   Wow.*
*   ... and lived experience.*
*   connected.*

Listening to the past with my eyes while looking at
PDFs and JPEGs. A séance of images, conjuring my
first encounter with your exhibition at an art fair in a
convention centre comprising works emerging from
your invitations to family and friends to 'tell me what
to paint'. Thinking and listening, my frontal cortex is
hacked by a mash-up of images: Instagramable
moments of Nadia and Jason Phu, an 'Oh-What-a-
Feeling-jumping-for-a-car' memory and paintings-
cum-drawing-as-poster-cum-speech. Listening to
the past with my eyes simultaneously looking out

and looking in, tracing narratives I am yet to know, by
a hand I am yet to meet.

    Cosas antes y después /
    things before and after.

Listening and reading; observing and hearing that I
am talking about writing behaving like painting.
Seventy-one pages, 15,000 words; the writing of
painting, the painting of writing. Text in your
paintings speaks to fragments I collect, fragments
we all collect – all-a-board movements for change;
saved chats, archived screenshots, notes from
overheard conversations, notes from conversations
had, glimpses shared, images distributed. While
nothing might be whole, the fragment is still
contained, even when your texts-cum-poems are cut
from canvas and hung tentatively, edges frayed.
There is an impossibility of being able to consume
the entirety. A language in circulation, swimming in
pools of meaning and farce – your colour bleached
and spritzed, light rendered in humble, zesty marks.
    I tweet: *photography is painting and painting is
writing and writing is data.* I know what I mean, but I
can't write what it is.
    Matrilinear and biographical, this is a relatively
young body of work conversing with millennia, myth
and a perplexing present. 'Chao, *mi vida* / Goodbye,
my life' your Aunt might say, and a collage it will
become. The phrasing of an ongoing ending in a
breath so cherished it prefaces a name.[2] We have
only met three and a half times: 'hello, hello, let's
walk, goodbye': a Collingwood café we
coincidentally share a love for, a road trip to Brighton
to see your work in a prize for women, and a trip to
the airport that doubles as a book exchange, food
rescue and farewell. You are off to Majorca to visit

your girlfriend, sharing a language and an intimacy of speech that parallels experience.

> *They were always there, intimate with each other in one way and intimate with me in another, as if I were a beloved sibling. They weren't watching over me, exactly; they were the protagonists of their own stories.*
> *But this story? This one's mine.*[3]

'No *corras. Que provocarás una estampida. Tienes que relajarte* / Don't run. You'll cause a stampede. You've got to chill.'[4] Your grandfather says this to you. A family protesting, your body on the street. To return to a home with intention. Your body on the line, the radical and the hopeful; a contribution to, well, any kind of shift. Economics. Environment. Politics. Oil. The familial and social bound by the conditional – place, history and colonisation. Home land. Homeland. All-a-boarding a movement for change, a confrontation, an encounter walked; an all-a-boarding the State attempts to intercept. Your body of work, their bodies on the street.

> *Cosas antes y después /*
> *things before and after.*

You are thinking about archives and the 200 or so drawings you will send over to Perth from your studio here in Melbourne. You tell me to read Carmen Maria Machado's *In the Dream House*. A semi-surreal break-up biography, *In the Dream House* is arranged in five parts containing 153 vignettes or lenses of experience and observations written under titles beginning with *Dream*. Some are as short as a single quote, others unravel as pick-a-path. *The Dream House as Prologue* riffs off Saidiya Hartman and her account of African slavery and the violence of the archive. You mention this containment of information: what is held, what spills out, the private and the shared. An archival silence, a screaming abyss. The archive, Carmen tells us via Jacques Derrida, comes from the ancient Greek ἀρχεῖος (arkheion), 'the house of the ruler'. Architecture and power, an authoritative voice whose completeness is mythological, whose femininity is discreet – the studio, a gallery, a museum, a vitrine; the family, a house, a suburb, a dream.

> *Places are never just places in a piece of writing. If they are, the author has failed. Setting is not inert. It is activated by point of view.* [5]

In conversation, you and I circle narratives about absence: a collage that will not be lent, a little-known father whose narrative can't be told. A question shared, DNA testing and genetic unknowns. Known unknowns. Or, we both ask, do we make do with the experience of the two sides we can know? What does science really reveal as it intersects with generational change? The multiple experiences had in places over time; an accumulation of memory and jumping through space. We segue to that movie: *Everything Everwhere All at Once.* I've written it before. Gestural sculptural movement markers guiding us between banners, psychological kitchenscapes, and pictographic scraps: a head of corn, your grandmother's arepa, the roof of a house. The everyday things we're made of; a broken timeline, a break in time.[6] *Cotidianidad* you say, everydayness. Colour keys in and icons prompt; the good, the bad, the ugly, us: aphoristic and memorable: *No pude recordar la casa, pero pude recordar mis sueños / I* couldn't remember the house, but I could remember my dreams.[7]

This prompts recollection of a sound work – you must remember to tell Robert. A compilation of cousins and aunts and extended family whistling your grandmother's whistle-while-she-waits-for-family-to-return-home. Paintings as hauntings, spiritual parlance; mediated by strange and familiar iconography – paper cuts, oil stick, linen. Textiles, text-tiles. Fiber, as noun, *la fibra* or *el carácter* – el personaje. Woven marks, a conversation with drawings and texts, a collection of poems by your grandfather, murals you have seen and speech you have stolen. Settler narratives shared, an energy and synergy. Image as language and language as image, beside your historical lineages nodding ... wait, cheering you along. A chorus of artists in reverence. Picture the Instagramable less probable: on a sunlit windowsill sits Sister Corina Kent chatting with Atelier Populaire looking to Nadia, coaxing her along. Pop and populous, Kent and the Atelier are born in times of radical change, conflicting ideals and productive contradictions. My crash course in Venezuelan history is an echo coalescing.

> *Así es la humanidad, compadre, que cuando uno quiere hacé una gracia le sale una morisqueta. Pero yo lo que digo es que si las cosas están malas, toavía se pueden poné más piores. / That's humanity for you compadre, you try to do something nice for folks and you end up falling on your face. What I always say is, things might be bad now, but they can sure get a whole lot worse.*[8]

It is a Saturday. I am a tourist at a conference on *Extractivism*. A background narrative in my head is

trying to process the brief but intense encounters
with you and my attempt to catch up on Venezuela-
as-Venezuela, mining resources and settler migrants;
bio-products of colonisation. Blinkered optimism. I
remember from afar, the early 2000's and Hugo
Chavez, red t-shirts and Socialism's hope. You were
young, but your politically progressive family was
already weary of the Chavez rule, aware of the
attempt to topple democracy in the 1992 coup
attempt.

    A century old petro-economy, its petro-
delerium and petro-excess-wealth. *Mene Grande*,
the name of the first oil well, still pumping. *Mene* – an
indigenous word for oil seep. At the conference I
write a note in my book asking if research is
extractive. Alejandro Haiek is speaking about water,
architecture and ecology. I am not paying enough
attention. He throws to an image of a drawing and
says: 'Amazon cosmology'. I stop running on my
floating world and think to your paintings,
cosmological in form. The antithesis of ecosystem,
cosmology negates the mechanical and questions
the industrial of arrangements categorised.
Cosmologies allow for gaps; in your work the need to
know is neither the imperative nor the drive behind
this placement of, then engagement with, form.

    A cosmological picture *plein air*. Your friend's
dog, and a worm that emerges from your Aunt's
nose, a serpent as border, the bridge for crossing. A
bridge for crossing. Fixed on this point, I recall more
refugees fled Venezuela than those that fled Syria –
social, economic and ecological wars. In these
paintings, your paintings, I find circulating gestures,
an energy of trying to hold narratives that might
easily disappear. The materiality of presence, a
rupture of loss. We have come to talk about painting
through what might be missing. To rend is to tear, as

tear might be to wound. I write this a lot. To heal a wound, to confront an animal: our bodies, our places, our cosmologies, our myth. Touch. To experience joy en route to transformation through struggle, the existential face of failure, the beauty of the local, yet spoken at a distance.

♥

Cosas antes y después /
things before and after.

I message Robert and thank him for introducing me to Nadia. We are women painters writing and painting a world we inhabit and encounter, intersections and vivisections, muddy puddles and deep ravines – listening with our eyes, seeing with our ears. There is a visceral in the cerebral, *en plein air* in the studio, the slogans of our regimes muralised by the poetry of our polis.

William Neuman ends his Venezuelan history by referring to the painter Armando Reverón. He lived on a beach near Caracas and painted a world drenched in the savage white light of the Caribbean, a light that seemed to chase away all colour from the landscape. 'Painting is truth', Reverón said once, 'but light blinds you, it drives you crazy, it torments you, because you cannot see light'. I think that Reverón meant that truth was elusive because you could approach it only through something you could not see.[9]

The afterword for *In the Dream House* references Joanna Russ and women's literary history as being 'written on sand'. There is a partiality in this observation. For Carmen Maria Machado, writing her

memoir felt like pinning down fragments of history,
as she describes it, with well-aimed throws of a knife.
Fragments pinned down before they could shift or
melt away.[10] There is a necessity in the Project, as
there is in Nadia's. Like writing on sand, she mediates
memories, negotiating distance and time, more
choral than coral. Her paintings write a fabric.

Lisa Radford

Lisa Radford is an artist who writes

Notes

1	Author's translation via Google. Nadia Hernández quoting her grandfather, from conversation with the author, Collingwood, July 06, 2022.
2	Nadia Hernández in conversation with the author, Collingwood, July 06, 2022: 'And then this was also part of that show. And it's this "chao mi vida", which is something my great aunt always says when she hangs up, she's like "goodbye my life." But I was like, "that's got a double meaning"'.
3	Carmen Maria Machado, *In the Dream House*, Serpent's Tail, London, 2020, p. 9.
4	Author's translation via google, Nadia Hernández in conversation with the author, Collingwood, July 06, 2022.
5	Machado, *In the Dream House*, p. 81.
6	Nadia Hernández in Emma Pegrum, 'How Nadia Hernàndez uses art to navigate intersecting identities and preserve cultural memory', *Harper's Bazaar*, June 2022, https://harpersbazaar.com.au/how-nadia-hernandez-uses-art-to-navigate-identities/.
7	*No pude rerdar la casa, pero pude recorder mis sueños / I couldn't remember the house, but I could remember my dreams*, 2021, paper cut, 71.0 × 90.0 cm.
8	Rómulo Gallegos, 'General Parmenión Cunaguaro' in *La Primera Versión de el Forastero, novela inédita*, written in approximately 1922 and published after the author's death in William Neuman, *The Collapse of Venezuela: Things are never so bad that they can't get worse: Inside the Collapse of Venezuela*, Macmillan, NY, 2021.
9	William Neuman, *Things Are Never So Bad That they Can't get Worse: Inside the Collapse of Venezuela*, 2022, Macmillan Audio.
10	Machado, *In the Dream House*, p. 279.

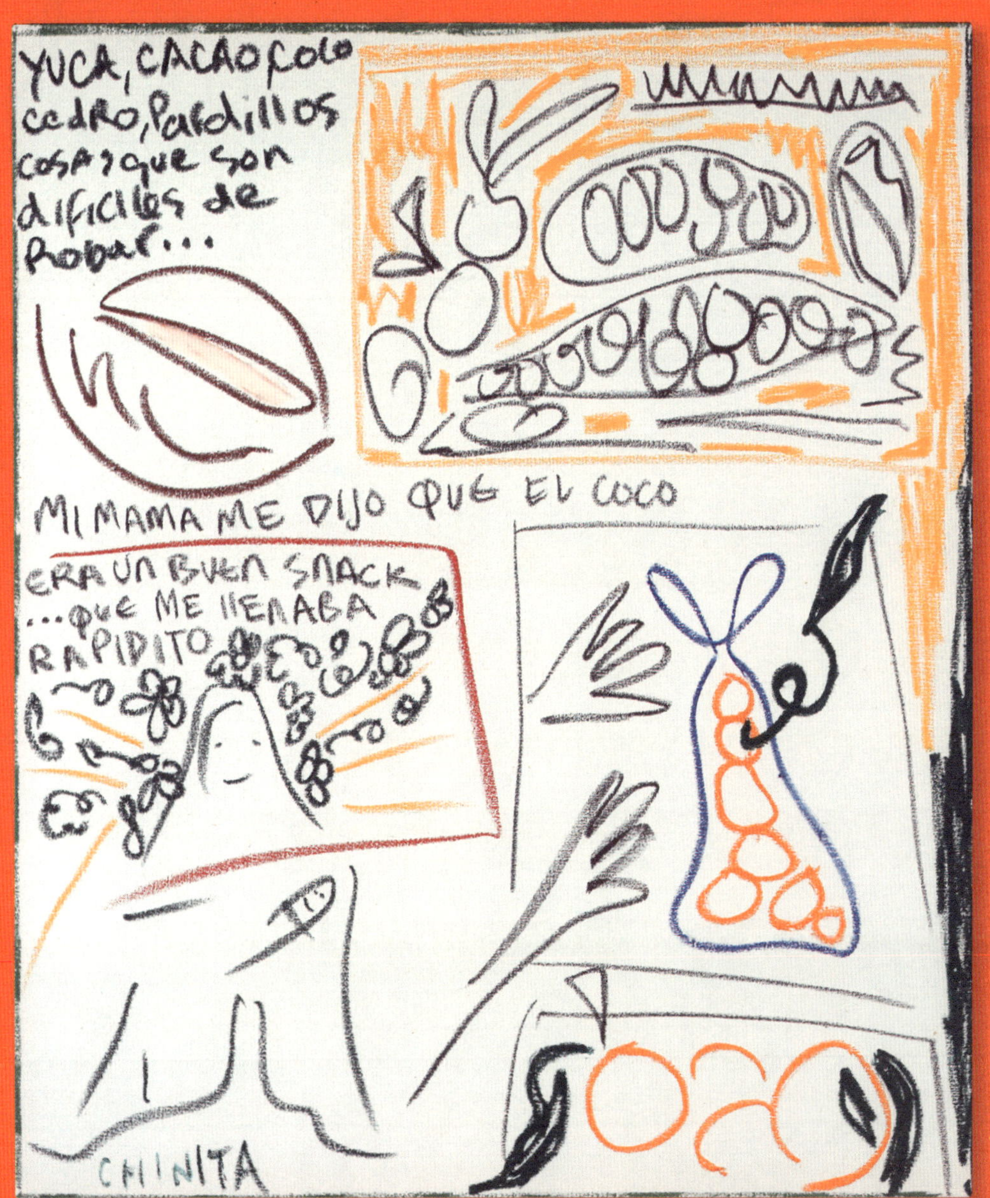

YUCA, CACAO, COLO
CEDRO, PARDILLOS
COSAS QUE SON
DIFICILES DE
ROBAR...
MI MAMA ME DIJO QUE EL COCO
ERA UN BUEN SNACK
...QUE ME llenaba
RAPIDITO
CHINITA

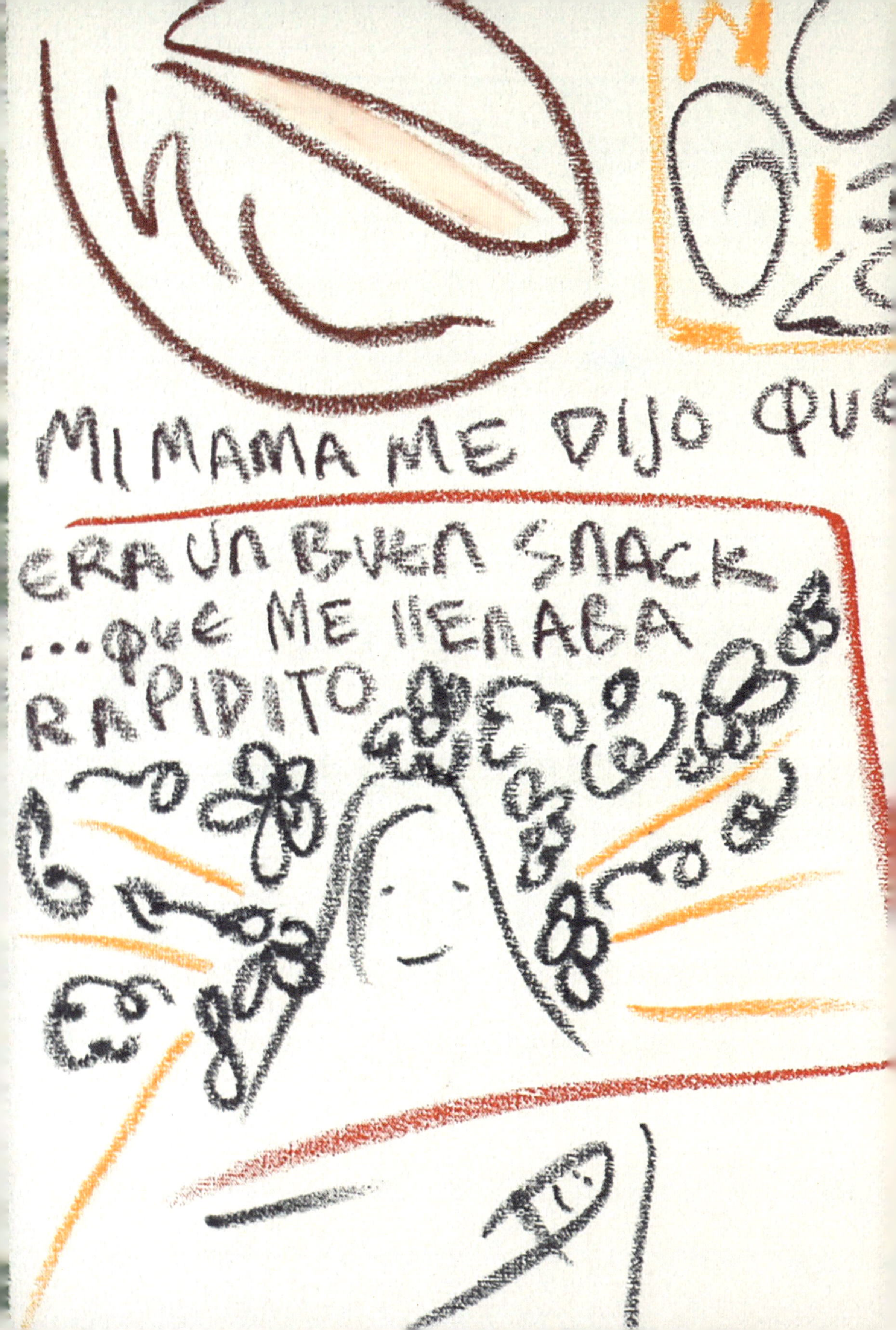
MI MAMA ME DIJO QUE
ERA UN BUEN SNACK
...QUE ME LLENABA
RAPIDITO

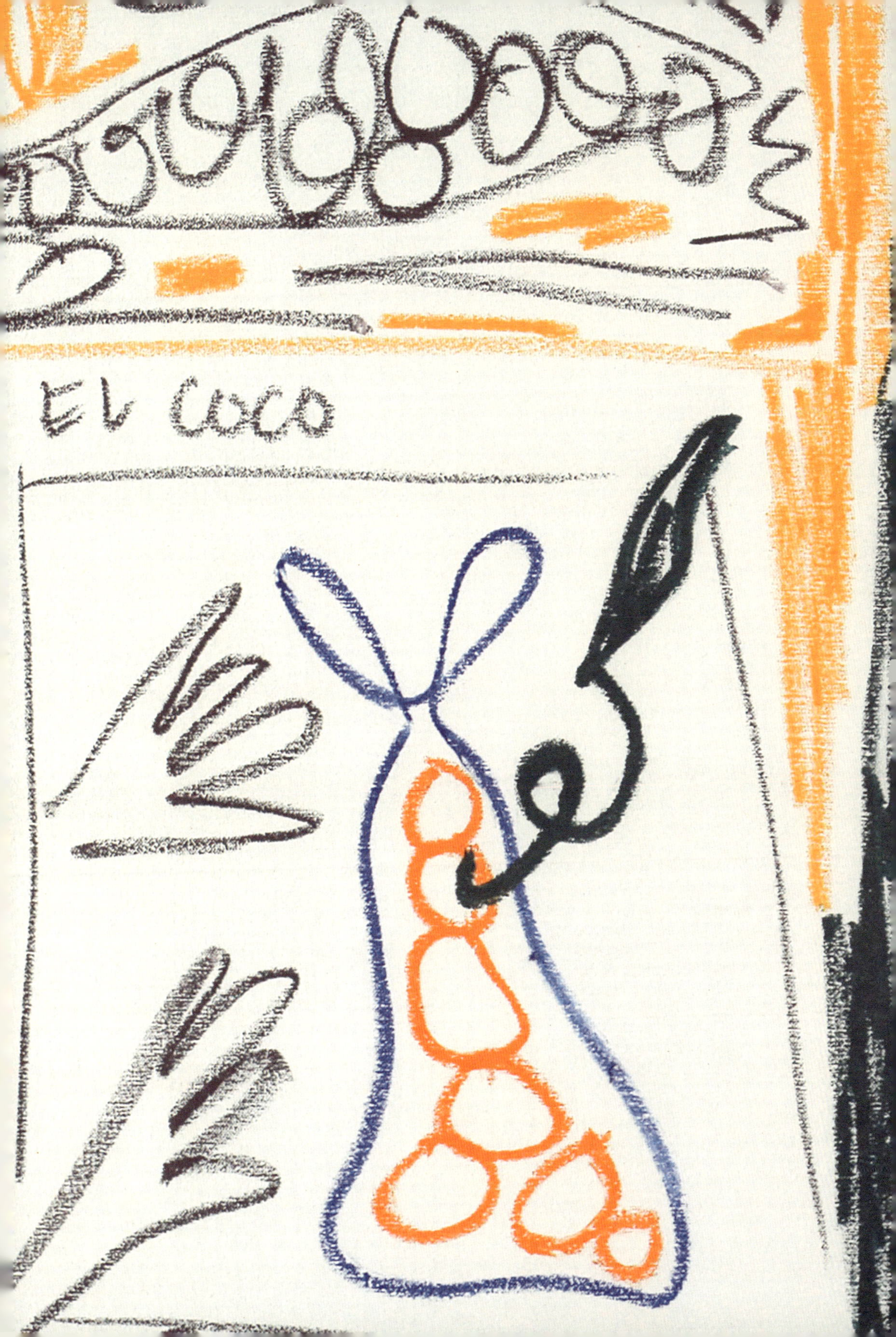
EL COCO

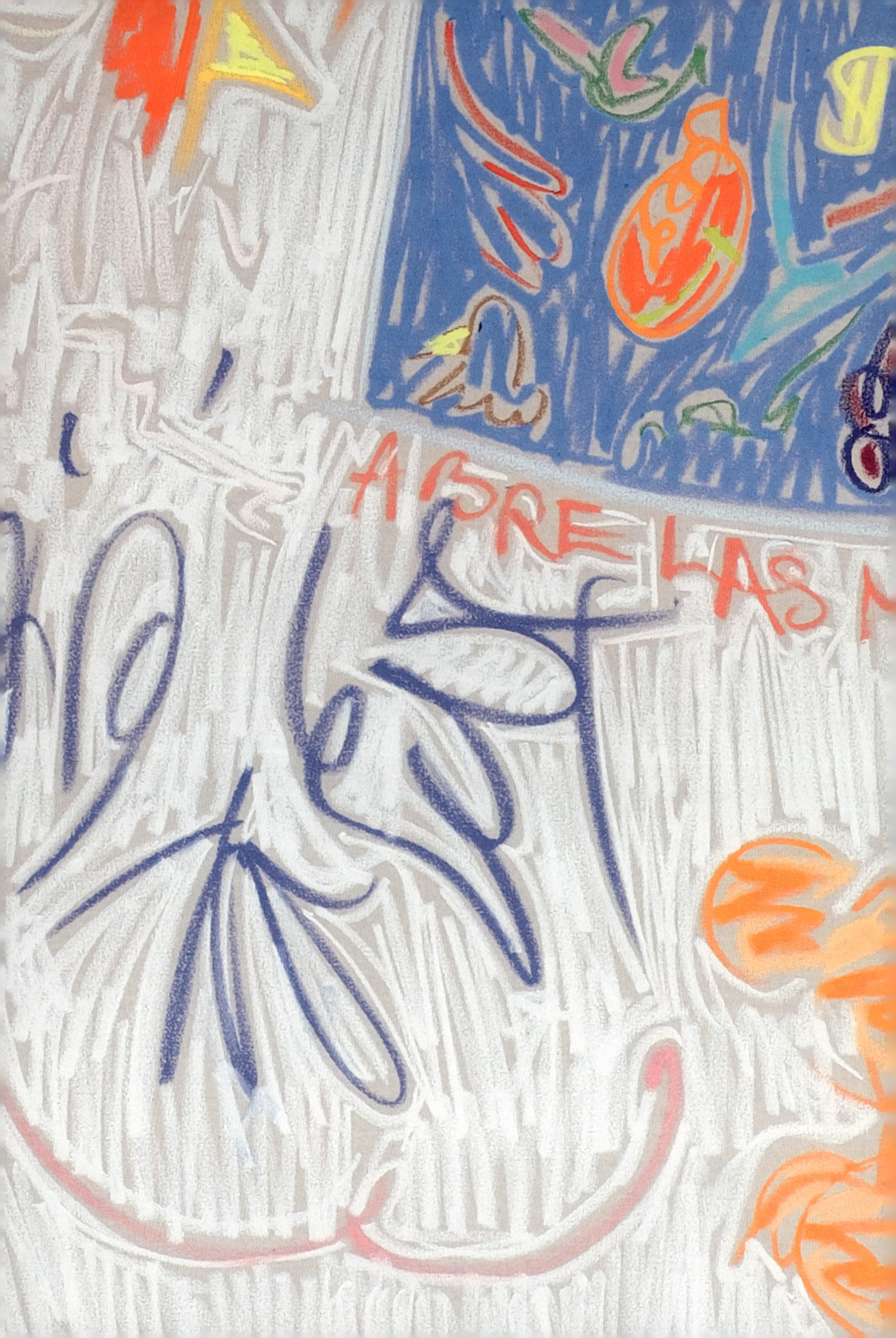

ABRE LAS

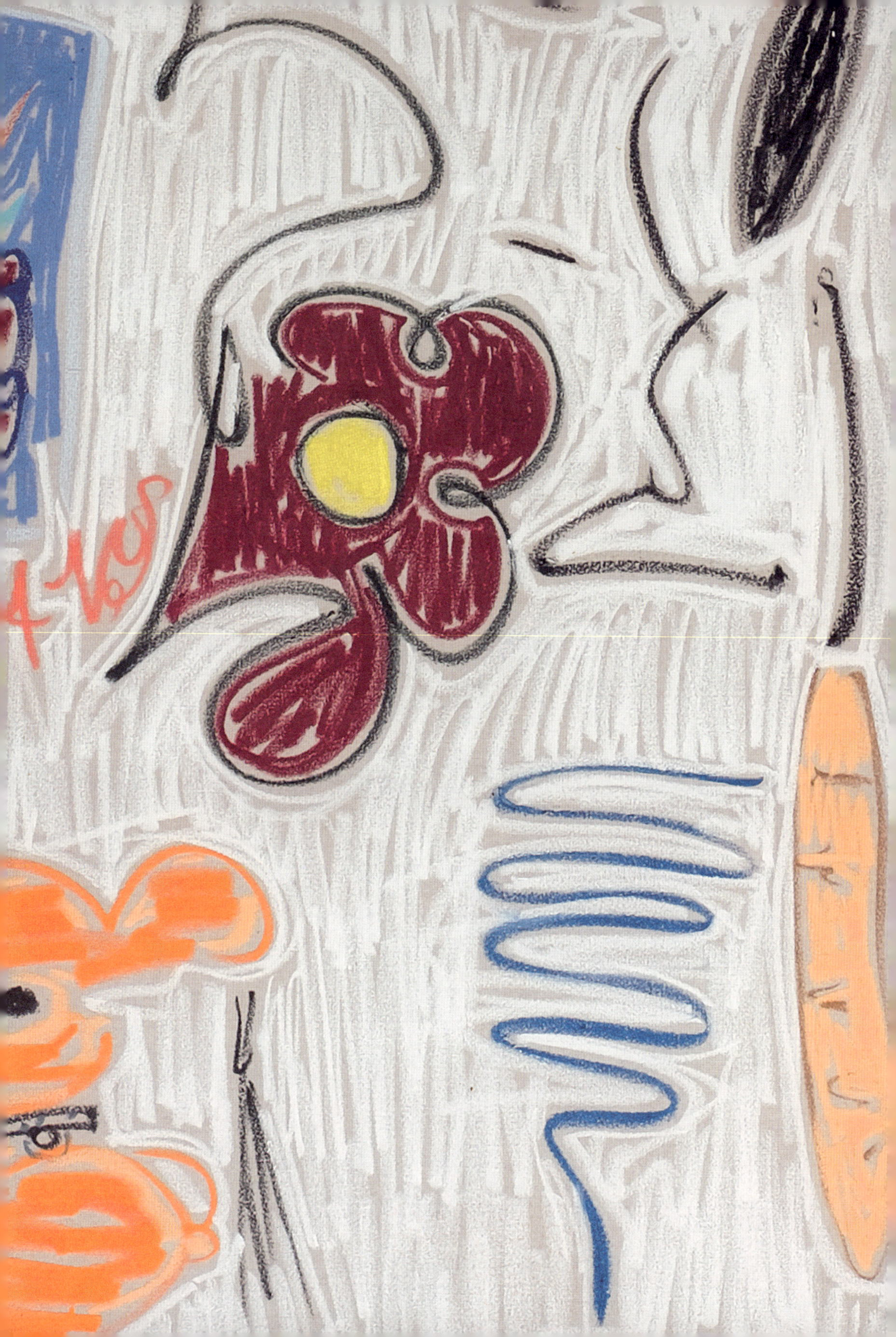

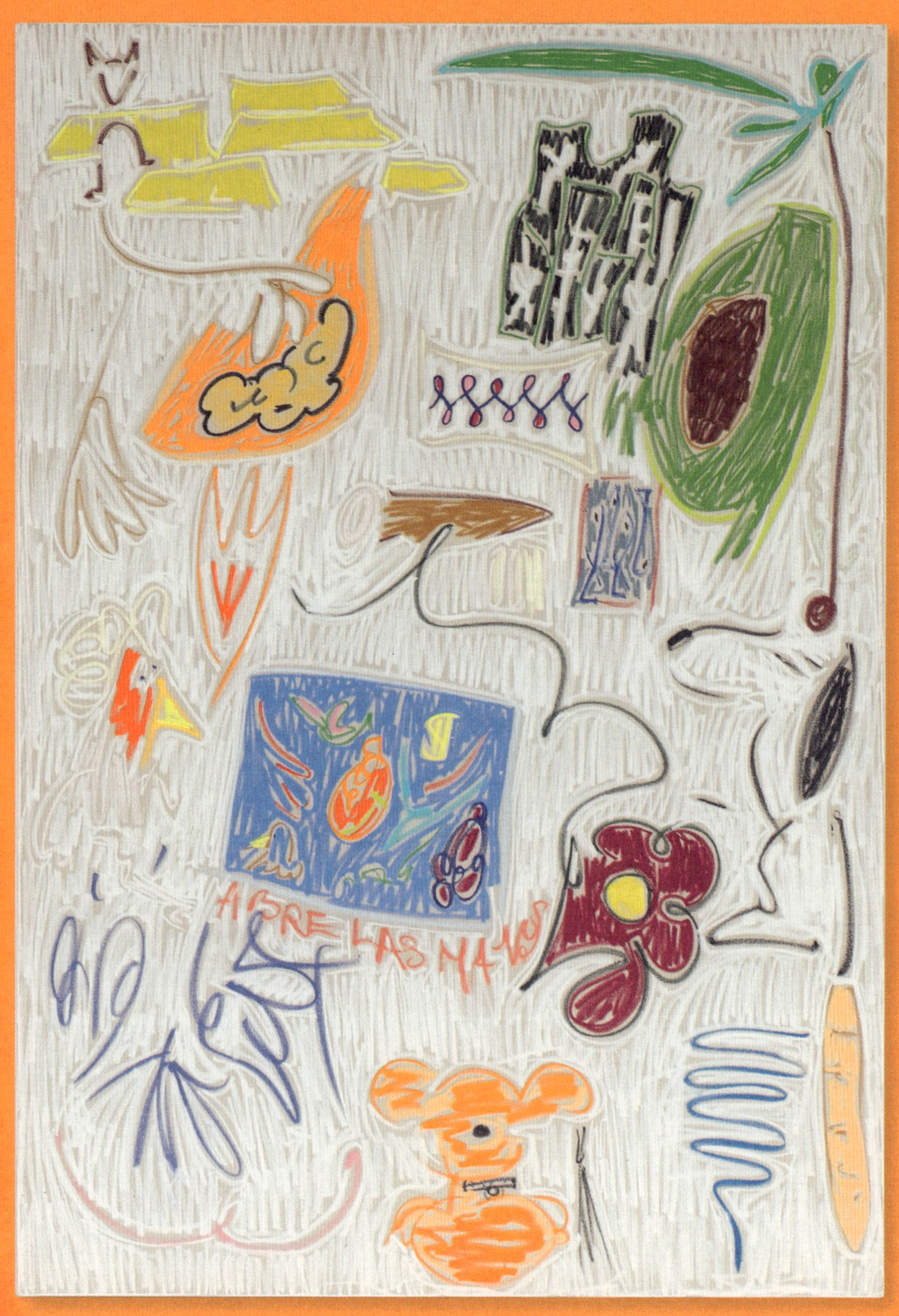
ABRE LAS MANOS

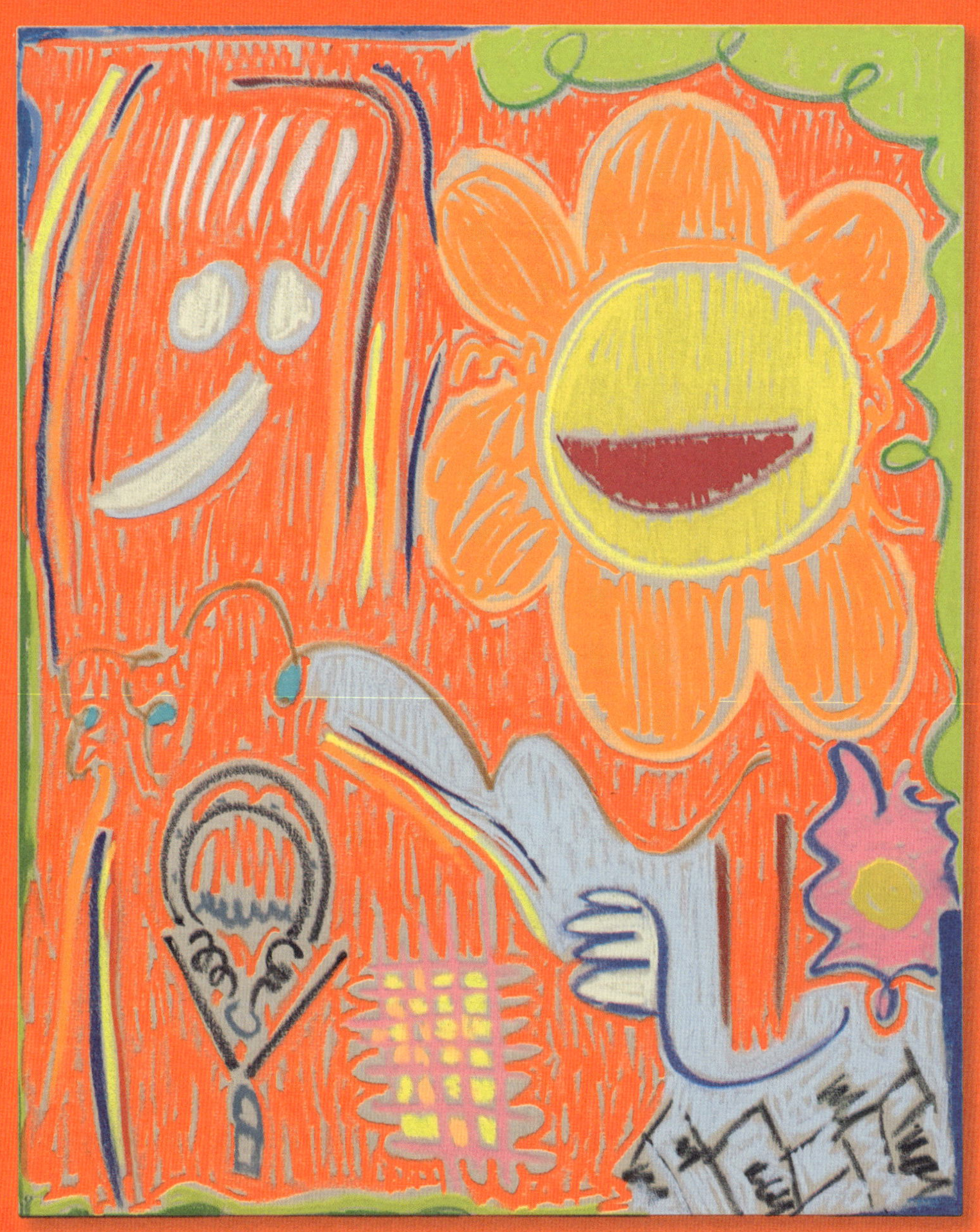

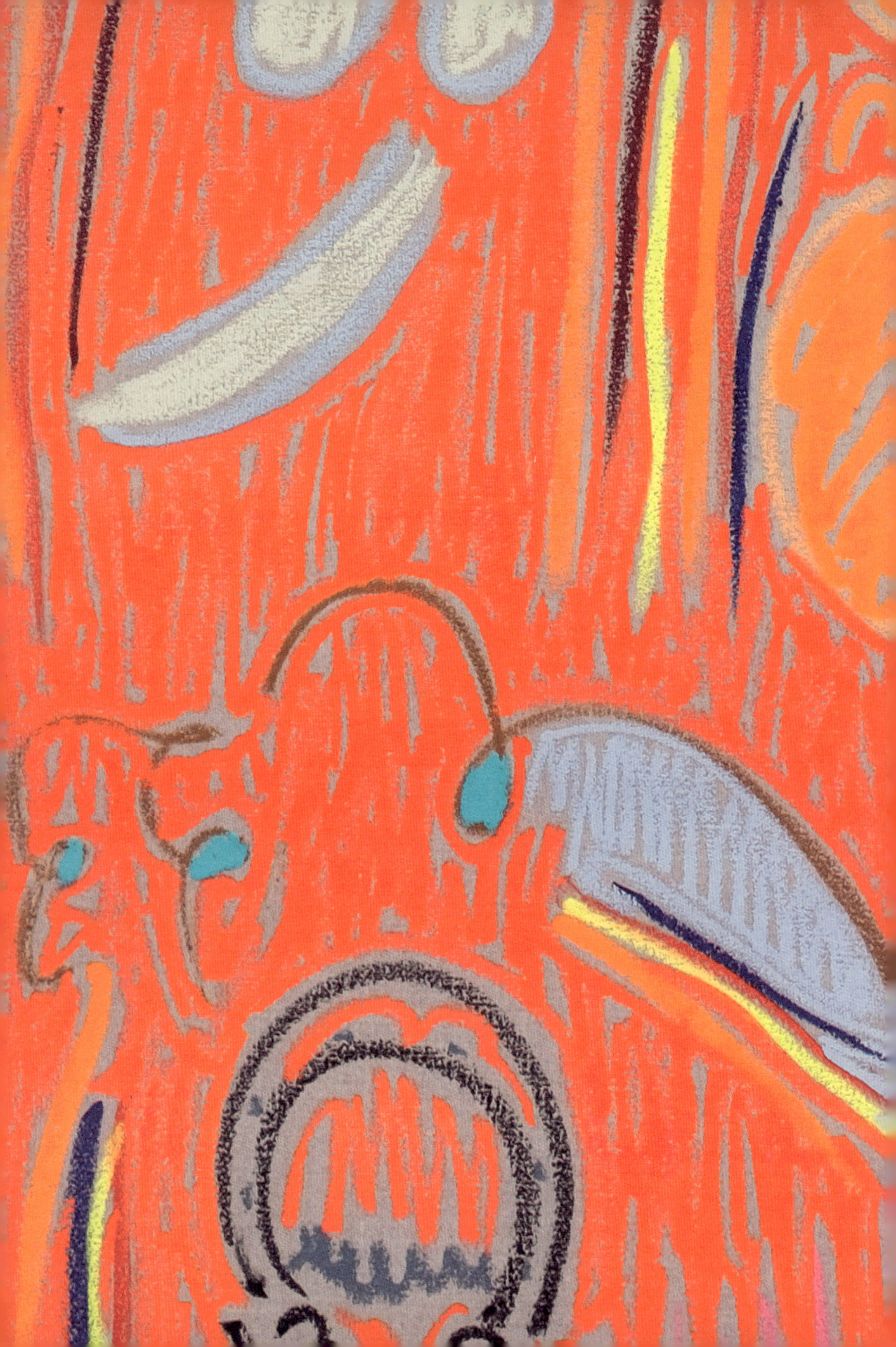

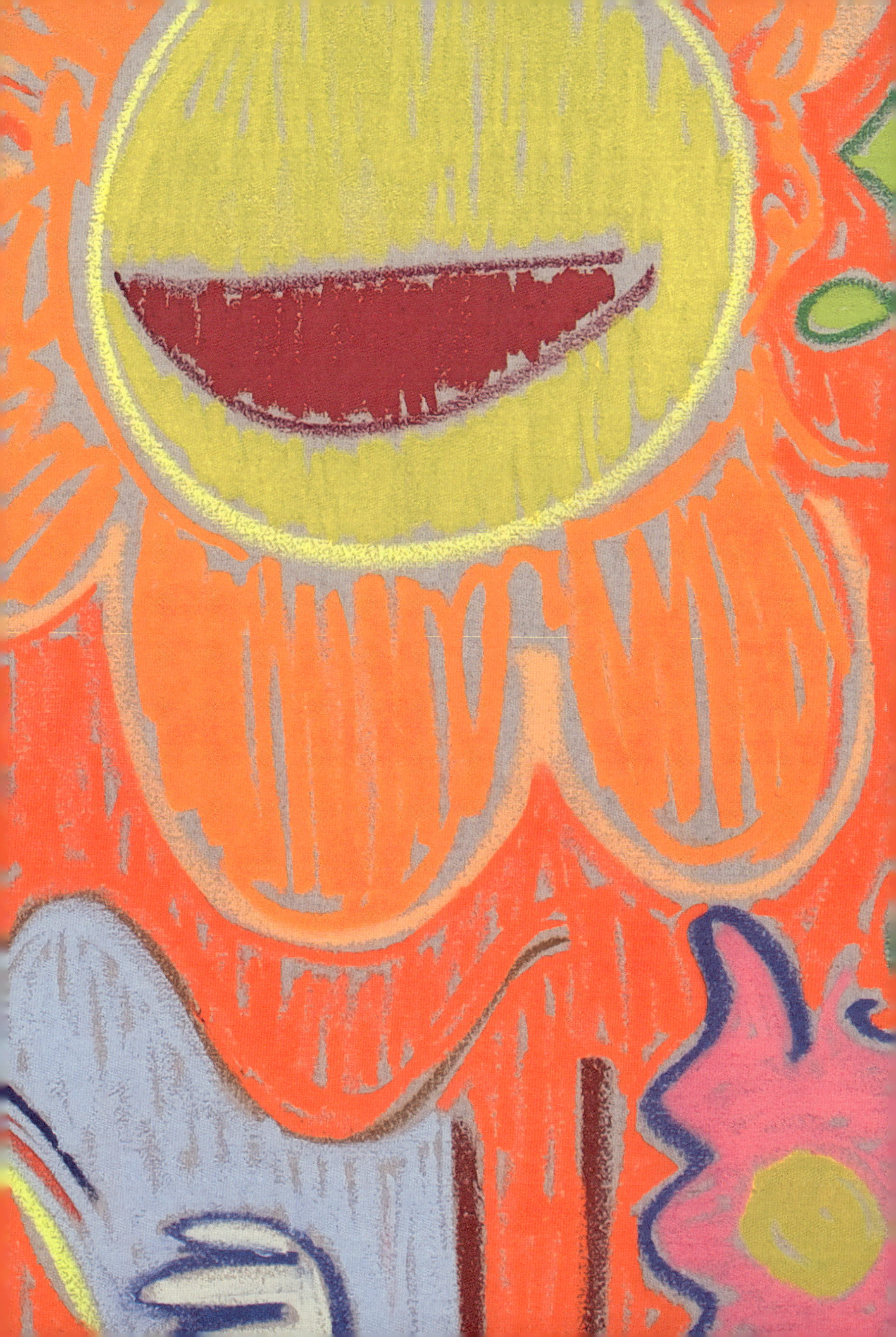

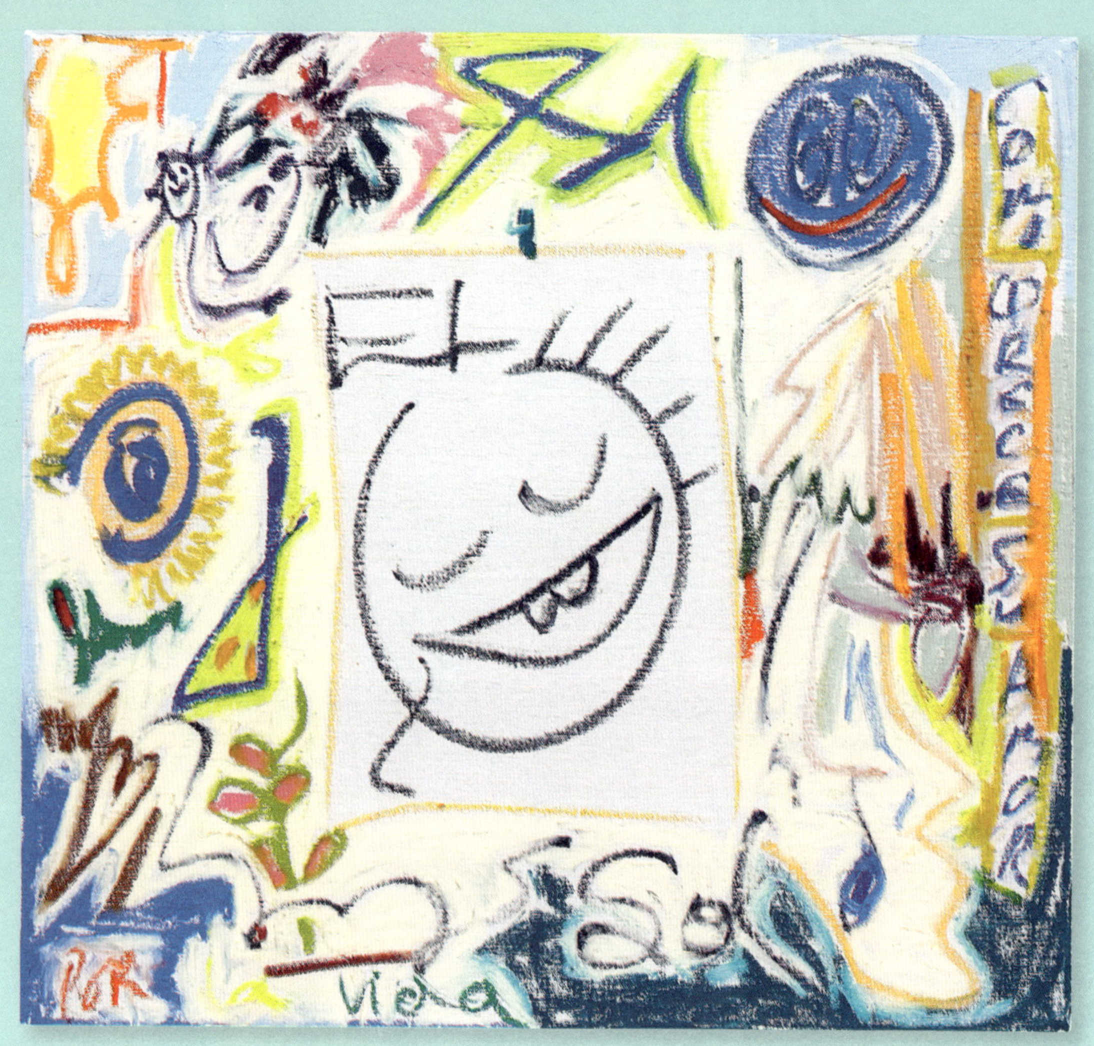

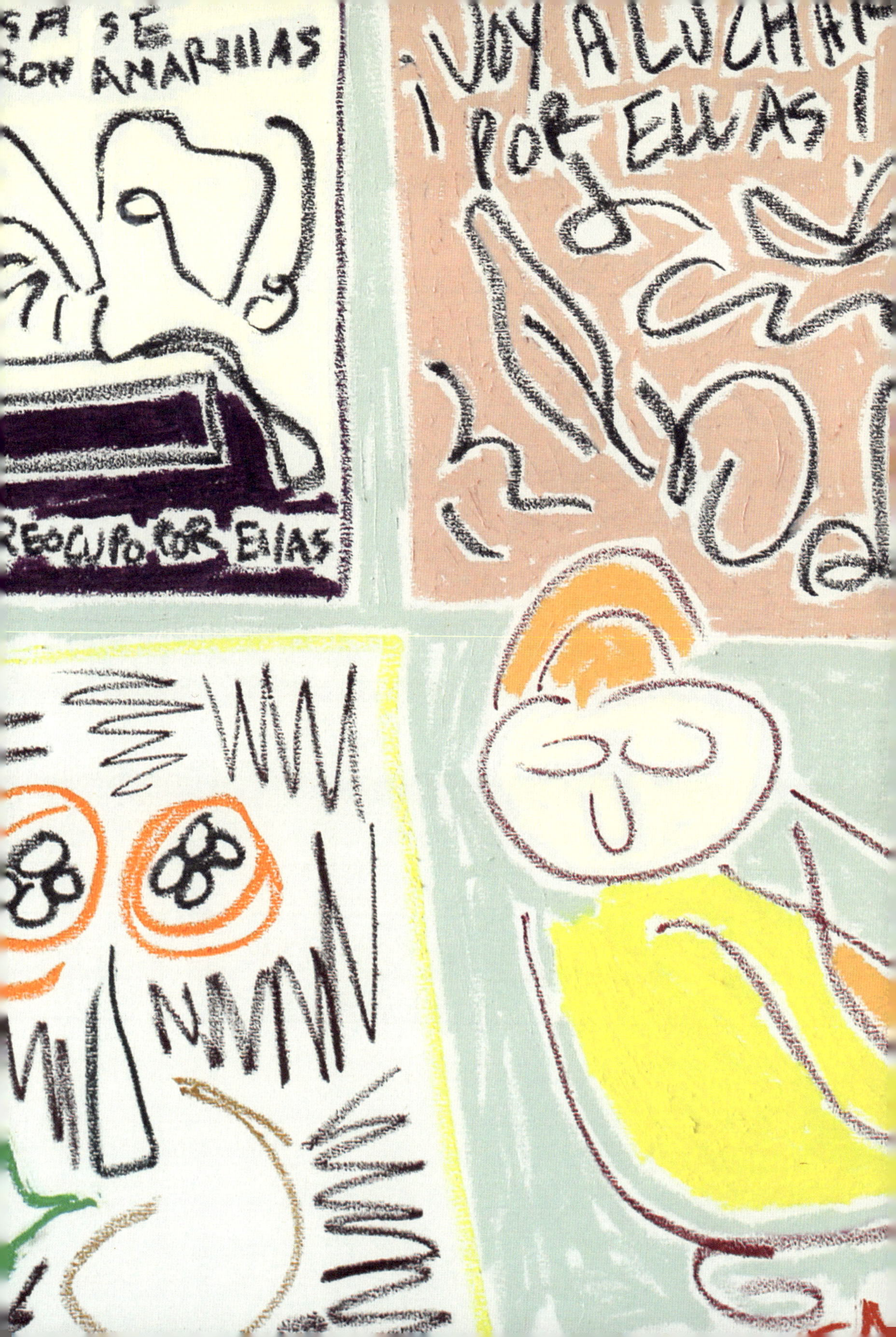
SA SE
RON AMARILLAS
REOCUPO POR ELLAS
¡VOY A LUCHAR
POR ELLAS!

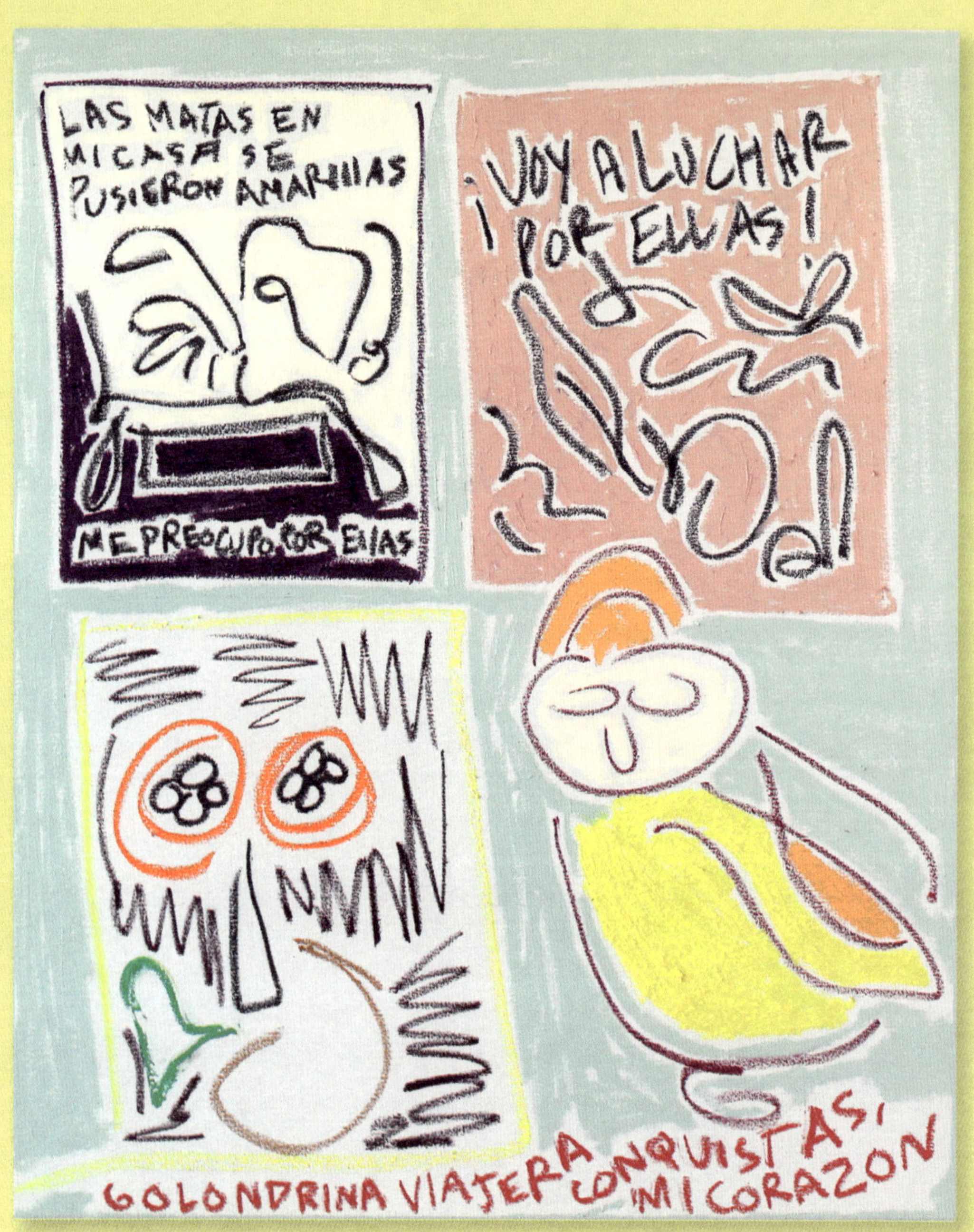

LAS MATAS EN MI CASA SE PUSIERON AMARILLAS
ME PREOCUPO POR ELLAS
¡VOY A LUCHAR POR ELLAS!
GOLONDRINA VIAJERA CONQUISTAS MI CORAZON

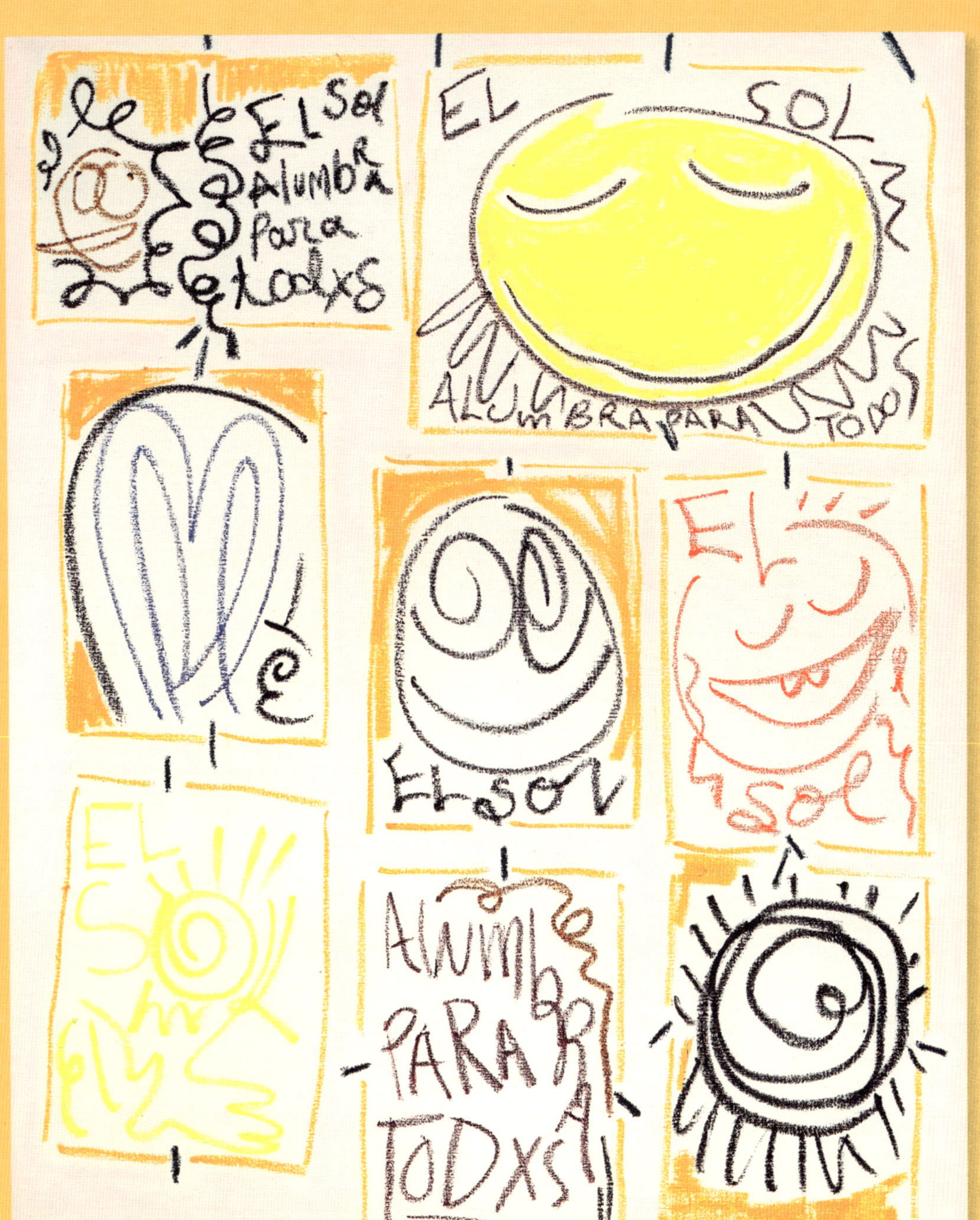

EL SOL ALUMBRA PARA TODXS
EL SOL
ALUMBRA PARA TODOS
EL SOL
EL SOL
EL SOL
ALUMBRA PARA TODXS

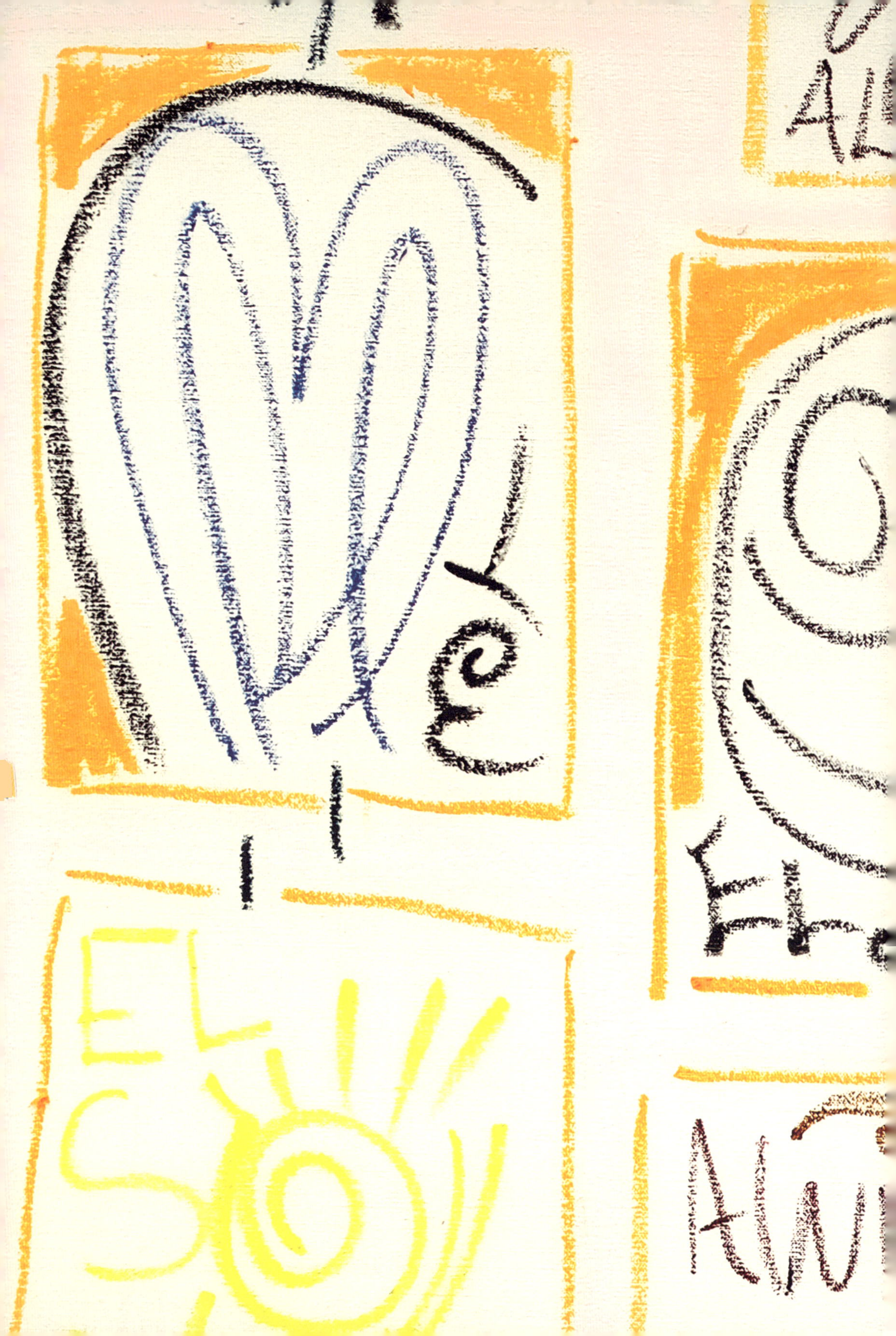
EL
SOL

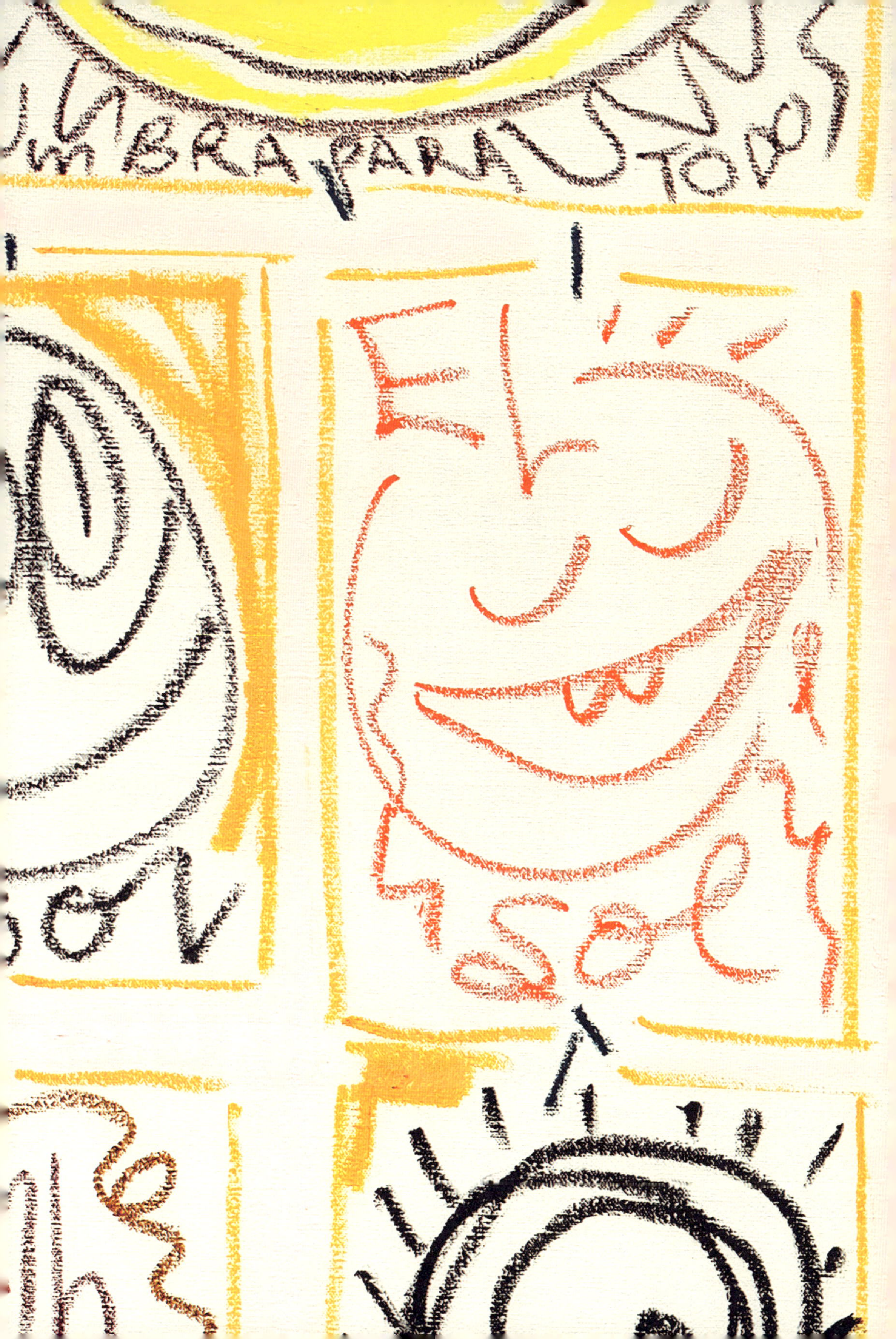
SOMBRA PARA TODOS

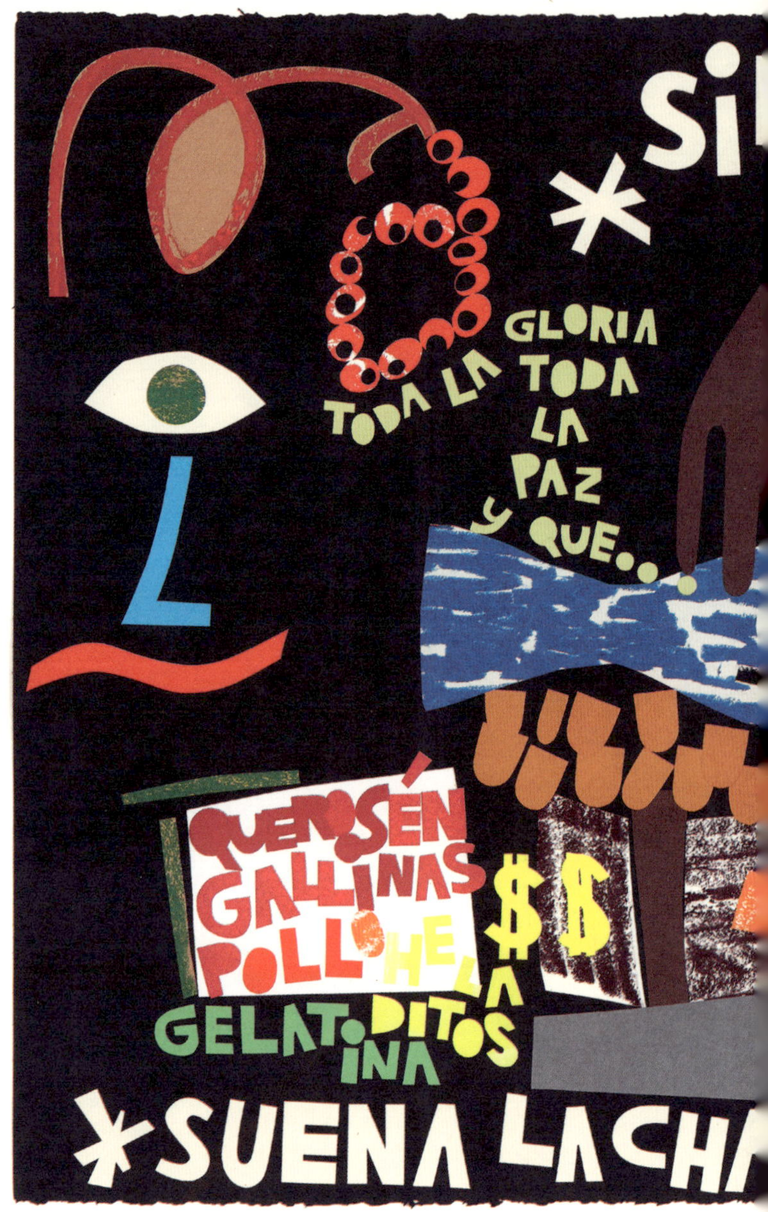

Si
TODA LA
GLORIA
TODA
LA
PAZ
Y QUE...
QUEDESEN
GALLINAS
POLLO HE
GELAT INA DITOS AS
*SUENA LA CHA

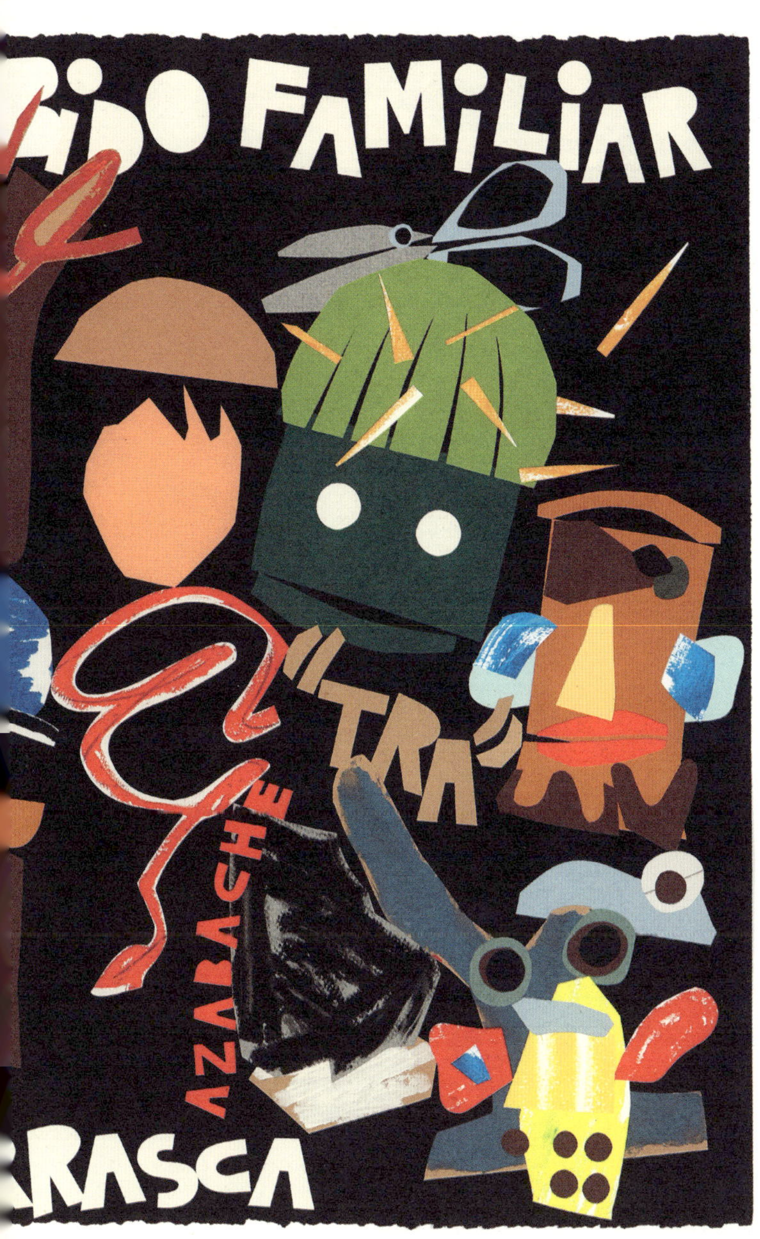
iDO FAMILIAR
"TRA
AZABACHE
RASCA

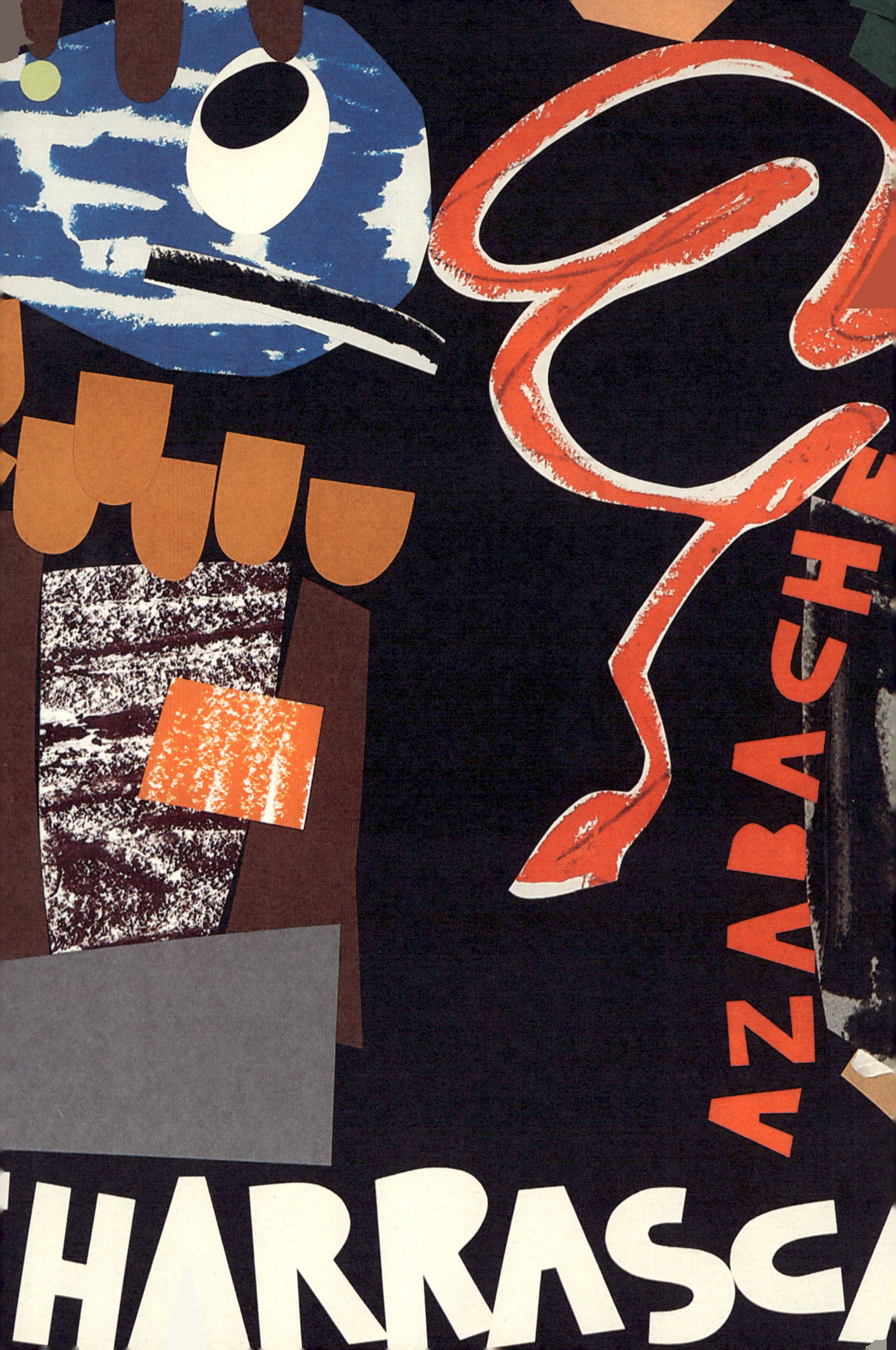

AZABACHE
CHARRASCA

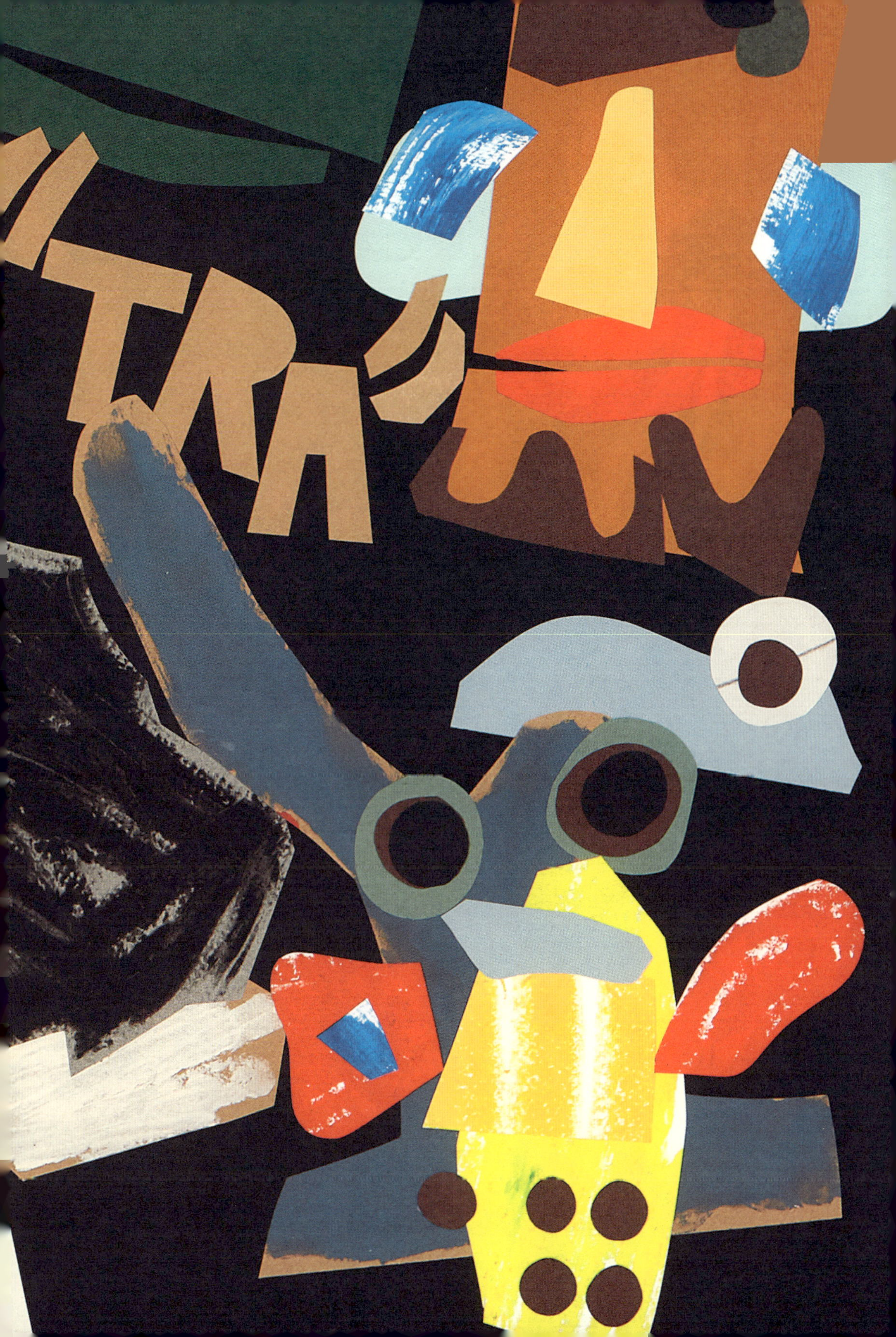

ULTRA

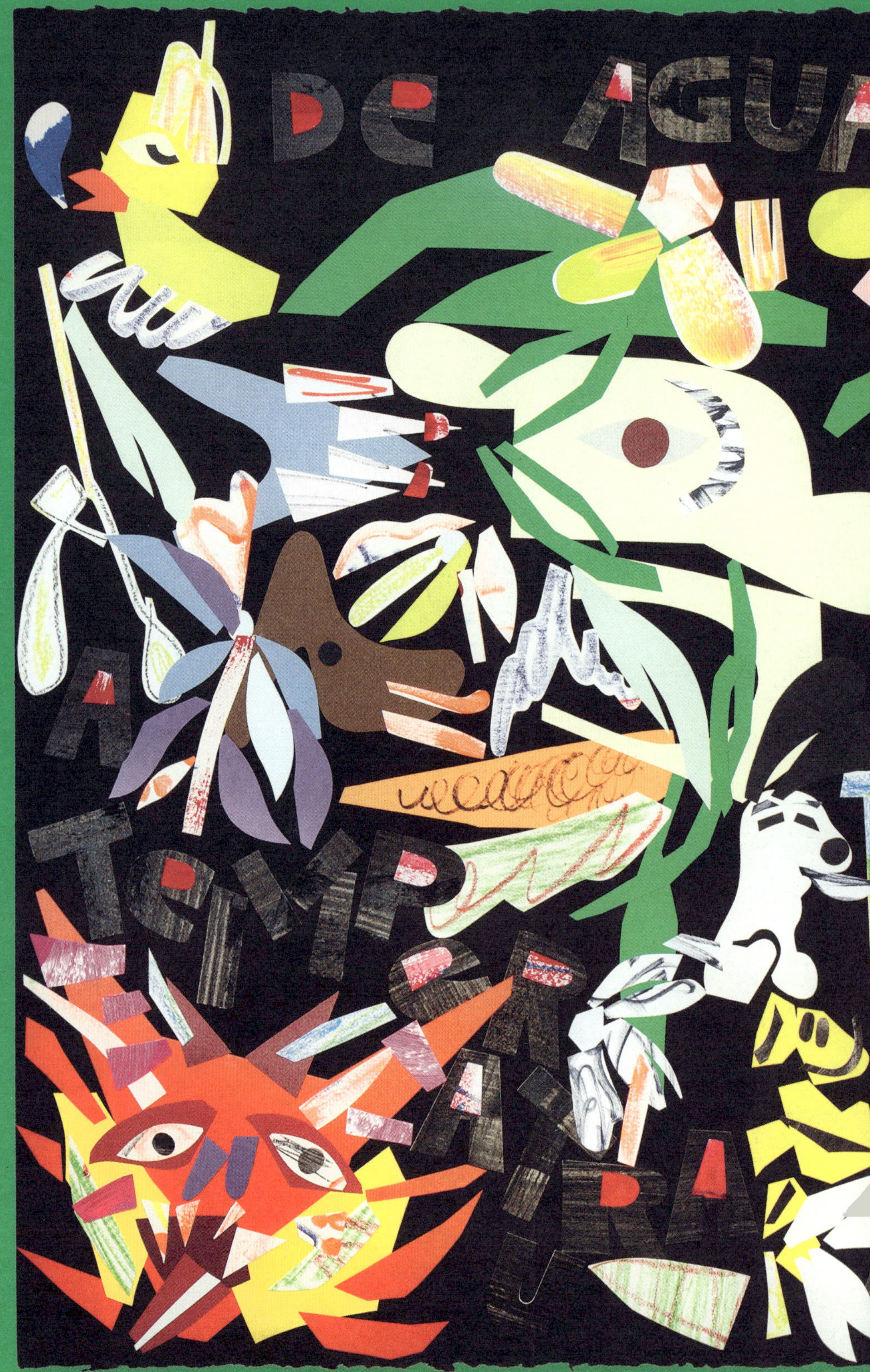
DE AGUA
A TEMPOR
A
RI

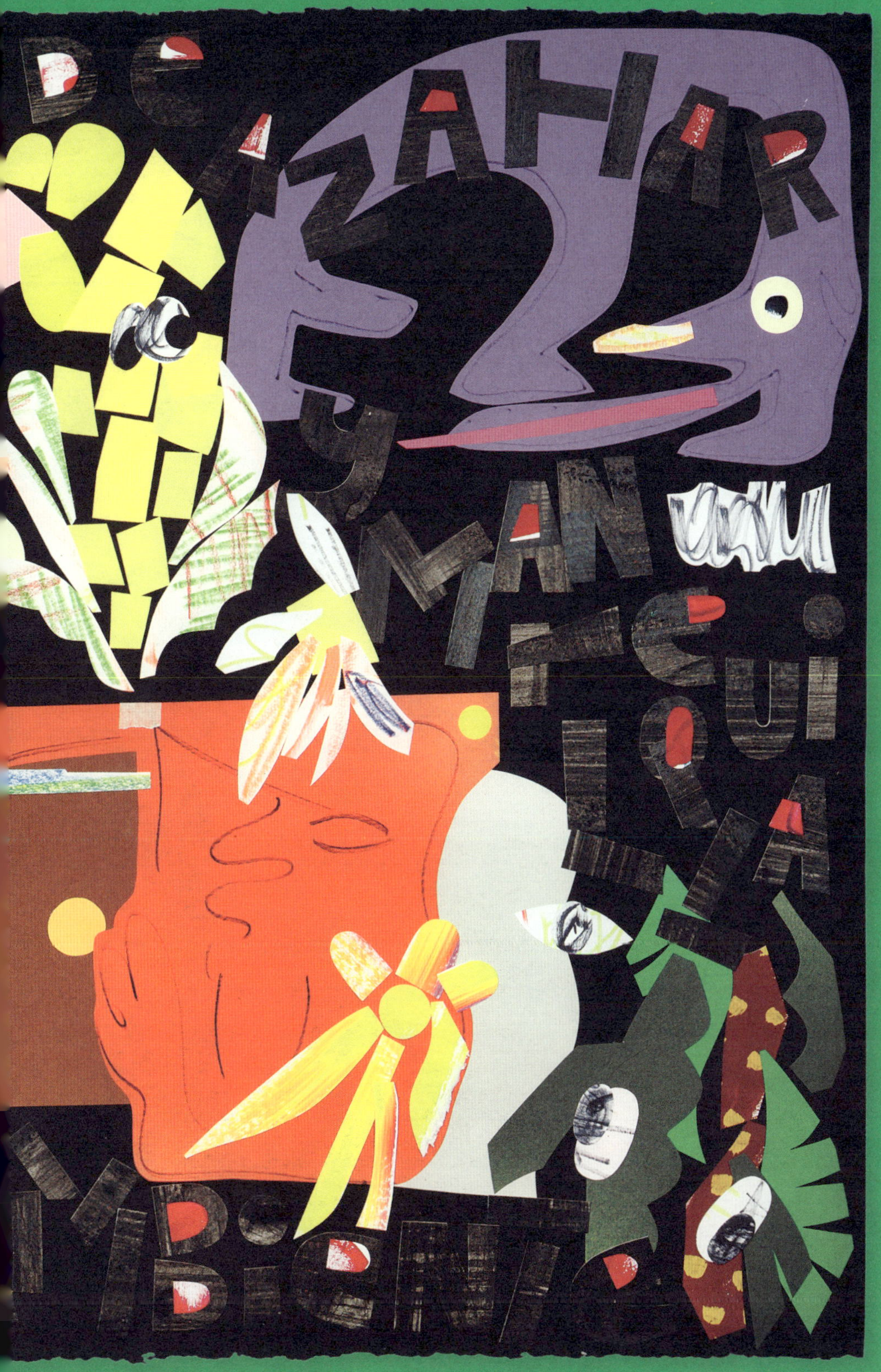

DE AZAHAR
Y MANTEQUILA
Y DICEN

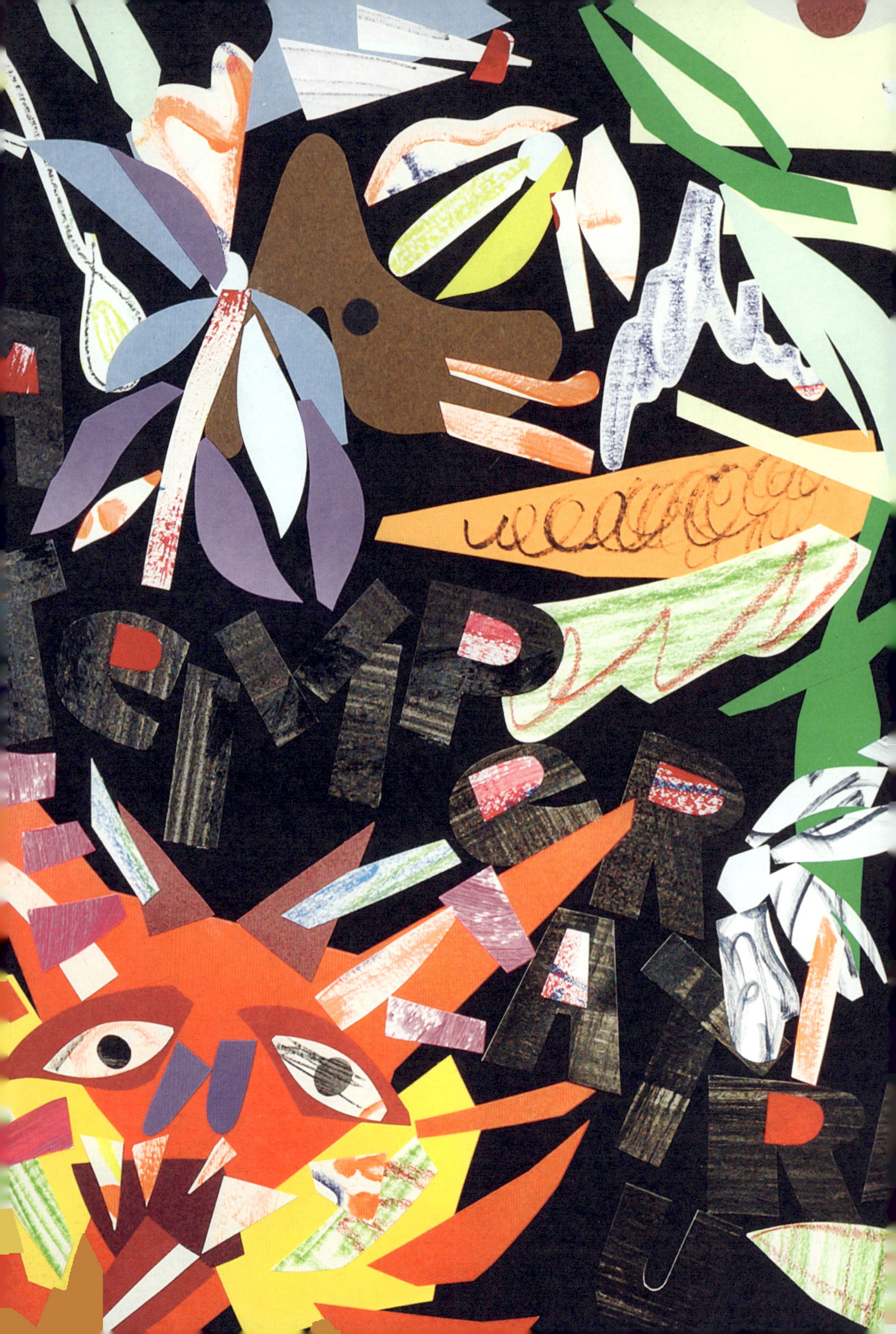

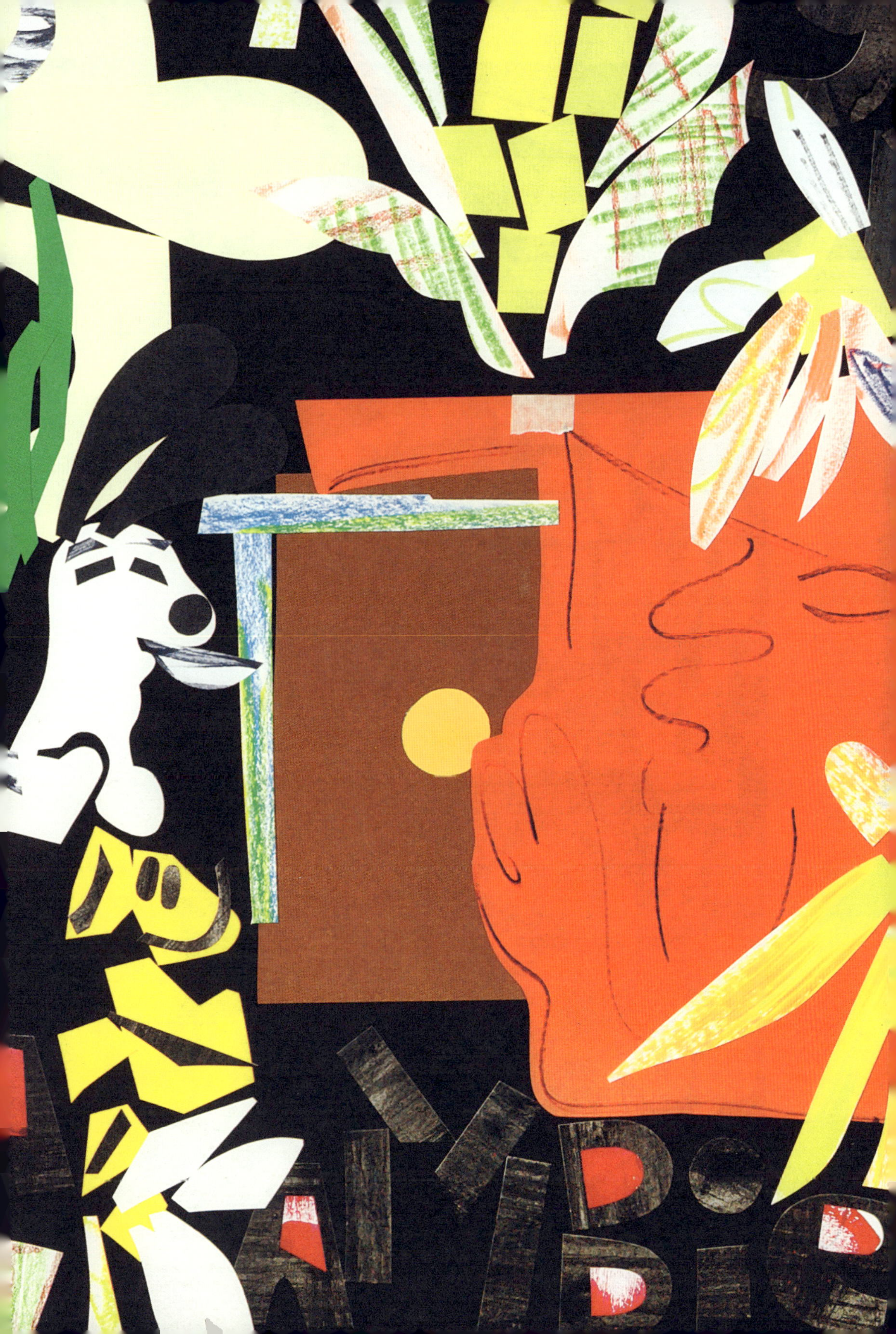

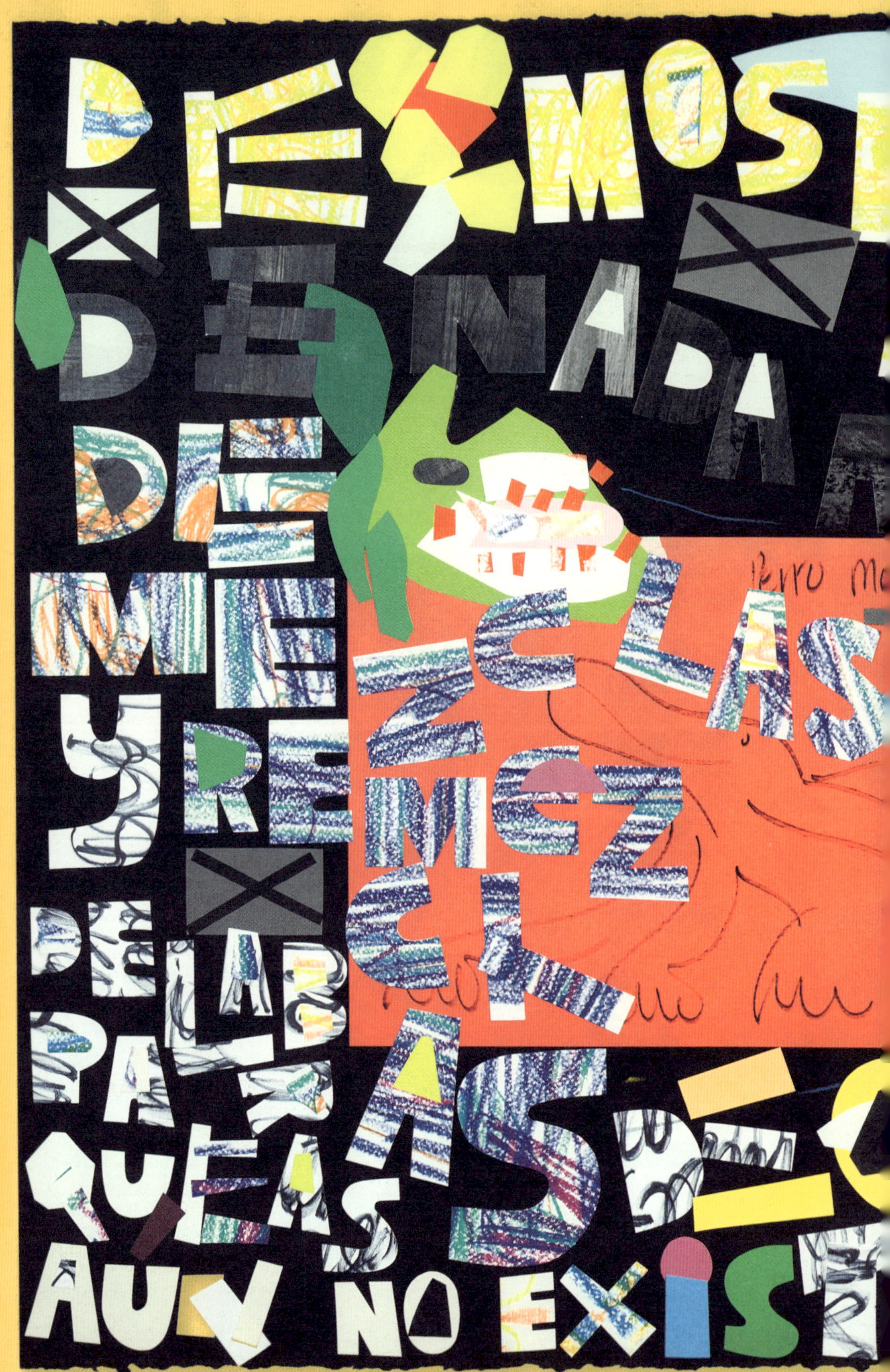

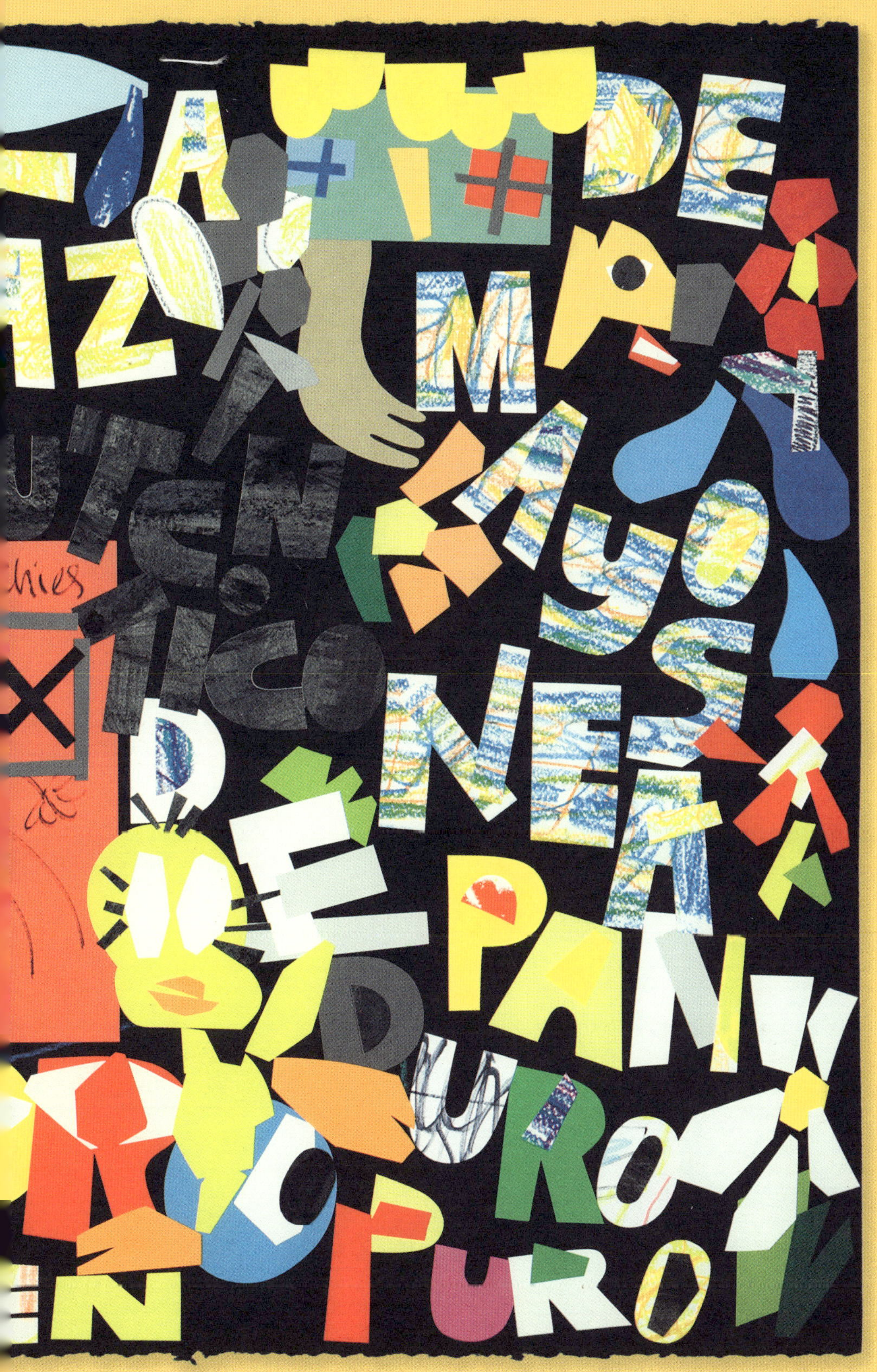

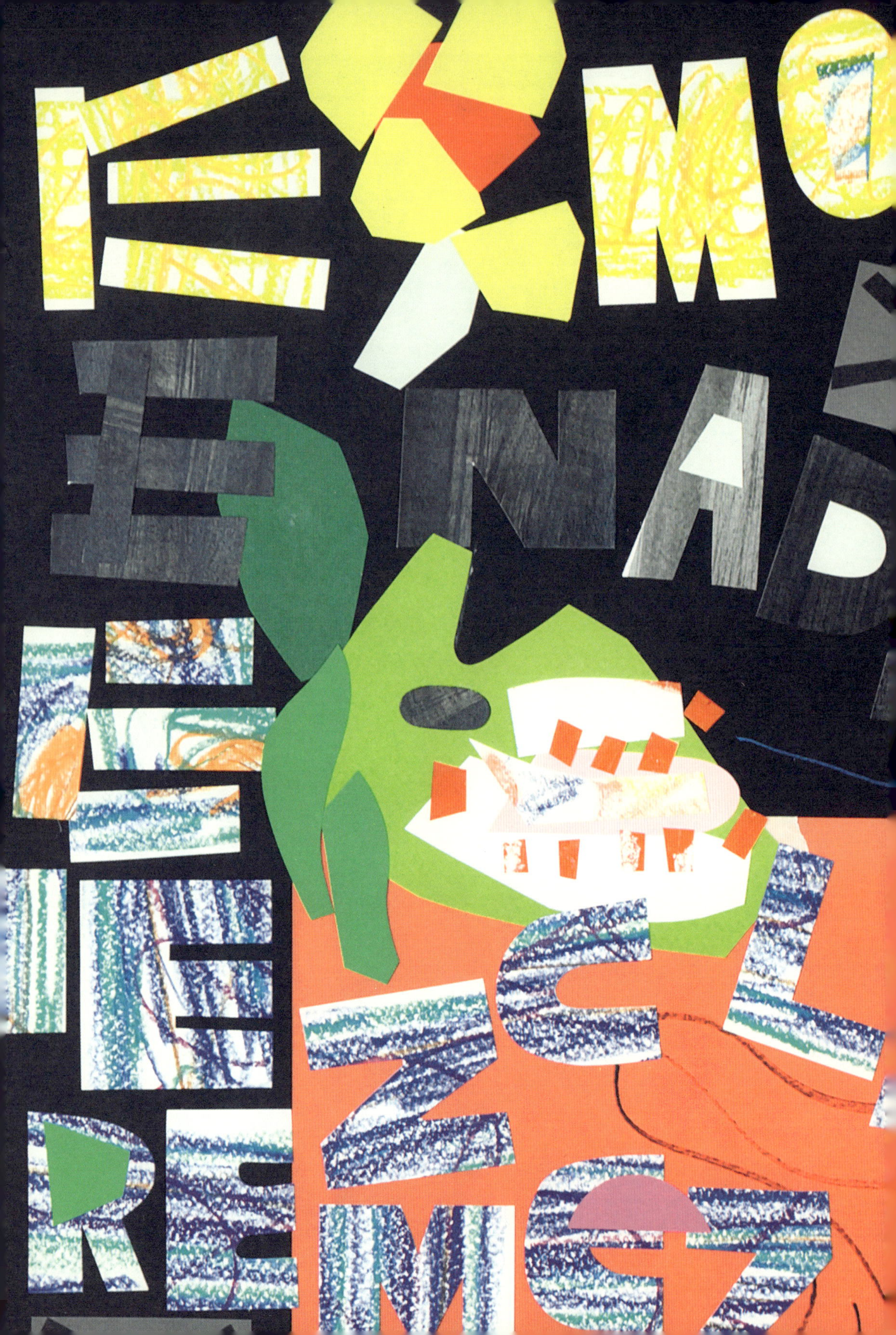

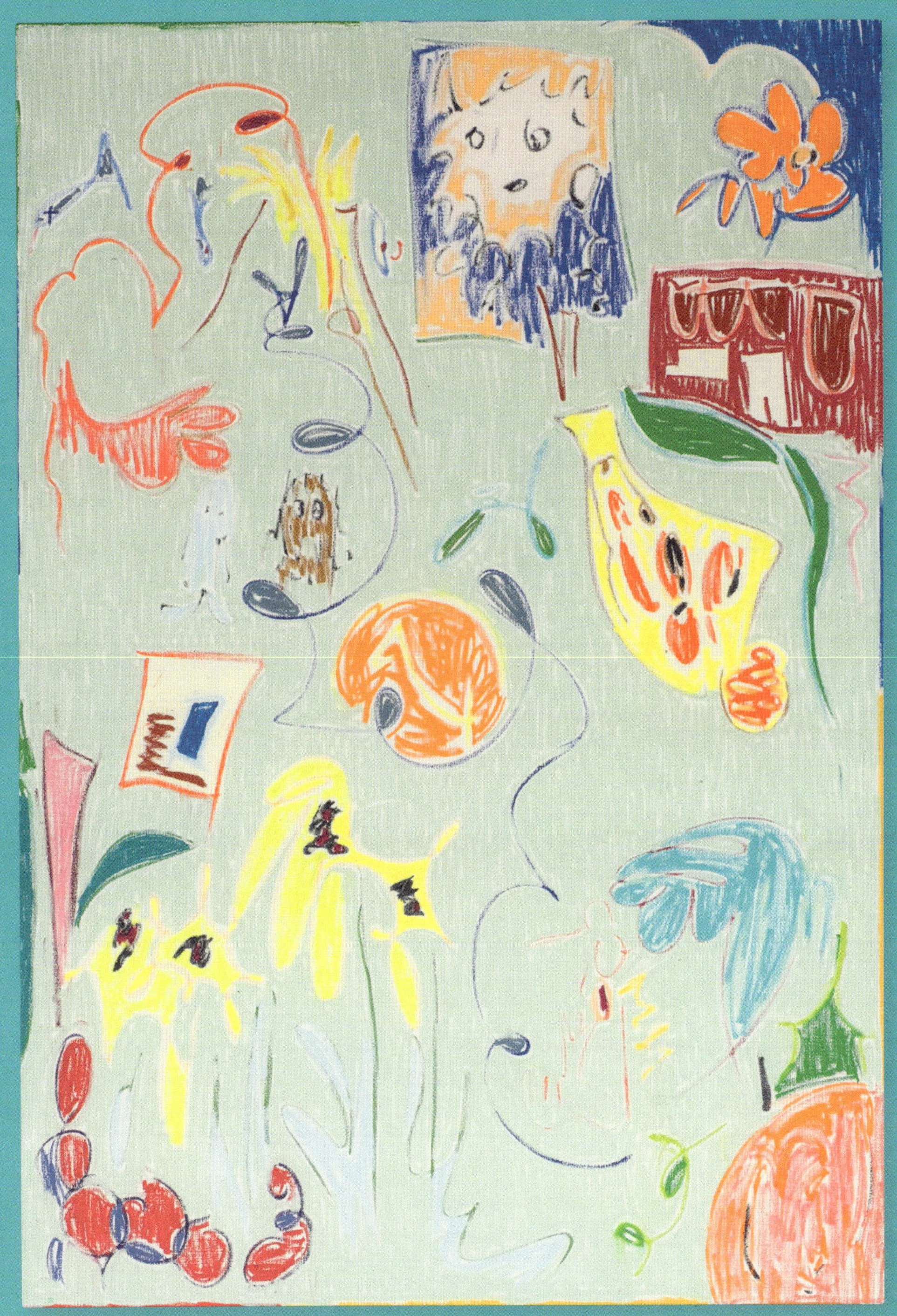

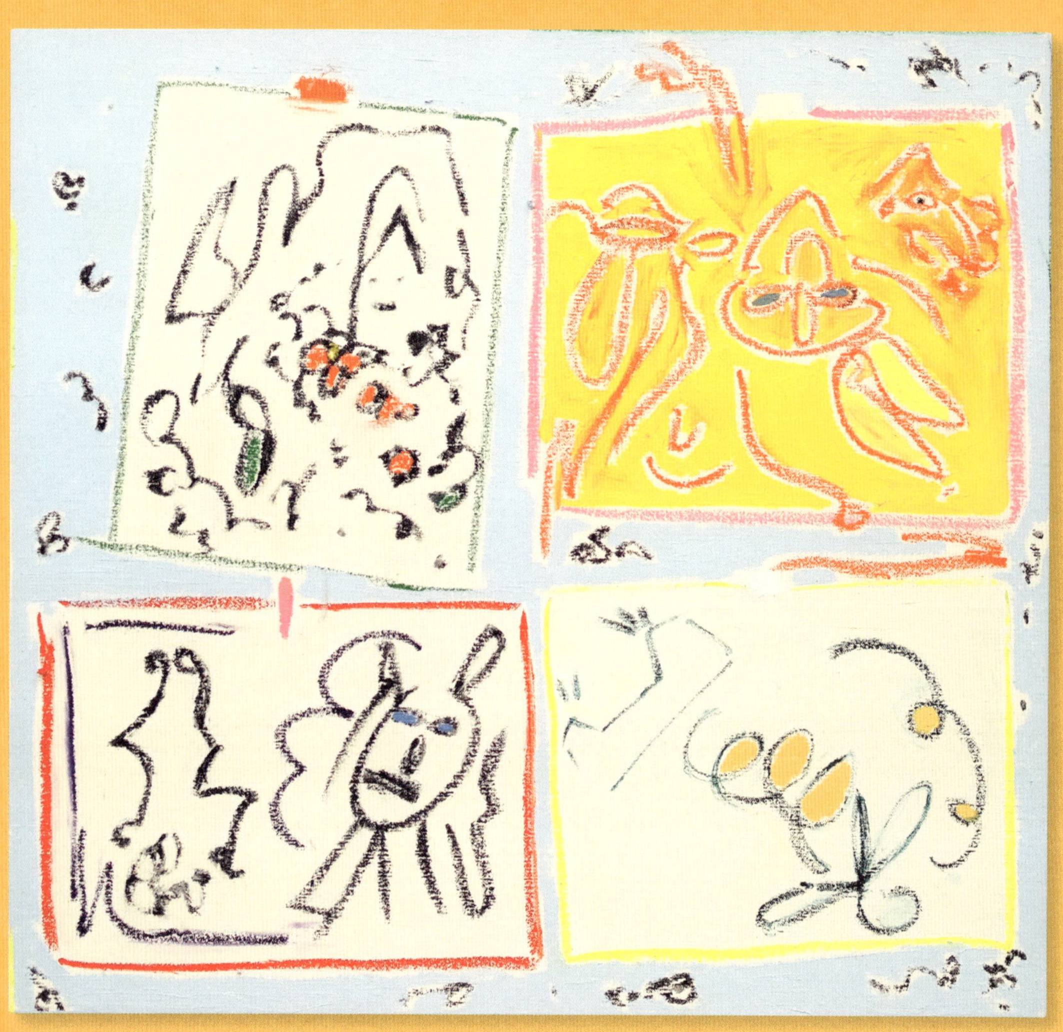

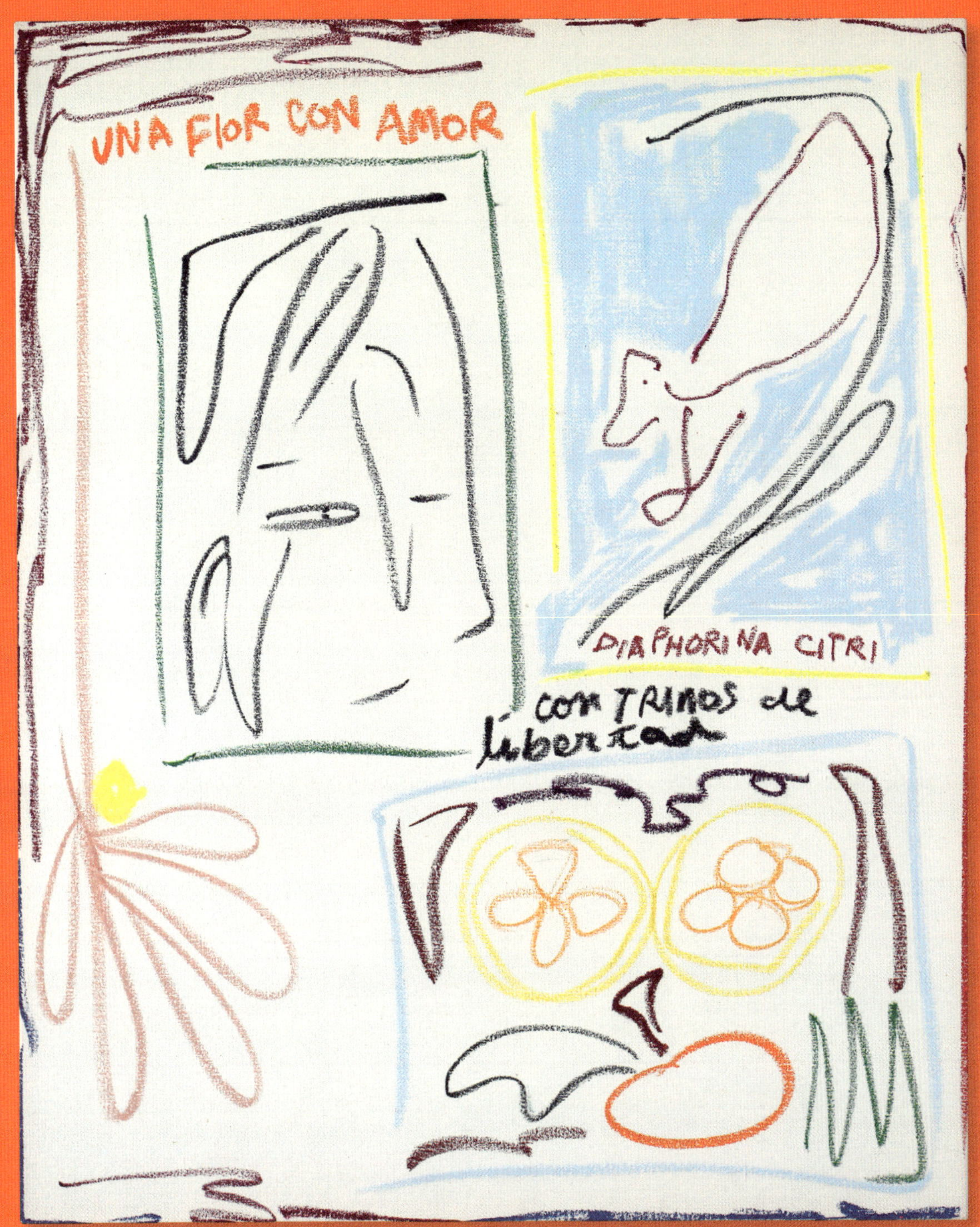

UNA FLOR CON AMOR
DIAPHORINA CITRI
con TRINOS de libertad

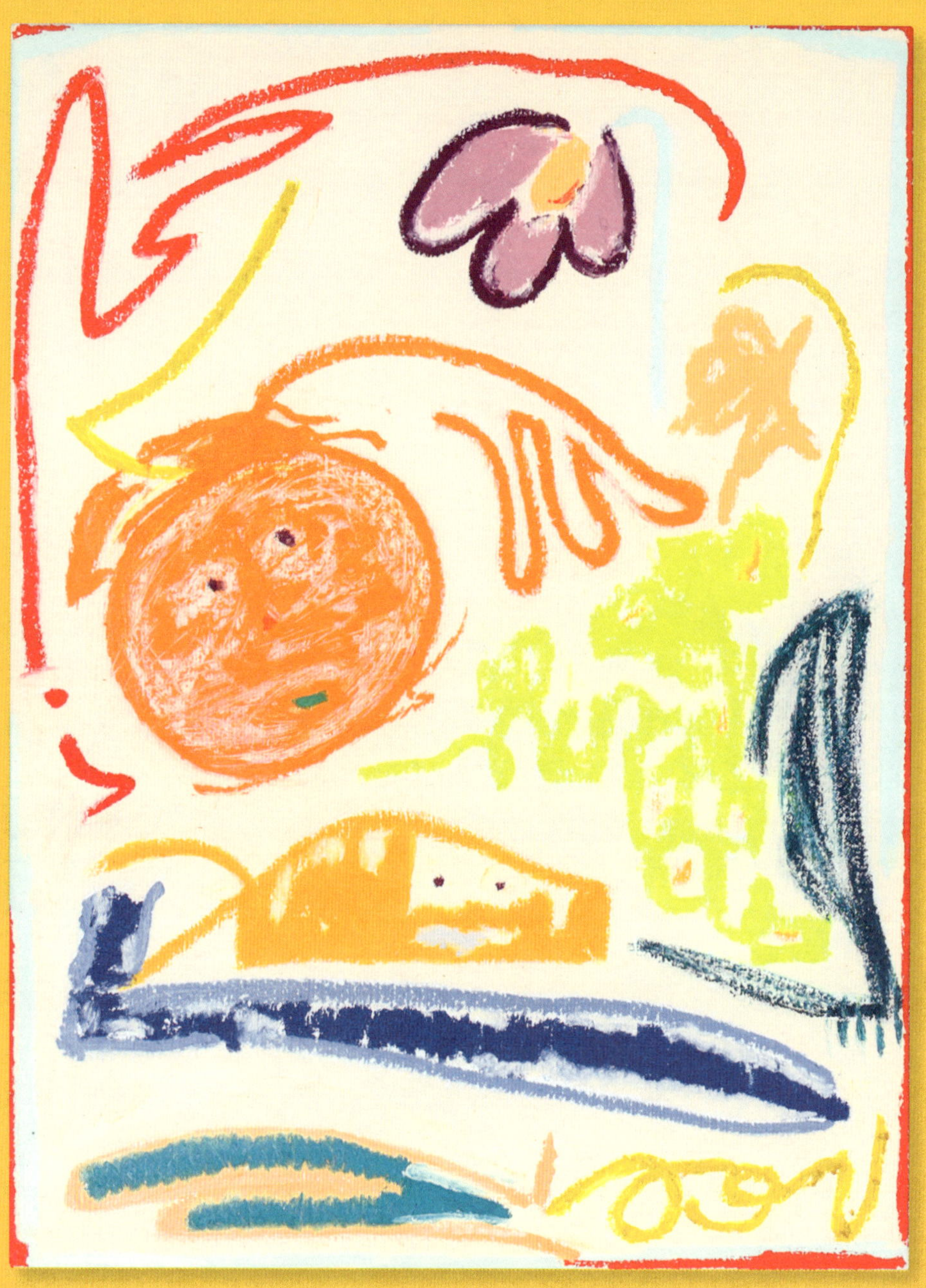

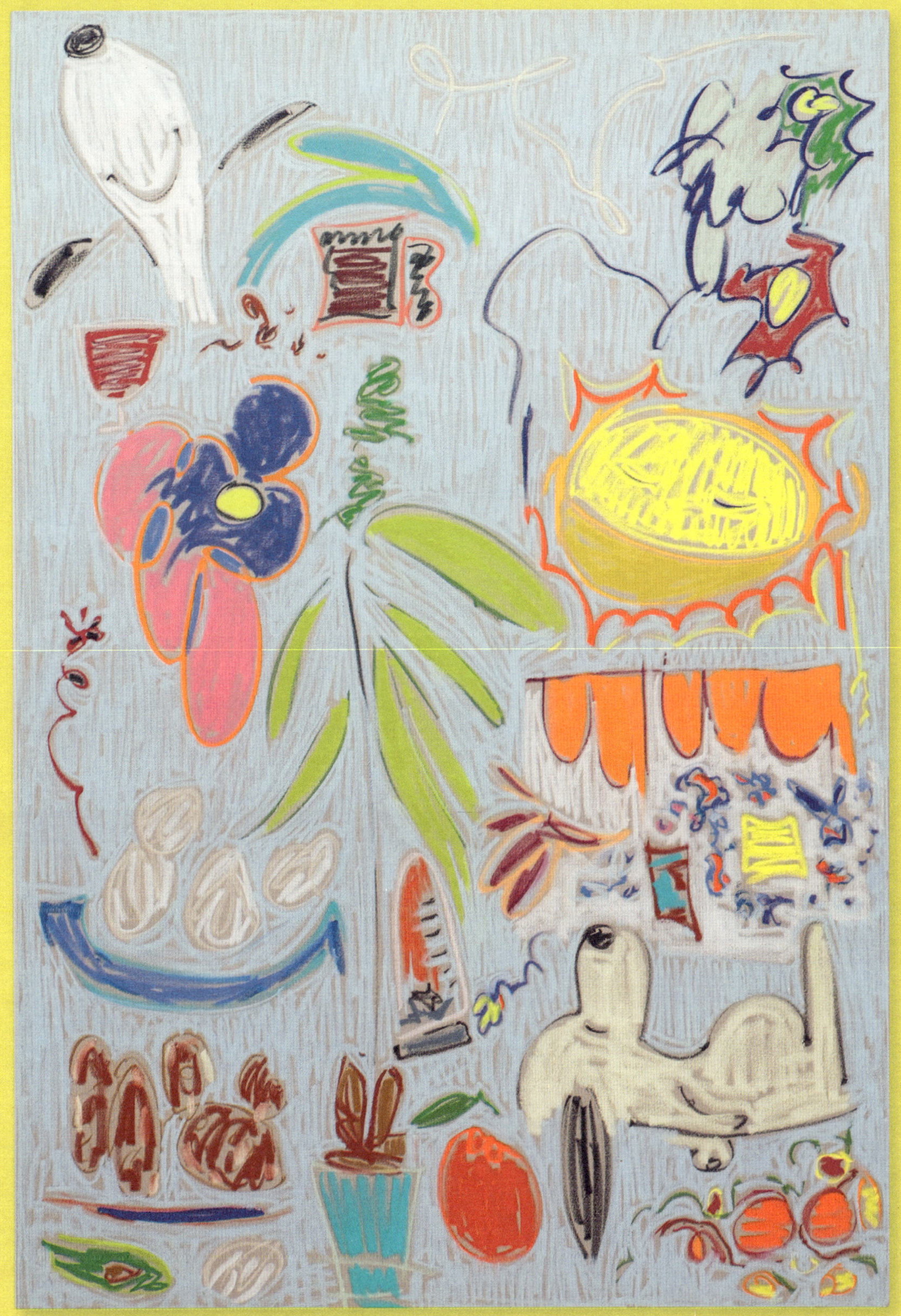

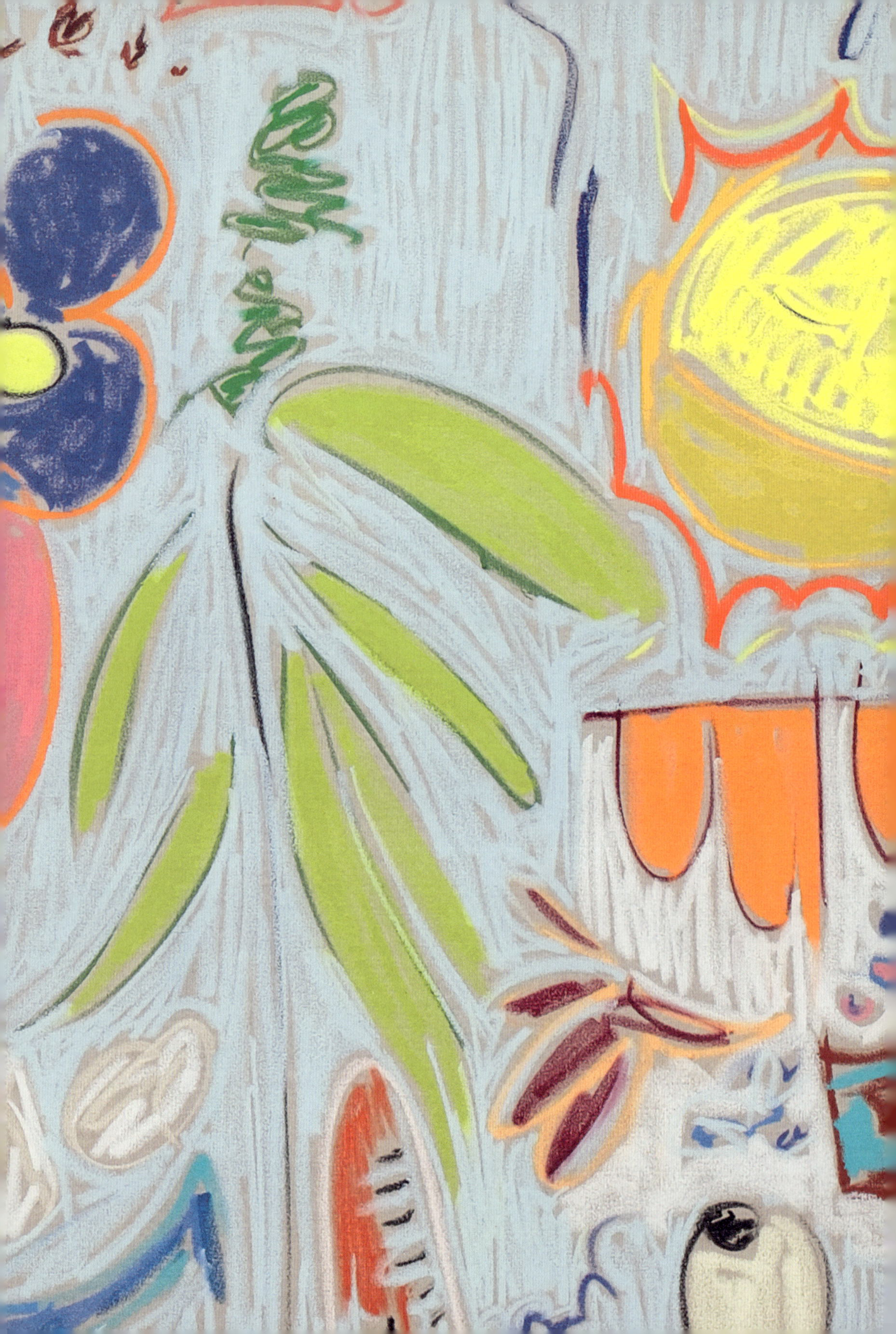

S

P

E   E

C

H

P   A   T

T   E   R

N

I   N

G

Speech Patterns is a cross-generational conversation between the practices of Nadia Hernández and Jon Campbell. Comprising material selected from across their careers, it is also a belated West Coast introduction to two of Australia's most vital artists. The spirit of the exhibition and book respects the differences between their practices while basing their meeting on affinities such as the ways they employ the aural, physical and material aspects of language. Neither formalist nor (explicitly) conceptual, their grounded outlooks pull words and commonly-used phrases from the people and artforms around them to float, protest and cope with personal and political concerns. They do so in dynamic relation to the ever-changing realm of pop and art cultures, while remaining deliberately in synch with the values of their social and family backgrounds.

Without getting too reductive, their methods of making and thinking might fit a label like 'poetic pragmatism'. By 'poetic', I mean that neither artist offers long-form, narrative-based or definitive summaries of experiences; they deal in fragments and evocation. By 'pragmatic', I am referring to philosopher and educator John Dewey's take on art, aesthetics and experience.[1] Holding no truck with 'museum art', Dewey considered art most favourably when it dealt with the grain of daily life. He understood 'aesthetics' as a mode of charged bracketing that amplifies our awareness of the sensations or structures of experience such that we might in fact identify them *as* distinctively meaningful experiences. An aesthetic experience, therefore, is a precise temporal articulation of an aspect of the world that distinguishes it from the regular stream of being/consciousness.[2] It doesn't have to be a peak experience; it can be quite ordinary.[3]

While Dewey's framing might not completely hold, it is pragmatically useful here because it helps us experience the manifold ways that Nadia and Jon's works catch, hold and reshape all manner of things (feelings, thoughts, ideologies, motifs, songs, poems) that might otherwise pass them (and us) by; and, in the process, distil their meanings in a fundamentally *relational* form. It makes lovely sense that Nadia refers to some of her works as 'field recordings' if we understand that recording is an active process that changes and reforms what has been collected and brings it into dialogue. In the work of Nadia and Jon we might consider the form of the recording to be a modernism they have co-opted as a medium or device to carry, embellish and heighten the intensity of their found materials. Though that's perhaps too strong an object–subject division. It may be better to say that they operate from within streams of consciousness shaped by layers of culture and experience, from which they creatively seize this element over that, translating them as they go and wrestling with their effects and affects. This all sounds rather too abstract – a matter that will be rectified, I hope, by listening-in to the signifying waves of several specific artworks.

♥

Since the beginning of her career, Nadia has arranged and recomposed voices of family and friends as a way of making room for the presences of those she is close to but far away from. Her works are gatherings in which singular authorship is not deconstructed but recalibrated from within a swirling collective that honours a multiplicity which is real and felt. Commentators of Nadia's work have typically (and correctly) noted that this quality is a response to her position as a queer Latinx woman residing in Australia. Yet it is not simply the result of her displacement from Venezuela, but a generative methodological platform that guides her work's unfolding within the complex pathways of dis- and inter-connection. In this regard, to consider Nadia's work is to be already inside it, to realise that one is somehow pitched within a tangle of people and places, hopes and sadness, alliances and losses. The work's difficult clarity comes from her ability to hold contradiction as she gathers the rush and pulse of the world in its bounds.[4]

In the trio of 2018 hanging textile works *Cae El Telón De La Noche, Un Ejército De Luces Entretejen La Ciudad (The Curtain Of The Night Falls, An Army Of Lights Interlace The City)*, *Arco Iris De Colores Alegran La Lejandad (Rainbow of Colours Brighten The Distance)* and *Bólidos Zizagueantes Atrapan La Soledad (Zigzagging Race Cars Trap Loneliness)* the bold shapes, bright colours and zesty phrasing stitch together a speech pattern based on one of her grandfather's poems. As an assemblage they evoke a sense of optimism *and* apprehension: *Rainbow of Colours Brighten The Distance* registers hope while *The Curtain Of The Night Falls, An Army of Lights Interlace the City* warns against the danger of illumination. Possibility and constriction address each phrase without cancelling themselves out. There is an opening and a folding-over that mirrors Nadia's relation to a political situation she emerges from yet is outside of. As she says:

These were the first works where I was looking at family connections while I wasn't physically present with them. We have lost so much from the regime. It has stripped from us so much of our relationships with each other. Culture and art gets lost, museums were being closed down and looted. In this context the poem is a tool, a non-violent weapon.[5]

The combination of words Nadia uses to describe the work – poem/tool, non-violent/weapon – reveal the spirit of a cultural revolutionary for whom creation must continue in order for her to critique, to disarm, to empower, and to think beyond the present antagonistic situation. She stages this mode of pressing against limits by stitching her grandfather's words into the semi-abstract hangings; words are blocked off against intrusion and their geometric form sharpens their declarative yet ambivalent communicative force. They proclaim, they hang, they evoke, they wait.

They also highlight a state of vulnerability. The three works can be seen as a hopeful yet mournful hymn about the ways visual art and poetry inhabit public and private space. Often brief, elliptical and ephemeral, poetry cannot be burned down; it can continue to exist in the writer's and reader's minds as they move through the world.[6] From this perspective, by transferring the poem into a three-dimensional realm, Nadia acts out its energetic freedom while making us aware that its new physical and artistic form is prey to potential destruction and ruin: textile poems can be torn down, stolen, burned.

The works stage both possibilities; the poem might still drift away from the work, become atmospherically poetic and fragmentarily non-linear, such that it continues its liberating and memorial function. This dynamic is the tacit background theatre of the work, its mode of gathering signifying momentum. Indeed, it's a dynamic that guides several of Nadia's works as her installations – staged as events more than exhibitions – are so clearly expectant spaces full of tragic buoyancy and optimistic despair about the past, the present and the coming thing. The focus on experiential encounter through material strategies of representation brings the body of the viewer fully into play, of course. As we walk around the works, understanding their physical presence, direct simplicity and evasive shades, we are aware that they do not merely signify their messages but perform them.

In *Como el sol y toda su energía (Like the sun and all its energy)*, 2020, Nadia uses this method in tribute to her great grandmother. The title phrase is an anecdote from one of Nadia's cousins who described their grandmother 'in the most beautiful and simple of ways: your great grandmother was like the sun and all its energy'. The work rains sunshine in words and in the shapes that frame them. And its arrangement of positive and negative space animates everything around it, creating a larger emotional weather pattern. Within its low and high pressure systems, language is sliced into the world as a bridge to becoming. Nadia links natural and generational orders, commingling their energies and capacities to enhance life.

Como el sol y toda su energía was made just before the COVID-19 pandemic and, unsurprisingly, the works completed in its wake employed growth motifs to keep this vital spirit in play. *Por la vida: El Sol, como crece su amor*, 2020, is a good example. In English, the title reads 'For life: the sun, how much its love grows'. Nadia says she made the work:

> when everything was shutting off and I didn't know what was going to happen. I fully freaked out, locked my studio and headed to Brisbane. I had a big impulse to sun symbolism; I wanted to flood the studio and myself with an extreme sense of positivity because I felt super helpless. The sun is important because it makes things grow; our planet turns around it. It is the optimism of being held in the patterns of growth, the cycles that we have known, that generate growth.

These works aim to create the means to remain part of the rhythmic pattern of life, a process that takes one forward within fields of relation. We see this too in *Una flor con amor, Diaphorina Citri, con trinos de libertad (A flower with love, Diaphorina Citri, with trills of freedom)*, 2019. The painting shows the interdependence between the state of Nadia's houseplants and her own emotional situation. Made during a breakup, this work features dispirited foliage with strange fruit that droop in solidarity with her spirit and from a period of relative neglect. The point here is that no event is isolated: everything ripples outwards, everything is a kind of companioning.

These ideas are forcefully present in the paper-cut works that were initially made to raise awareness about political issues in Venezuela. Bringing forth the legacy of the political poster, their

high-contrast intensity depicts the agitated and enervated bustle of a people speaking back to the regime. *La Fuerza Es La Unión / Strength Comes From Union*, for instance, was created in 2015 after Nadia had just come back from a visit to her home town. Arguing against the government's efforts to polarise the population in order to weaken its ability to form a strong oppositional force, the work expresses her fundamental solidarity with her family and the people who remained.

The punchy focus of this (and other early works) are complemented by recent paper-cuts that are rather more tumultuous, such as *De pan duro, de oro puro / Of stale bread, of pure gold*, 2021. The text here is based on a tongue-twister Nadia learned as a child. Its densely layered spray of words and letters visually matches the sensation of trying to keep up with a complicated rhyme that is seemingly forever escaping us. Importantly, this failure is creative: the impending breakdown of meaning in the tongue-twister form offers a space for a new story to be composed. The original verse simply conveys the wonders of pure gold, but her tweaked version holds the aspirational trope in ethical check against the context of people living in an oil-rich country who can't afford stale bread. The hectic feel of the work alludes to a possible failure to process, or keep up with, this fact. The 'X' in the piece, for Nadia, represents a file or an image which can't be loaded on a computer – processing power has failed; there is too much complexity to allow the item to reveal itself. Accordingly, the words are massively animated yet caught in the equally immense static of expectation. The work as a whole jitters in sympathy, attempting to hold the shaken fullness of the matter.

This is not a tangential or incidental occurrence in Nadia's practice. On the contrary, *active holding patterns* are a major part of her productive management of ambivalence and ambiguity. This approach is present in the overloaded precision of her maximalist paper-cuts, but is most clearly articulated in the paintings in which a sketchy flurry typically troubles the surface while also acting as a unifying force for component motifs. Within the bounds of these paintings symbols cohere then decay as the eye darts around the canvas, never quite finding a place to rest. In this manner, Nadia fashions places to attend to the rhythms and tumult of life, and its modes of temporality. There is the time of remembering, the time of forgetting, of noticing, of moving on, of return – all of which are subtly different experiences, none of which are fixed in place or privileged over another.

At times, Nadia refers to the segmentations that animate several of these paintings as vignettes. This is particularly the case in *Consejos, cosas que son difíciles de robar, y 'Chinita' (Nuestra Señora de Chiquinquirá)* / (Advice, things that are difficult to steal and *'Chinita' (Our Lady of Chiquinquirá)*), 2019. The painting came into being when she was doing online research about a disease affecting citrus plants in Venezuela: 'I had a huge array of open tabs and I was overwhelmed about how to process the information'. This matched how she felt about addressing all the other issues facing people 'back home': 'I found it impossible to find one word or sentence to simplify things; the only way I could process it all was in a series of vignettes'. This led her to create cartoon-like sections portraying a loose story about a bug and the virgin of Chiquinquirá reaching her hand into a bag of citrus fruit. The story symbolises the binding of contemporary issues and traditional cultural forms. The vignette structure does not offer stability (or reduction) of meaning but makes us aware of the ongoing flow of the intermingling itself. It speaks as much about imaginary future relations as it does about what is actually presented within the frames.

The point is that her canvases are porous fields of encounter, and increasingly so. The large paintings from 2022, *Entre otras cosas ...*, *Pinta flores, pinta aguacates ...*, *and Pinta ... cacao, chocolate ...*, are each composed from motifs, symbols and characters from popular culture and everyday life that were suggested by people close to Nadia, including her mother, grandmother, girlfriend and best friend.[7] Some items were chosen because they were subjects Nadia is known to enjoy, while some were random ideas about other things they really wanted her to paint. In each instance, Nadia rendered these sketchy, open motifs into new dialogues with each other. In this zone, there is a quality of imaginary translation in play, as if she is imbuing the ideas with the traits of their passage from person to person to person. In this way they are brought to life in an amorphous state that is close and distant at the same time, and, again, in a state of continual creation and recreation. This is dramatised by the familiar strangeness of popular culture characters in particular, like Snoopy and Tweety. Such North American fictional figures were part of her childhood – friends in a way. They express familiarity, and therefore family. These works honour the significance of these 'actors' in our minds as well as how, in their new guises, they become chimeric energies that bind us in shared

recollection *and* in the gum of change. The past is present but never as it was. The world is mutable, fundamentally in flux.

It's worth pausing here to consider the presence of the grand, looping, highly poetic titles that pulse ahead of and around Nadia's works. Often these are handwritten on the works themselves in such a way that they render her words as pictorial, rhythmic threads in the world that she is holding space for. This is reminiscent of Louis Marin's evocative description of a sequence of 11 poems handwritten by Picasso about the weather. He suggests they open up:

> a present-time I call intensive; it is the time of poetic creation, or, to put it more precisely, that of the pregnancy of the visual in the textual, the eruption of the gaze in the reading of letters, the germination of a cosmic, solar eye in the gray and white flux, the snow of signs.[8]

This is all so pertinent – the snow of signs, the time of poetic creation, the visual in the textual; the systems of meaning becoming matter that scatters through us, communicating physically. Nadia's work *Mantequilla a temperatura ambiente / Of butter at room temperature*, 2021, uses this approach quite specifically. It was initially inspired by one of her mother's recipes that she 'found too much poetry in'. She intended to use a line from the recipe in the form of a banner in order to release that format from its solely protest-oriented role, while still keeping the collective in play. Nadia considers the work to be about 'a state of union, in the way butter melts and fuses with the other ingredients to shift and change things'. Its titular phrase states what it represents and expressively signals it. But new meaning springs from the coming together of the elements – a newly flavoured whole emerges that is about what it is to feel hope, physically and emotionally; what it is to yearn for transition.

Again, this is underwritten by an attempt to process, and to hold, the difficulty of living while the processing occurs. In a certain manner Nadia's work here enacts the extreme difficulty of the 'relational position' articulated by Édouard Glissant, who argued that the mode:

> is linked not to a creation of the world but to the conscious and contradictory experience of contacts among cultures; is produced in the chaotic network of Relation and not in the hidden violence of filiation;

does not think of a land as a territory from which to project toward other territories but as a place where one gives-on-and-with rather than grasps.[9]

He proposes a way of thinking beyond ownership and the essentialism of place – but surely this enterprise is incredibly hard to achieve in real life? It exists as an ideal, but when one has no place, no ground, it might at times (or continually for some) be just too much to bear. Even so, this is in part what many of Nadia's works deal with: the effort to give-on-and-with, to not grasp, and yet to still hold on to things … because if one doesn't, what is left? If there is no future unity, even as an idea, might one just drift away?

♥

With the potency of that question in mind, I turn to Jon's practice and begin with a painting that sums up one of his key aesthetic attributes. His work, like Nadia's, uses expressive letters that riff off the visual in the textual and that situate themselves as performances of meaning. They are also often celebratory, which is rare in contemporary art – though Jon's works are never as straightforwardly 'up' as they might appear. We can see this use of lettering in *Fuck Yeah (Matisse)*, 2015. Incorporating the phrase 'fuck yeah' and visual references to Henri Matisse's cut-outs, Jon's painting is a peppy homage which distils the French modernist's late style and congratulates him for it at the same time. At this level it is simple enough, and has a terrifically open-hearted charm. Yet part of this charm comes from the force with which the work breaks a social convention. It is not the swearing that's so powerful, it's that it is a full-voiced personal address. There is body and an implied loudness in play that feels transgressive in an artworld context; the work speaks against expectations that art appreciation should be physically detached and silent. Jon pitches the idea that genuine, impulsive liking could be a unifying force between artist and audience. The jolt of this might make us wonder how Henri would react; would he become puffed up and proud, or bashfully demure? Jon would probably be excited to see this response, but he also makes it okay for his own reaction to stand alone – it's cool to be excited, buzzed by an encounter with an artwork or an artist. And as he gives no reasons for Matisse's greatness, he creates a space where we can just spontaneously

dig stuff. By apparently disregarding the restrictions that might dampen our responses, Jon also flattens the hierarchies that keep high art separate from real life. In this way, the work is also a meditation on rules of behaviour that equally frames the flipside: if art can be everything, and is everywhere, must we *always* be silently engaged, critically alert, careful of treading on, or bumping into it? This question posits an oddly panoptical reading of art as a system of emotional and physical regulation and governance.[10]

This can be seen in relief in *Yeah / Mr. Football*, 2009. The banner depicts 'Mr. Football' (Ted Whitten) leaping up to take a mark for his team, Footscray. Jon made the work to honour a local hero, in a working class area that has had few. Its celebratory tone feels natural because boisterous fandom is expected in sport, and is sanctioned for emotional release. Whitten's mastery is more easily taken as a given than the prowess of the modernist work itself which might be described as 'something my child could have done'. That noted, the reverse idea is in play too: football is constantly critiqued by professional and amateur commentators across all platforms. Could an artist cope with the pressure of a talk-back-radio sledging session of a hundred callers? It is clear that Jon is honouring the confidence to leap, to take a risk, to do your own thing in spite of who the crowd is barracking for. By extension, he is also fashioning his own extended sense of excellence in popular culture which entails works we can take into ourselves without fear of being wrong about them; works that we can drop our guards around because we feel them and encounter them as equals. And we can get beyond ourselves in the process. Even if we don't share the same love of Matisse or Whitten we can liberate ourselves from a contained passion by going hard at what we enjoy.

What are you fuckin lookin at, 2014, however, probably makes us put our guards right back up again. Typically, these words are spat out by someone looking for a fight (which is why there is no question mark in the work). It is impossible to reply to them. If you respond with 'Oh nothing', the rejoinder would be 'You saying I'm nothin are ya?'. If you say 'sorry', they could reply 'so you *were* looking?' If you remain silent, it'd be 'I asked, what are you FUCKIN LOOKIN AT!' We can see this work as the airing of ambient hostility, a ferocity that lies beneath the surface or around the next corner. Yet it also has an art meaning: it might open up wounds from our lack of trust in our ability to have a correct, satisfying, ameliorating response in the face of an artwork. Jon says the piece is also about making us question what we are in fact looking at in the off-kilter state generated by the work – can we look harder? see a bit deeper? could we have missed the point? The work slaps us, and in a way that is not entirely at odds with the works addressed above: if artists and footballers have to put themselves on the line, audiences might also be expected to do so.

Still, it's destabilising, and the fact that there's a few ways to understand it, adds to its punch – there's no right or wrong, just baiting and wrong-footing. Realising this should make us cautious about Jon's broader interest in truth and lying, as is indicated by the work *It's a world full of lying bastards*, 2017/2020. He has used this phrase in various works, and in this painting it reads more or less like a basic statement of fact. Its abstracted form (with each letter on it's own individual canvas) and indirect address makes it less harsh than *What are you fuckin lookin at*. We can let this work's sentiment hang in the air. Depending on our mood, we can take it personally, even as a warning. Or we could enter into a tedious philosophical debate about whether a person who says they are lying is telling the truth. As with much of Jon's work we can take it all ways at the same time.

The same unsettlingly ambiguous quality is present in otherwise direct works like *Fuck Knuckle*, 2019. Our responses to the questions inherent in the work frame *us*: Who is? Why are they? Am I? Are you? Am not! You are!!! This dialogue comes from the distinct idiom of 'Australian egalitarianism', a culture based on expectations of transparency, of fairness, of not putting yourself above others, of joining in, of being a team player. In Jon's work this not-quite-past idiom waves the liberating *and* antagonistic elements of its value system in front of us. We feel located by sentiments that are sometimes happily down-to-earth and open-hearted and sometimes cajoling, viscous and belligerent. Often both at the same time. Even if we know where we stand within these codes, we know that we are required to continually account for why and how we are standing. Works like *Fuck Knuckle* evidence a watchful cultural self-policing that makes sure we're all behaving in the correct way.

This diffuse critical bent extends to Jon's Don Watson-styled weasel-word critique of administrative culture – of those who do not say things clearly, who hide behind jargon. *Your Application Was Unsuccessful*, 2022, is an example that is brilliantly of this moment. It captures the sting of rejection

exaggerated by the blandness of bureaucratic response. Its gleeful tone even seems to celebrate the rejection; we can imagine the administrative officer, section head or agency CEO nonchalantly signing away an artist's dreams. But we can also imagine the artist who suddenly finds themself unburdened from having to deliver on the vision they hustled together under extreme stress for a grant application. Freed also from the civil servitude of accounting for one's practice to funding bodies.

The liberation of failure is differently expressed in *Up Shit Creek*, 2014, a slight abstraction of those very words. Similar to *Your Application Was Unsuccessful,* the painting has a fresh, modern pep. Perhaps this optimism implies that we're not alone, and that, having acknowledged we are in a pretty bad spot, we can focus solely on getting out of it. There's a relief in getting to this point and sharing the knowledge – a relief that is akin to pleasure. This work flirts with the compulsion to repeat traumatic events, and to get an elevated existential pleasure from complaint – a thrill akin to taking the mark or making the incredible painting. As practically-minded and sensible as Jon's work might seem, it is perhaps mostly about the joy of feeling things intensely; he wants us all to leap, to extend ourselves and the world.

Of course, his attitude is based on a politics focused on the better elements of the egalitarian frame he holds up to scrutiny. At times, this is focused on particular issues. In one of his first paintings incorporating text, *Peace and Love*, 1991, his wife, Annie, is depicted taking on a boxer's pose above a scene of American troops entering Iraq during the first Gulf War. The image channels Jon's awareness of the ever-present war which broke out while he was in New York; it is also a homage to Alex Katz's frequent depictions of his wife Ada, and is imbued with the feel of 1960's radicalism. Annie's chic vibe and clenched fists call for calm above the strife that rolls underneath her. As well as imbuing a kind of hopefulness, there is an ironic awareness that, despite the achievements of the 1960s peace movement, the American war machine had become even more powerful.

Nonetheless, Jon retains his faith in collective action, for battles both big and small. This is seen in *Let the Franklin flow*, 2009, that refers to demonstrations against the damming of the Franklin River in Tasmania, and takes its title from a 1982 song by the Australian activist band Goanna. The dam was being planned to support mining activity in an area of Tasmania with a delicate and rich ecosystem. Between 1978 and 1982, environmentalists, politicians and the general public joined to protest against the inevitable impact on the forest and wildlife. More than two decades later, Jon made the work to remind himself that groups can indeed come together to effect change; he needed this fillip as he and his colleagues protested new management structures at the Victorian College of the Arts where he was teaching. The work *Group Tutorial*, 2013, is about this moment, and is based on a flyer made to bring staff and students together to address the matter. Like *Your Application Was Unsuccessful*, the work expresses frustration with the nature of bureaucracies: he believed that new university protocols would compromise the school's practical, artist-led culture.

This concern indicates a vital thread that runs through much of Jon's work. We can see it as a study of energies, their release, their damming. He delineates how types of casual and formal governance operate, but he doesn't claim one freedom is better than another. He leans against, and pushes at restraints to make their restraining nature visible. This tactic is clear in *Undressing in Public Prohibited*, 2019, based on a photograph, by surf photographer John Witzig, of a graffitied beachside sign in Byron Bay. It speaks of too many laws, or the wrong laws, and a libertarian attitude that is oddly found in the more conservative parts of the country. The letters have an upright stuffiness to them, and are a bit spikey. We feel like we are being told off by both of its messages: the one telling us to obey and the one telling us there's too many people telling us what to do. The work holds these elements of the 'Australian character' in interplay: on the one hand there's larrikinism, 'she'll be right mate' and letting go; on the other, there is the wowser, the town clerk and the public servant.

This interpretation demonstrates how Jon's work operates. He doesn't offer a (fully fledged) critique of a particular issue. He rouses responses but does not attach an argument. Because of this, we can provide no excuses for failing to measure up. Moreover, Jon's works reverse our typical understandings about pictorial perspective. Instead of guiding the gaze of the viewer through a scene to a single point that may or may not represent infinity like traditional perspectival paintings, Jon's work gazes at *us*, holding us in its thrall with an infinitely receding field behind us.

This requires that there is little perspective in the work itself, that we do not sink into it. In order for the work to speak of and from the world, it must not represent it as such. This

flattening of the picture-plane began early in Jon's practice and we can see its presence in works from the eighties such as *All the Boys*, 1984; *Firetruck*, 1984 and *The Party*, 1986. Celebrating the places and people he came from, these works indicate that where he was moving to would incorporate the past. Their shallow depth of field coincides with a shift from representing a particular social world to relating what that cultural and social realm might say.

By making different kinds of images out of outlines and words, and letting them hover, Jon depicts universal pictures in the sense we might glean from Wittgenstein:

> But I did not get my picture of the world by satisfying myself of its correctness; nor do I have it because I am satisfied of its correctness. No: it is the background against which I distinguish between true and false.[11]

Jon's work has always been about making the background active, making it a thing we can't avoid. His continuing interest in the concepts of true and false as floating 'problems' which have energies we need to negotiate (but with no fixed coordinates to do so), gives us insight into the language games we are often unwittingly involved in.[12]

♥

This sense of involvement – of how, if, where, why one is involved in the work, in one's life, in the world at large – is a fundamental aspect of both Nadia and Jon's practices. The point is not necessarily to find a path to fixity, but to be in the flow of the problem and therefore to be in the world as much as possible. As visual artists, their material working-through of this challenge, aligns with Raymond Williams' theory about how the world's more complex elements and forces can be expressed:

> Practical consciousness is almost always different from official consciousness, and this is not only a matter of relative freedom or control. For practical consciousness is what is actually being lived, and not only what it is thought is being lived. Yet the actual alternative to the received and produced fixed forms is not silence: not the absence, the unconscious, which bourgeois culture has mythologised. It is a kind

of feeling and thinking which is indeed social and material, but each in an embryonic phase before it can become a fully articulate and defined exchange.[13]

While they draw from the tropes of modernism that render their works legible, both artists create ways to remain in this embryonic space, as they consciously *and* intuitively work towards picturing their practically felt experiences in play with the world around them. At the same time, each use their practical consciousness to unpick existing official cultural forms to critique and to reveal what is still possible.

Robert Cook

Robert Cook is a curator at the Art Gallery of Western Australia

Notes

1   See John Dewey, 'Experience as Aesthetic', in *The Philosophy of
        John Dewey*, The University of Chicago Press, Chicago, 1981. The
        word 'pragmatic' also conveys the down-to-earth feeling that both
        artists evoke.
2   'Stream of consciousness' is a phrase taken from psychologist and
        philosopher William James. With Dewey and Charles Sander Pierce,
        James was one of the founders of the pragmatist school of thought.
3   Equally, it does not privilege the creator, but makes the same room for
        the viewer. Moreover, by engaging with the work, the viewer is a
        necessary co-creator of the aesthetic experience.
4   This matches Frank Kermode's description of Marianne Moore's
        poems: 'Anything could get into them, including all the chosen
        pleasures of her life, the ballgames and prize fights, the paintings and
        exotic animals'. Frank Kermode, 'First Pitch', *London Review of Books*,
        Vol. 20, No. 8, 16 April 1998.
5   All quotes from Nadia are from a phone conversation with the author
        on 8 July 2022.
6   Psychoanalyst Jacques Lacan noted that 'The signifier presents itself
        both as being able to be effaced and as being able, in the very
        operation of effacement, to subsist as such. I mean that the signifier
        presents itself as already endowed with the properties characteristic
        of the unsaid'. Jacques Lacan, *Desire and Its Interpretation: the
        seminar of Jacques Lacan Book VI*, (translator Bruce Fink), Polity,
        Cambridge, UK, 2009, p80.
7   The full titles of these works are: *Pinta ... cacao, chocolate, Chocolate
        el perrito, el asado negro, los gusanos colgando cuando caminamos,
        las matas y la parrilla y la hamaca*; *Pinta flores, pinta aguacates, pinta
        un bodegón lleno de cosas que te gustan, pinta algo que hayas
        cocinado con tu madre, pinta ...* ; *Entre otras cosas ... es verdad que
        Rocky se comió un ganso.*
8   Louis Marin, 'Picasso: Image Writing in Process', *October*, Summer
        1993, Vol 65, MIT Press.
9   Édouard Glissant, *Poetics of Relation*, (translation Betsy Wing),
        University of Michigan Press, Ann Arbor, p144.
10   As Allan Kaprow put it in a 1964 essay, 'reverent manners are still
        confused with reverence for art'. Allan Kaprow, *Essays on the blurring
        of art and life*, University of California Press, Berkeley and Los
        Angeles, p56.
11   In Everett J. Tarbox Jr., 'Linguistic Pragmatism: William James and
        Ludwig Wittgenstein', *American Journal of Theology & Philosophy*,
        January, 1994, Vol 15, No 1.
12   Moreover, as Tarbox Jr. observes: 'One of Wittgenstein's central
        insights ... was his recognition of the 'projective nature' of our
        language, especially philosophical language. Once taken captive by a
        picture, one thinks one is tracing nature, but one is only tracing the
        frame through which we look'.
13   Raymond Williams, *Marxism and Literature*, 1977, Verso: London
        pp130–31.

DRIVING DOWN TO WYE RIVER ABOUT 1978 TO GO SURFING. HITCHY, BEAKY, MARTY, MORRY, WAYNE BOY & ME. HITCHY'S BEHIND THE WHEEL OF HIS FALCON WAGON. I'M SITTING IN THE MIDDLE IN THE FRONT. SOMETIMES I TAKE HOLD OF THE WHEEL & STEER WHILE HITCHY SMOKES A BONG. WE'RE ALL DRINKING AND SINGING 'IT AINT ME BABE' FLATTER THAN BOB DYLAN EVER DID.

ME. HITCHY'S
THE WHEEL O
WAGON. I'M
THE MIDDLE I
SOMETIMES I
OF THE WHEEL &
WHILE HITCHY
A BONG. WE'

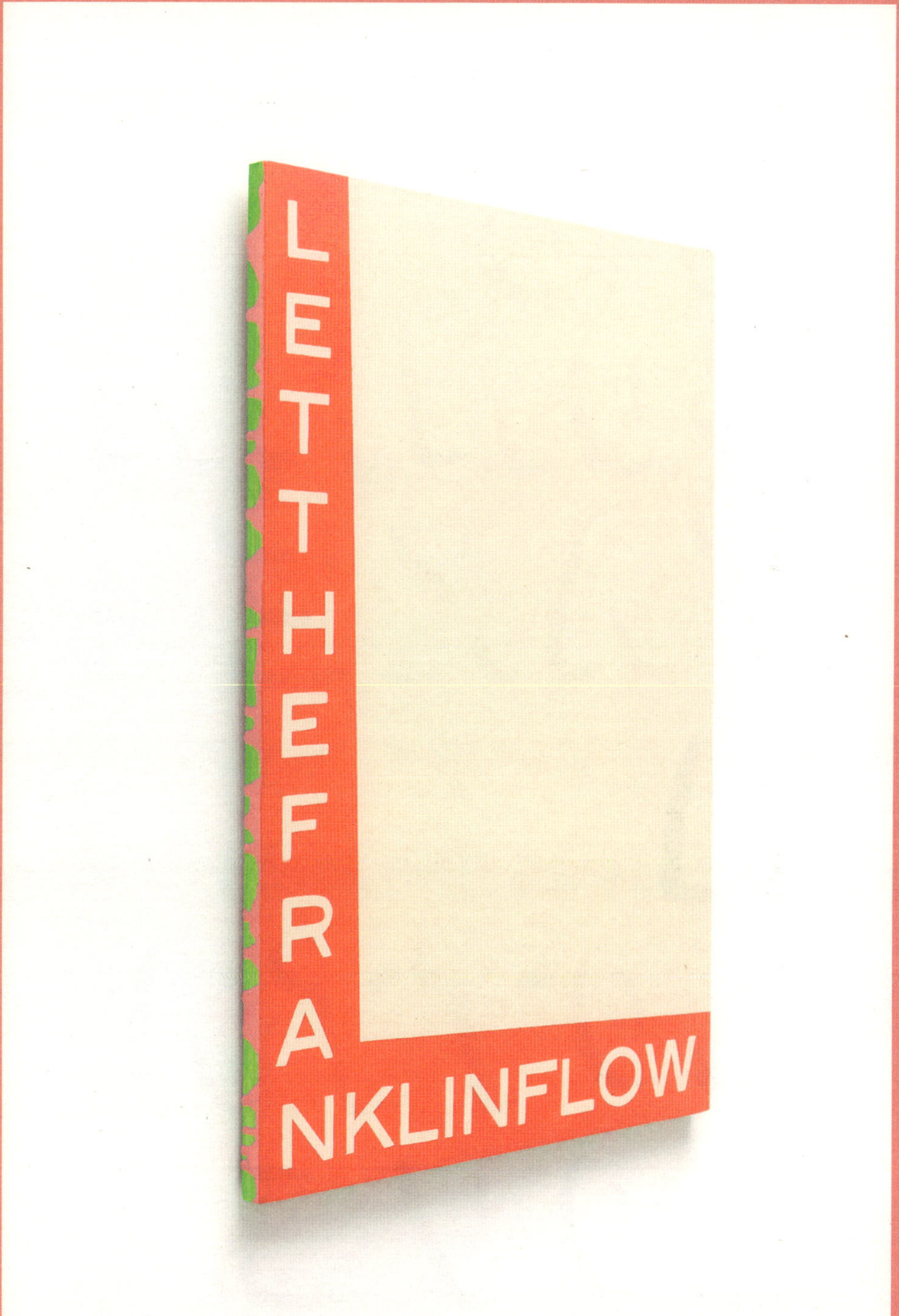

LET THE FRANKLINFLOW

IT'S
GONNA
TAKE
A
LOTTA
LOVE

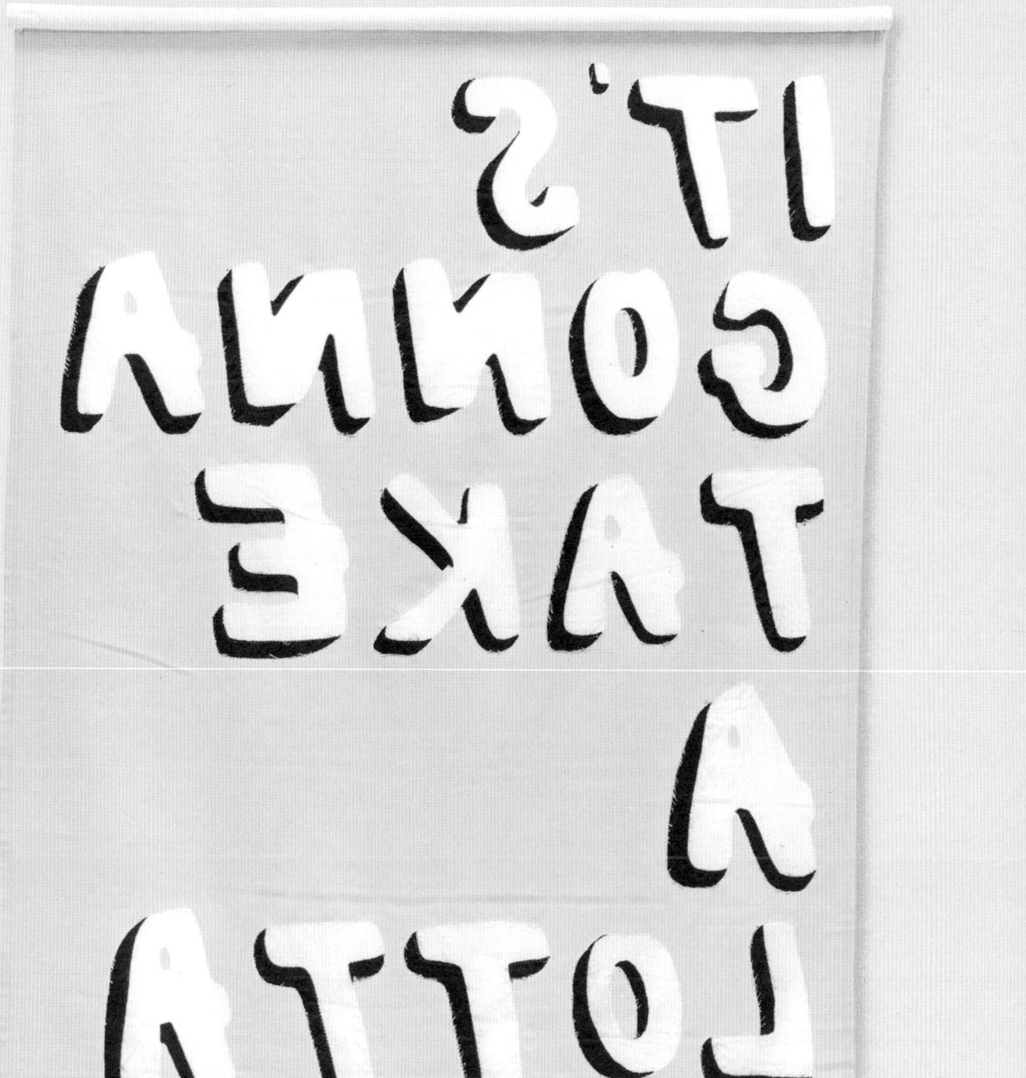

IT'S GONNA TAKE A LOTTA LOVE

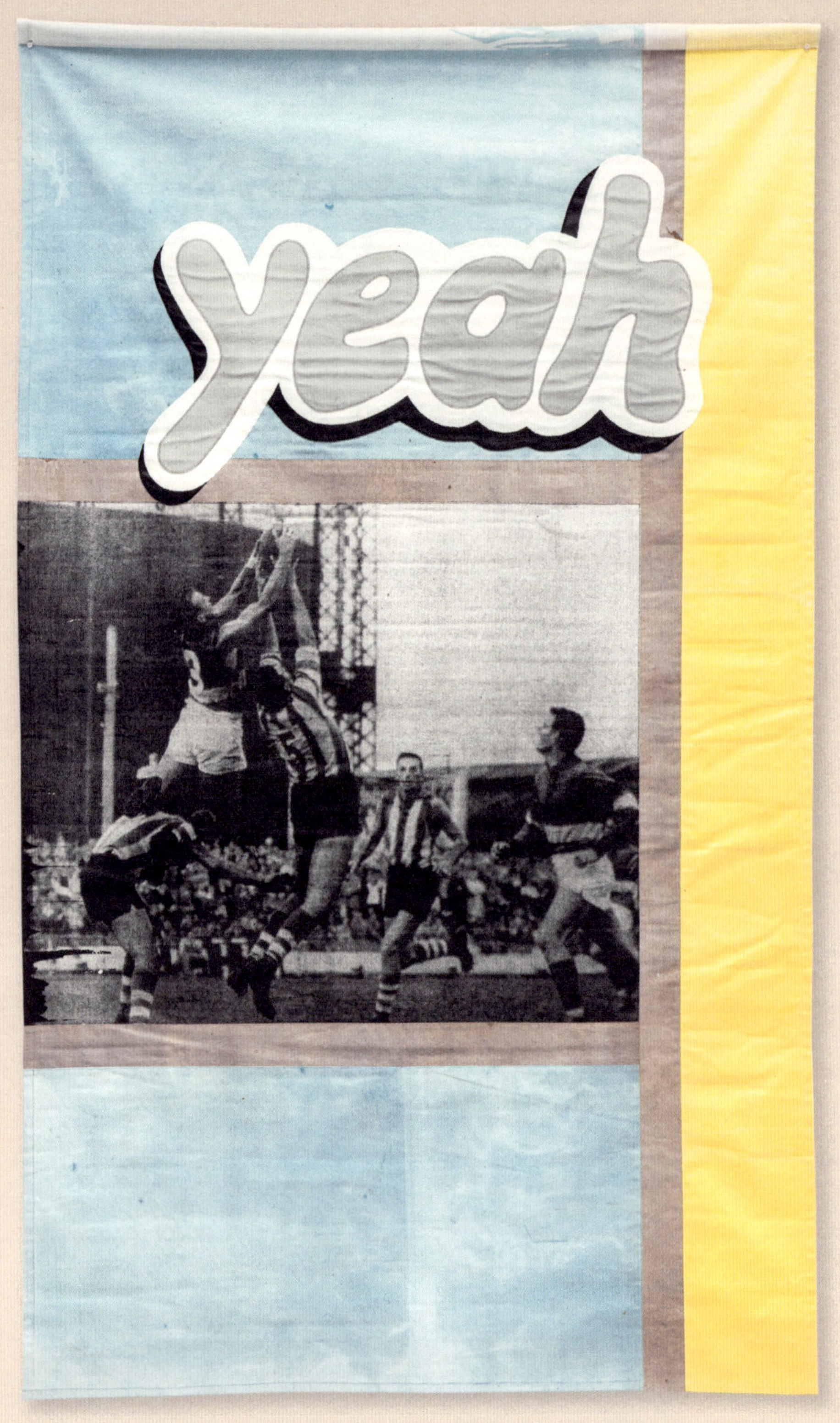
yeah

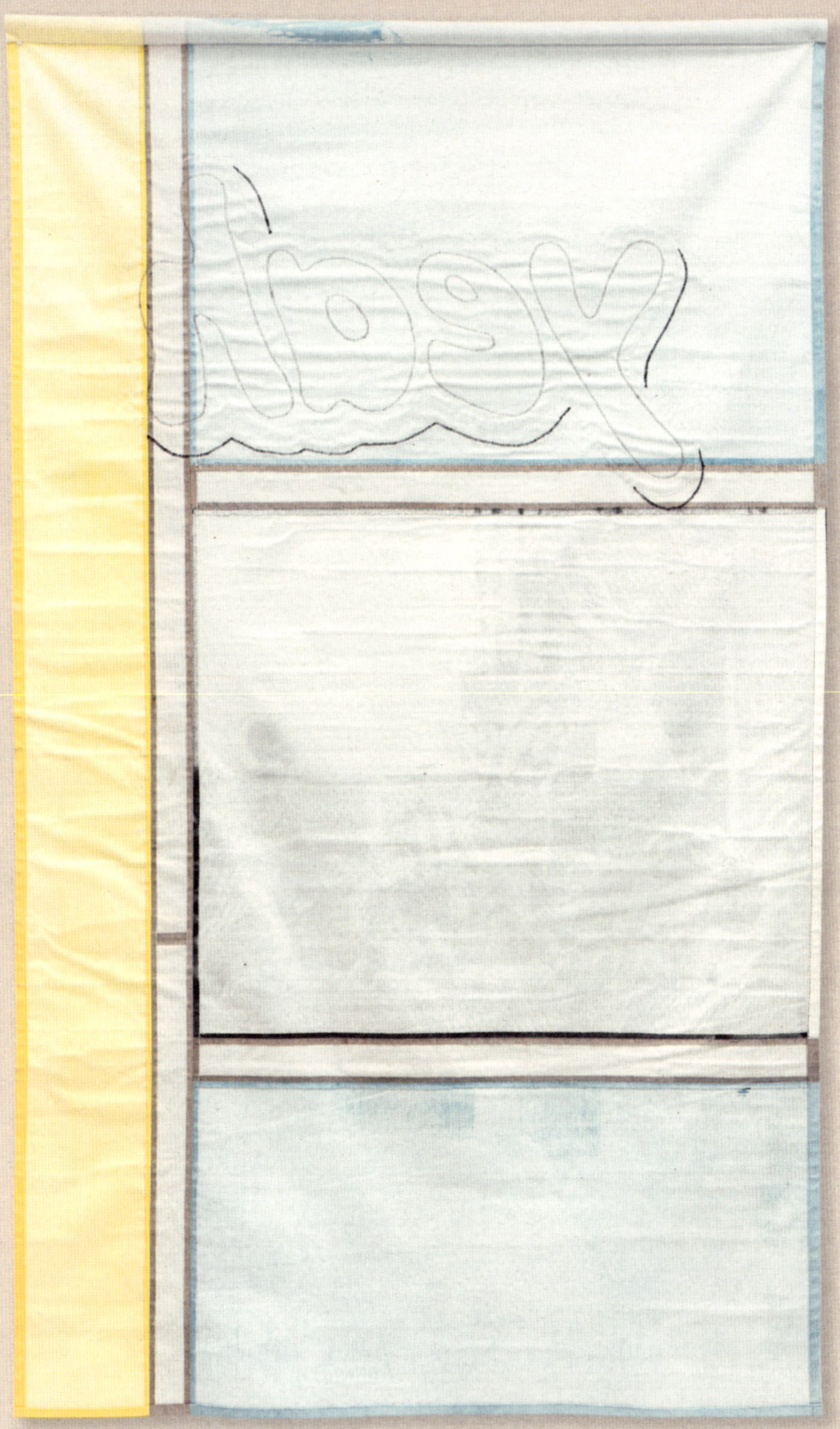

FUC
LOO
AT

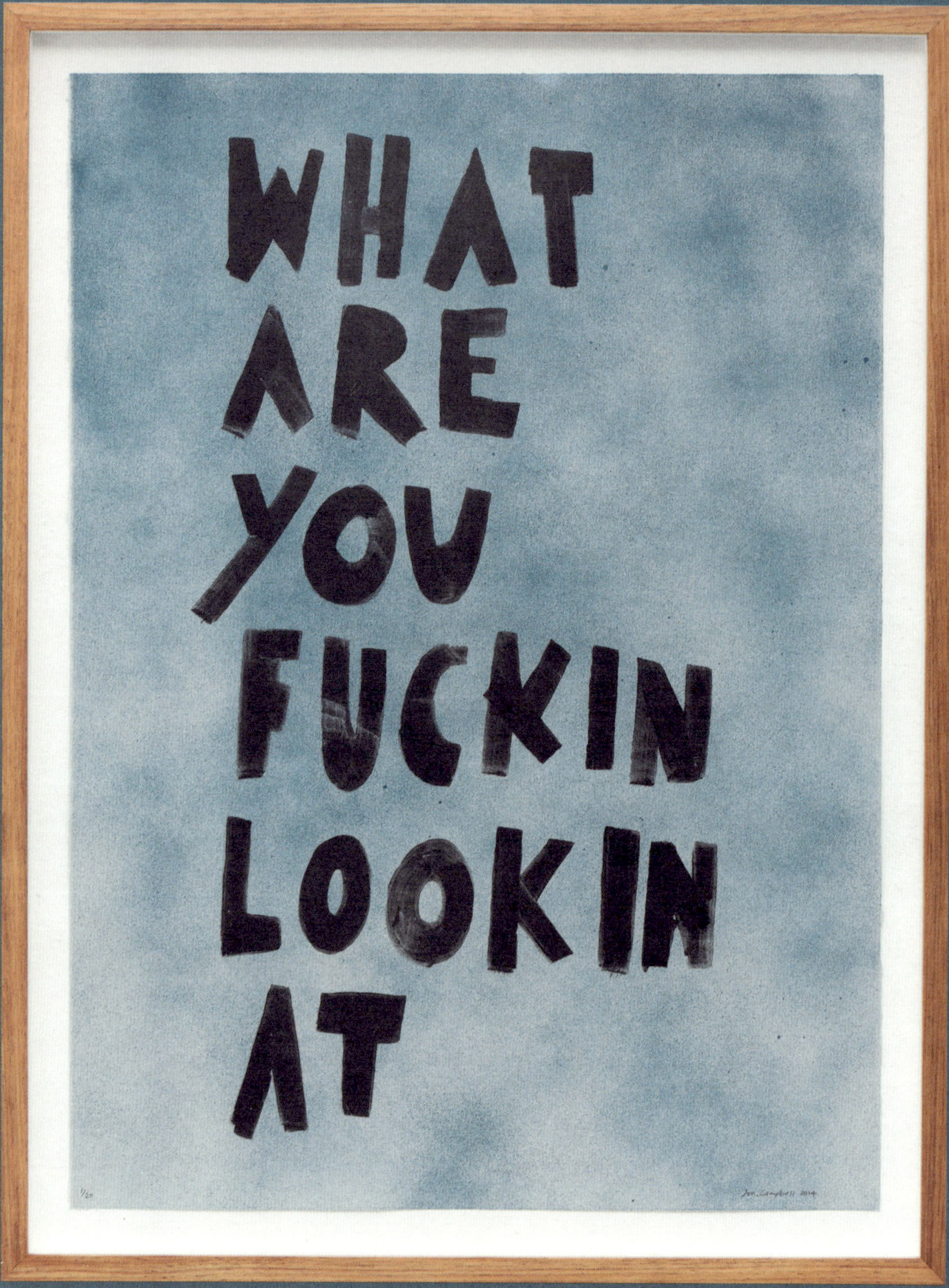

WHAT
ARE
YOU
FUCKIN
LOOKIN
AT

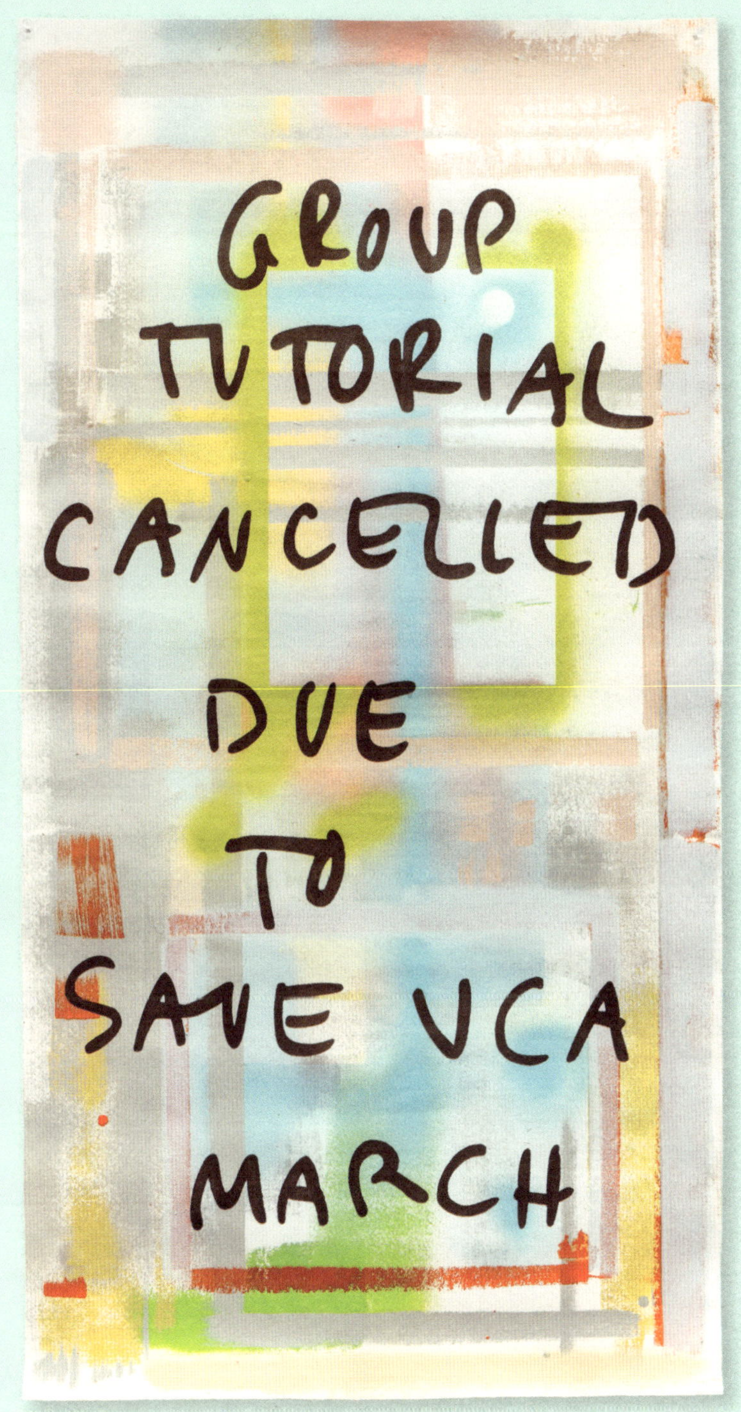

GROUP
TUTORIAL
CANCELLED
DUE
TO
SAVE VCA
MARCH

CAN C

DU

TO

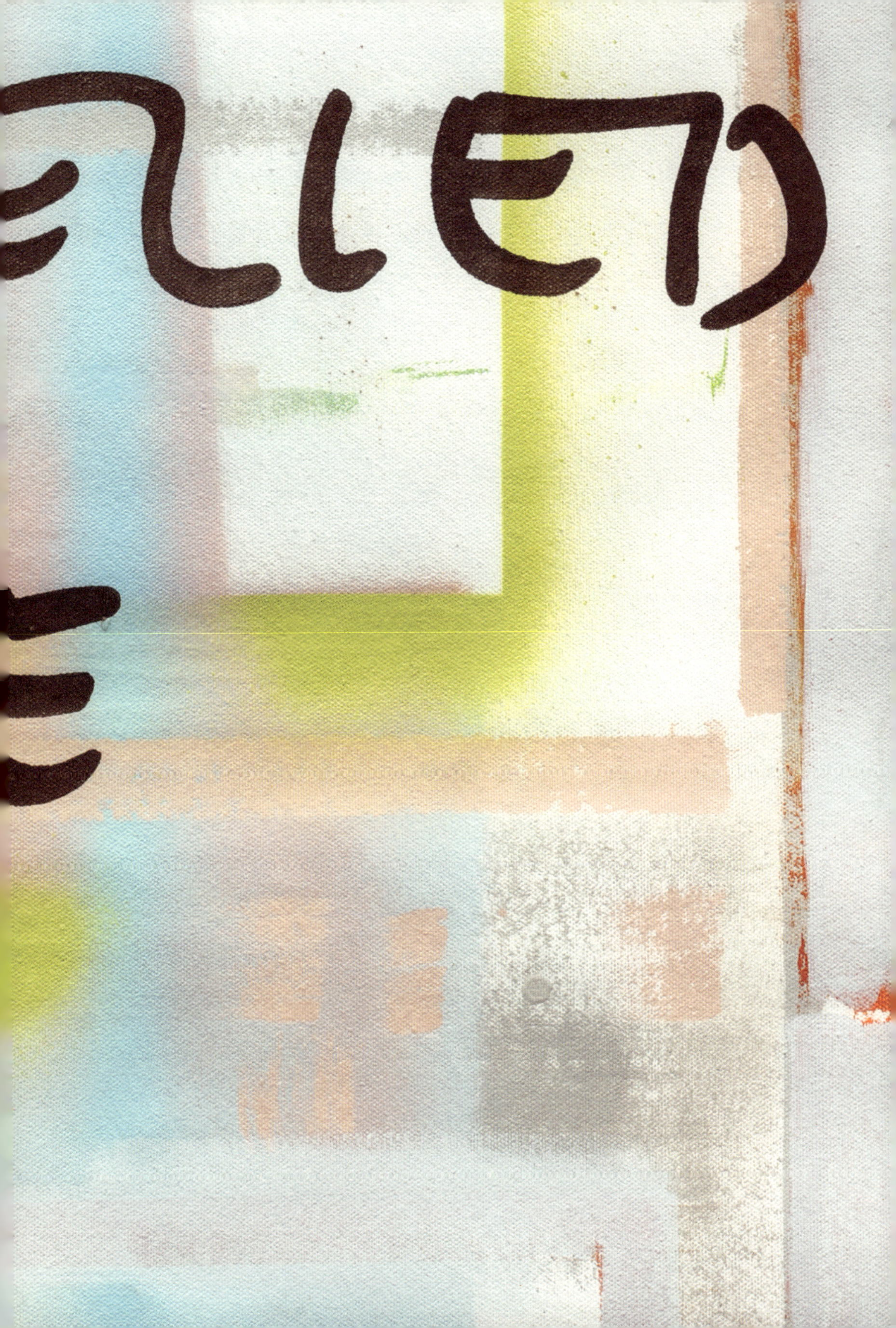

UNDRESSING IN PUB
PROHIBITED
THE MORE RULES AND
LAWS SOCIETY MAKES
THE MORE SOCIETY
REVOLUTION

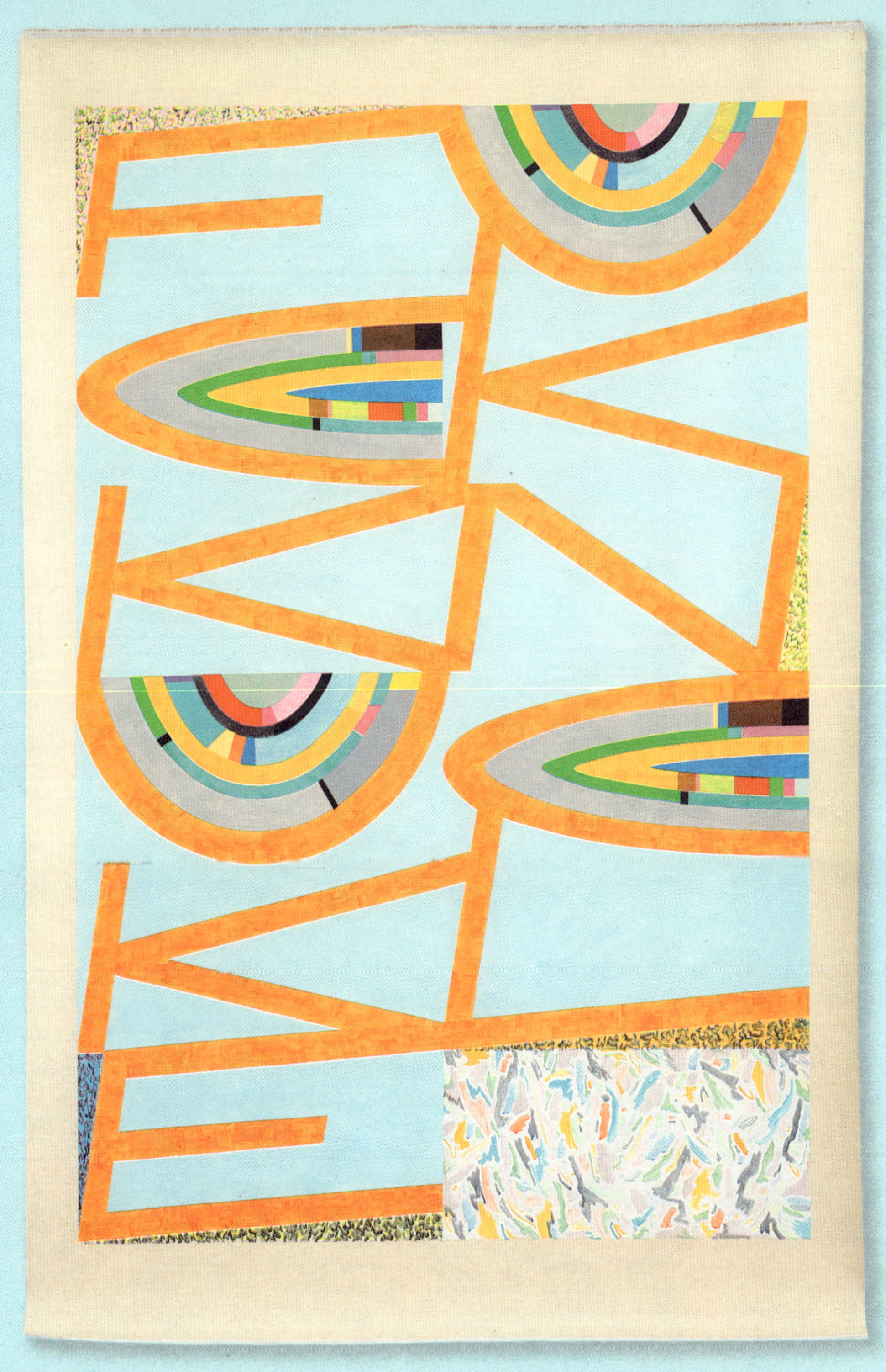

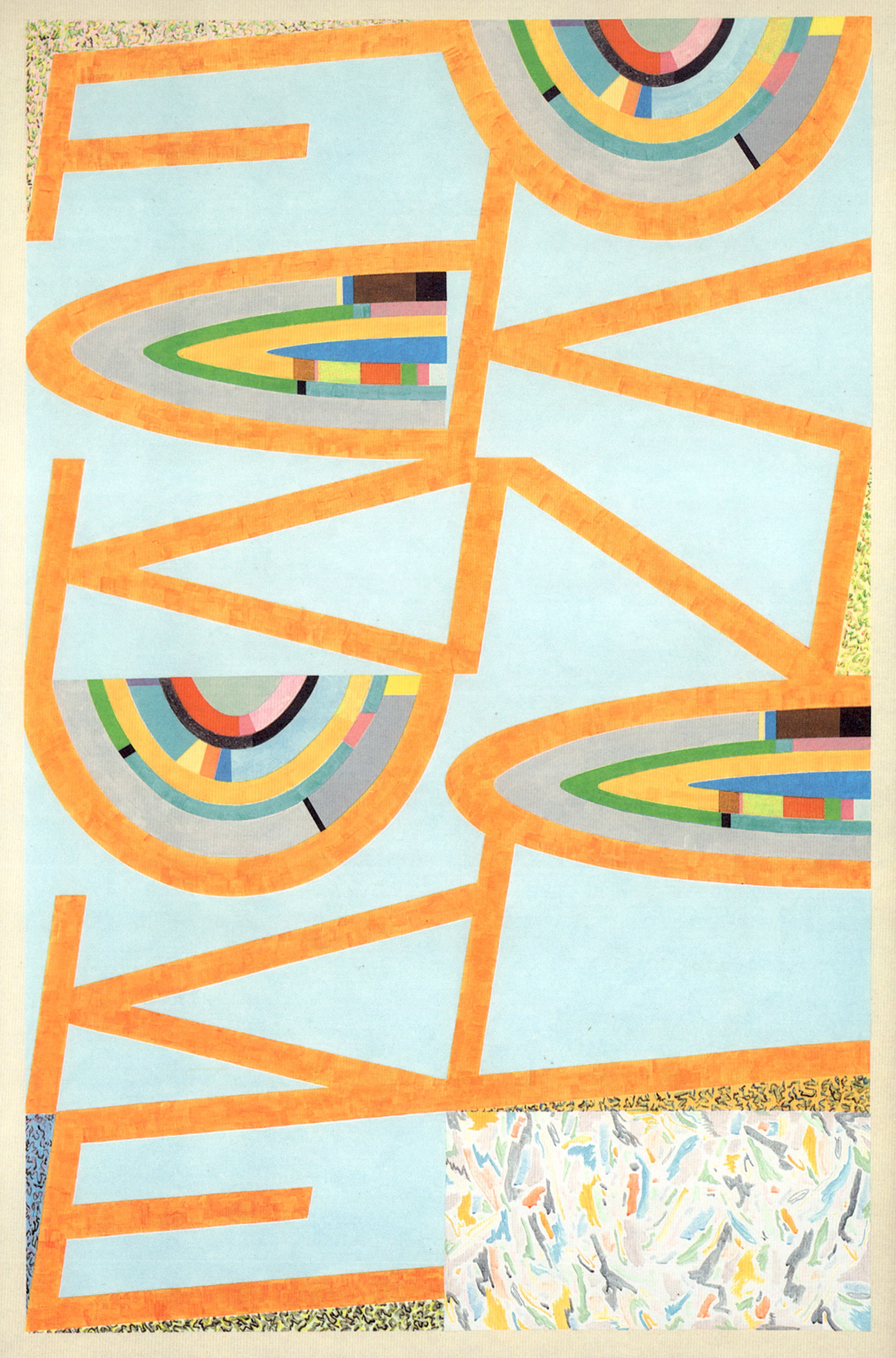

You

are

looking at

a

fucking
catalogue
essay

I am walking down High Street in the gentrified suburb of Northcote in Melbourne, thinking about the structure of this essay for Jon Campbell. Histrionic people and little dogs inspire me in the context of shop fronts displaying trinkets made of resin and conscientious tears. Sometimes I feel like tapping on random vitrines and positioning my face between the hot yoga flyers sticky-taped to the glass. Pressing my cheeks there until they look like Pipilotti Rist's *Be Nice To Me (Flatten 04)*, 2000. Puffing and huffing, with everyone looking, to yell, 'Hey! Your splash pastel aesthetic is giving me a rash, losers'. Ugh, the idea of wasting a second of my life with these people, who probably play UNO high on ketamine, makes me yearn for global warming. Anyway, I am meant to be relaxing right now, making space in my mind for what I love, not what I hate. Cowabunga turtles. I mean, Ohmmm.

The plan for this catalogue is to write an introduction stating my position, then move on to three paragraphs which unpack form, content and context; followed by a conclusion. I wrote an opening sentence to keep me focused:

> *What are you fuckin lookin at* is a lithograph by Jon Campbell that shows this colloquialism painted in an abrasive font above a nebulous backdrop, to occupy the totality of the image.

I like this line because it self-consciously addresses mediums with an economic language that also favours lively adjectives that help to capture the energy of a single artwork that is representative of Jon's wider approach. The tone has to be serious to demonstrate that I am really engaged, but a bit quirky so as to signal creativity, like shaggy hair after 8am. Within this tonal region, I want to focus my critical attention on *What are you fuckin lookin at*, 2015, while drawing from other pieces to consolidate my view. The idea is that words are more illicit than images because we have a Judeo-Christian legacy of 'the word' as creation and heresy in the West. Jon's work trades in this primordial sense of danger-as-style to incite suggestive images in our heads, rather than on the canvas, and to establish an aesthetic of efficiency. This precedent makes phrases like 'fuck yeah' in *Fuck Yeah (Australian sing along)*, 2018 – where Jon placed this slogan on top of a record cover – more rousing and direct than figuration or abstraction. His work is quick to unpack but its longevity relies on a mental picture, a semiotic residue that lashes onto a myriad of associations through time; it circumvents the dearth of tautology by relying on the surplus of visual culture.

I need a structure to unpack these ideas because I am playing it safe. It is the first time that I have been asked to write for a museum and it is important that I come across as sympathetic. Hence, I have to victimise myself in one full paragraph to elicit a symbolic hug. Something that makes everyone feel like good people for giving me a platform. But the piece also has to be angry to fit with the Buzzfeed/Junkee stereotype that a millennial writer with a foreign name in the arts conveys: the whole tamale of safe spaces, trigger warnings and micro aggressions. While 'the conversation has shifted' – this outdated delivery is so 2015 – subtler forms of anger remain. Grumpy cat mode is a crowd pleaser for the Professional Managerial Class, Northcoteans, Arrested Development Folk – whatever you want to call this demographic, who refuse complexity in favour of simplistic optics.

Thus, I want to talk about how the hand-brushed lettering of Jon's lithograph *What are you fuckin lookin at* invokes the iconic Sex Pistols font, to convey a state of rage with its bold and uneven strokes. I am interested in how the cloudy texture in the background, made with blue spray-paint then printed, resembles the ethereal imaginings that we reserve to express inner speech – such as the ubiquitous thought bubble in cartoon language. I want to describe a disgruntled state of rumination: a choleric reaction to an other, most likely a stranger, that is kept within the bounds of the mind, without necessarily reaching the external realm of speech. It represents that fuming reaction that we indulge in when someone decides to look at us at the wrong time, in the wrong place …

'Hwuar arrre yoo fukin lukin at.'

… I suddenly tell myself, when a creative type, dressed in an orange Carhartt WIP jumper and a blue Uniqlo beanie, comes out of the organic grocer Terra Madre, interrupting my concentration as I stroll along. His demeanour bothers me, as it painfully suggests that he is one of those people that leave their car with the engine on 'just for 5 minutes' in the oddly reliable streets of Northcote. He looks like the cartoon *Hey Arnold!* went to film school, and is now watching Mubi wearing a fucking headpiece from Muji, high on the CBD oil that he stole from grandma who has insomnia. He makes lists about obscure cinema with the public setting turned on because he wants to die. But Nickelodeon won't let him. This dork believes high culture is his human right because he was born a few days before the fall of the Berlin wall – making him an embodiment of democracy and free expression. I suspect *theholisticpsychologist* and *The Empaths' Survival Guide* taught him pissy language like 'co-regulation' on Instagram. Yet he accuses other people of using wellness vernacular when they try to establish a genuine connection because he is projecting his own emotional mediocrity onto others. Everyone is a narcissist, except him. In the last election, he surely turned his Instagram stories into a campaign for the Greens, targeting everyone that is already voting Green. Vice Media and Mexican skull tattoos are not embarrassing in his 'friendship group'. Smoking was cool in high school but now his breath stinks because he neglects hygiene, and his hair is full of knots. I want to brush it but I'd rather touch hot lava from El Popocatépetl than his head. Somebody cuddle him, please.

'Hey DYE-go', he says out of nowhere, 'how are ya doin mate?'

God, be merciful to me, it turns out I know him from somewhere. I've forgotten his name but can't tell him because I am a people pleaser: I don't want him to stop liking me. Or worse, get angry at me. I need to exit the situation politely and return to Jon's catalogue. So I reply, 'Your presence is like a hammer-drill trepanning my skull. I obliterated you from my memory as a coping mechanism', then I mumble with a tense jaw, 'remind me who you are if you must?' Oops, that came out the wrong way. His face now looks like cheese melting in the microwave, so I say 'I am sorry ... sorry that you are a turd'. Oops, that came out the wrong way too, 'my bad, a dog's turd'. This must be fawning – when one ignores one's own needs to avoid conflict and becomes overtly apologetic. But I am in therapy now, doing a mix of ACT and CBT, and I am healing, 'what I need from you right now is to get the fuck out of here, I am busy'. Oof, I think he is crying now. It is true what they say about toxic people resisting boundaries; doing the work is hard. But it feels good to communicate my needs to this fuck knuckle.

I learnt this term in Jon Campbell's acrylic painting *Fuck Knuckle*, 2019, where the artist painted these words in orange over electric blue, similar to the colour palette of surf music. The skewness of the letters in *Fuck Knuckle* brings to mind Kurt Cobain's Jag-Stang guitar, which follows the Fender Jaguar (traditionally associated with surf) but displays a more crooked shape than the original guitar (suggesting dissent). Jon also filled the letters 'u' and 'c' with circular shapes that reference the colourfulness of 60s post-painterly abstraction to encapsulate the visual culture of this era. The painting hangs on unstretched linen, like a flag, to synthesise a complex sentiment with minimal symbolism; the incensed connotations of its words ('fuck knuckle') are complicated by the upbeatness of its enunciation (colour palette). It looks like someone added the word 'fuck' to the lyrics of The Beach Boys' 'Surfin' USA', and blasted it during a museum opening, to make a misfit statement. More than a political stance, the painting conveys an attitude that is both antagonistic and carefree, like a pelican stealing a sandwich at the beach. Once again, it is an efficient deployment of words that become poeticised once they swirl in the mind, where they find references to lash onto within a shared pop cultural reality.

While *What are you fuckin lookin at* conveys inner speech with its semblance to a cartoon bubble, the banner quality of *Fuck Knuckle* implies a public uttering. Both paintings deliver a rude address to the spectator by commenting on the status of the works as art, to create the impression of a subject presented in fragments (what a person thinks, then articulates). The former does this by provoking the viewer, asking them to consider the object of their gaze or look somewhere else; and the latter by 'offending' the viewer, or suggesting the painting is twittish in content or style. This device grants the illusion of agency, for these works appear to speak as if they were alive. However, rather than invoking the horror of possession, where a demon inundates speech with murderous obscenity, Jon imbues the words with the comedy of anthropomorphism, making the inanimate become sentient. One feels like Ben Stiller in *Night at the Museum* (2006) in which displays come to life at night to initiate obnoxious exchanges. But in Jon's critical zone, rather than soliciting a PG-13 adventure like Stiller, we are invited to consider what is within the mind of visual culture by listening to the way the objects speak.

Jon's work motivates me to think about Northcote because it has a local feel; it is deeply rooted in Naarm/Melbourne's urban landscape. His imagery resembles commercial graphics – the lettering that populates the suburbs. It is like hearing a place talk in a vocabulary that is duplicitous, for it is word and image at once, and generative, as it evolves through time. Yet it is accessible, since it communicates with a language that is readily available and easily understood. Jon's work is brief because pop culture is expansive and its associations are infinite. It crawls in our heads with ciphers that find their coding in personal messages within. Channelling a working-class upbringing, his address makes me wonder what an older version of Northcote would say if it could speak back to the excesses of monstera plants and melodramatic

creatives who go bouldering as soft therapy because
they are suffering from First World atrophy. Would
yesterday's Northcote ask 'What are you fuckin
lookin at?' I bet today's Northcote would answer
something pissy, like 'I am an empath' or 'my inner
child'. I wonder what the equivalent of Northcote in
Perth is, and if the intelligentsia in that suburb sucks
too. If they only eat bread from bakeries with heavily
tattooed staff and are capable of understanding just
as many perspectives (sourdough worldview). While
promoting themselves as the embodiment of
inclusivity, even though they quickly reveal
themselves to be punishing and intolerant. Thank
god no one can read my thoughts, and I never
committed this essay to the screen, because these
streets are made of eggshells. The conclusion is that
I would get exiled to Fremantle.

Diego Ramírez

Diego Ramírez is an artist, writer and arts
worker with h0p3s and dr3ams

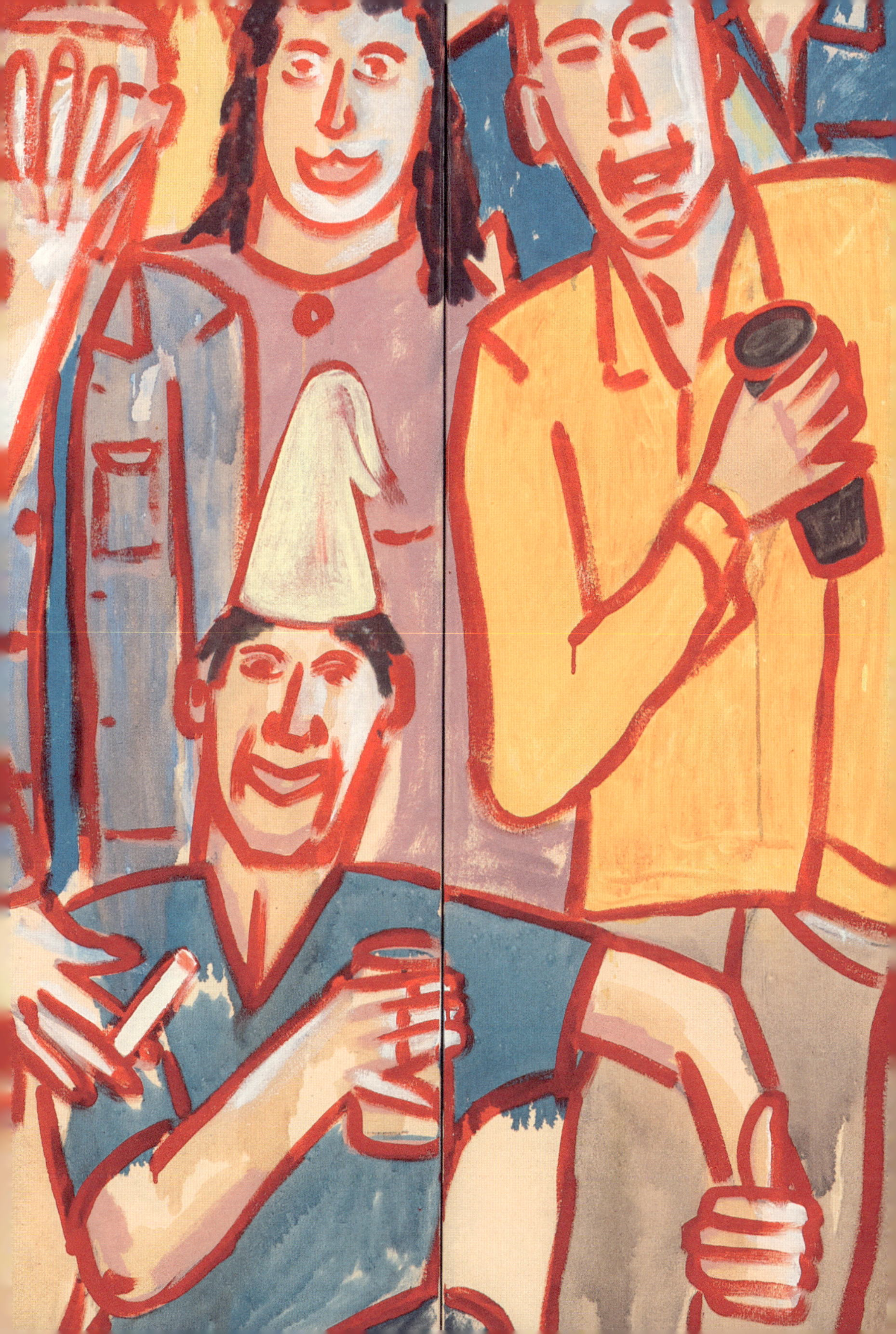

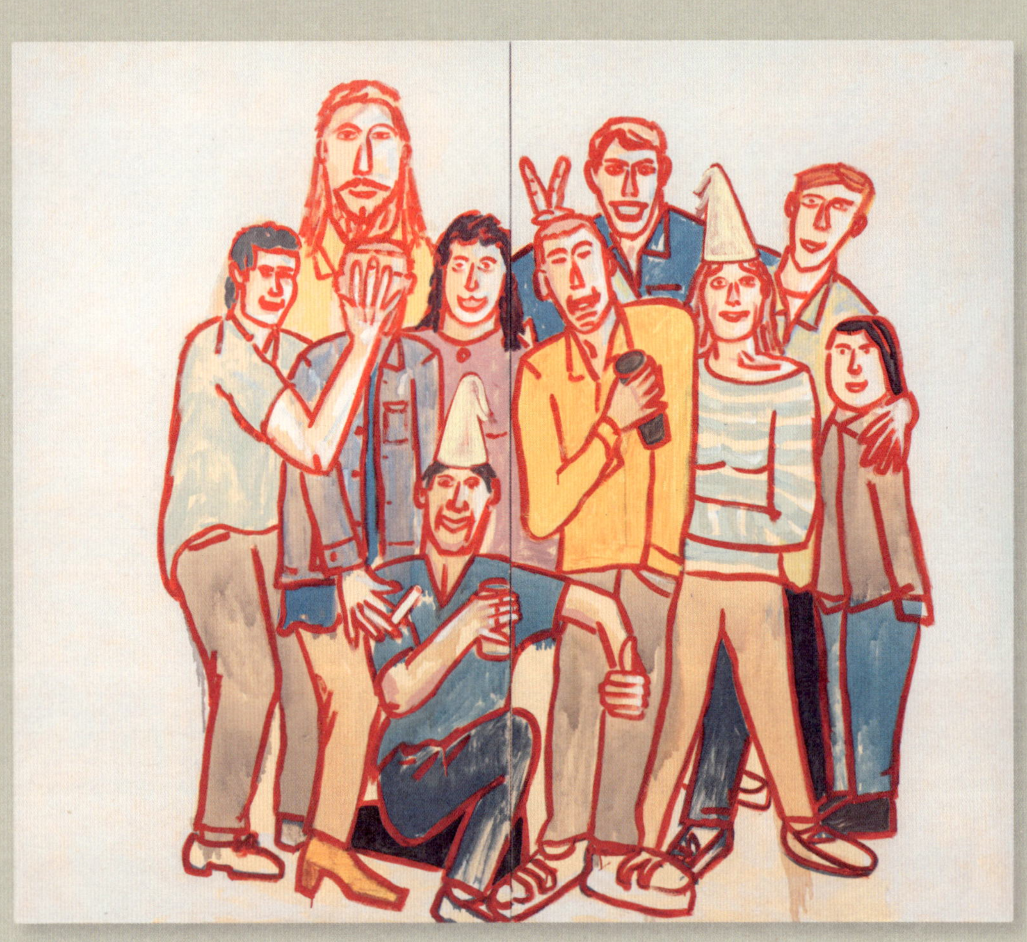

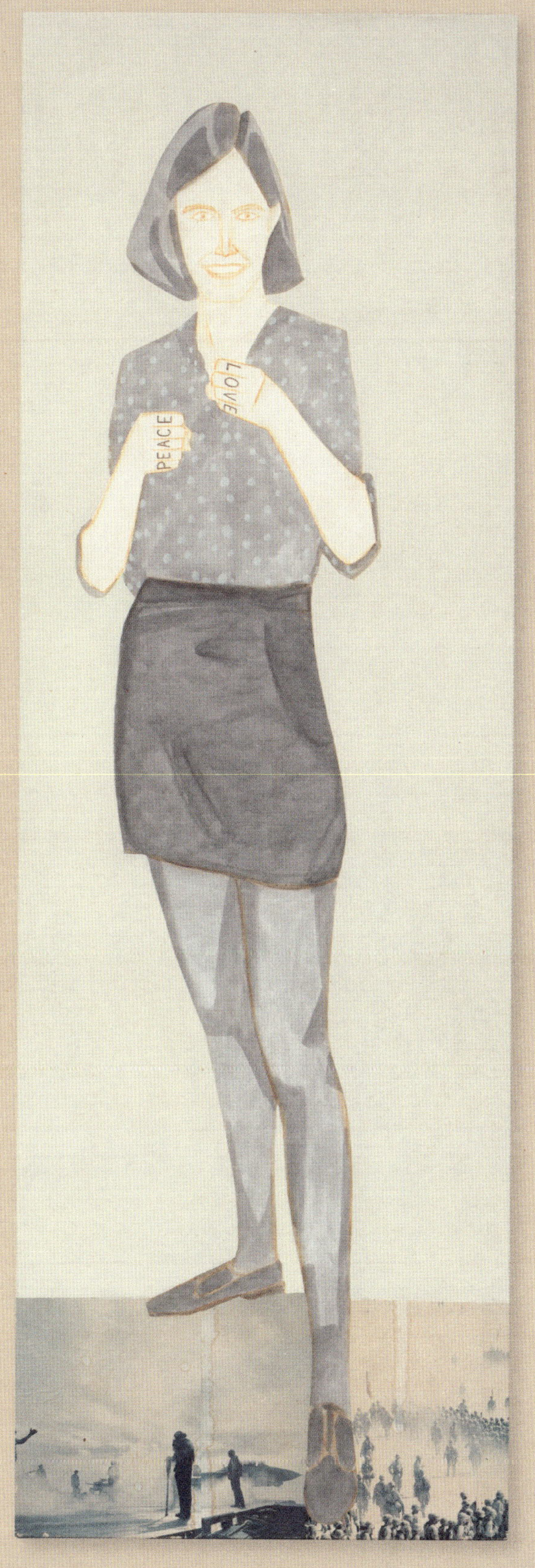

LOVE
PEACE

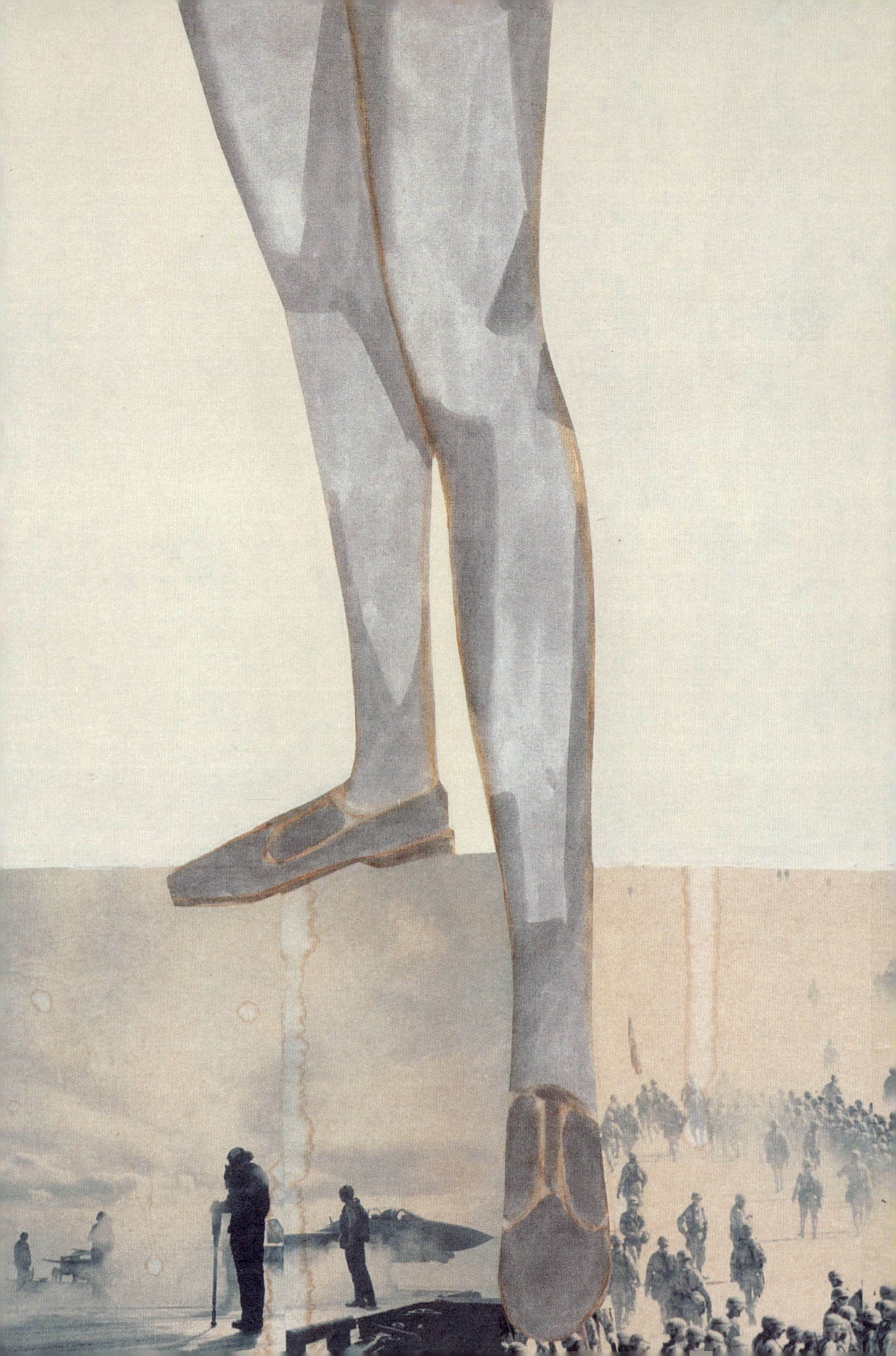

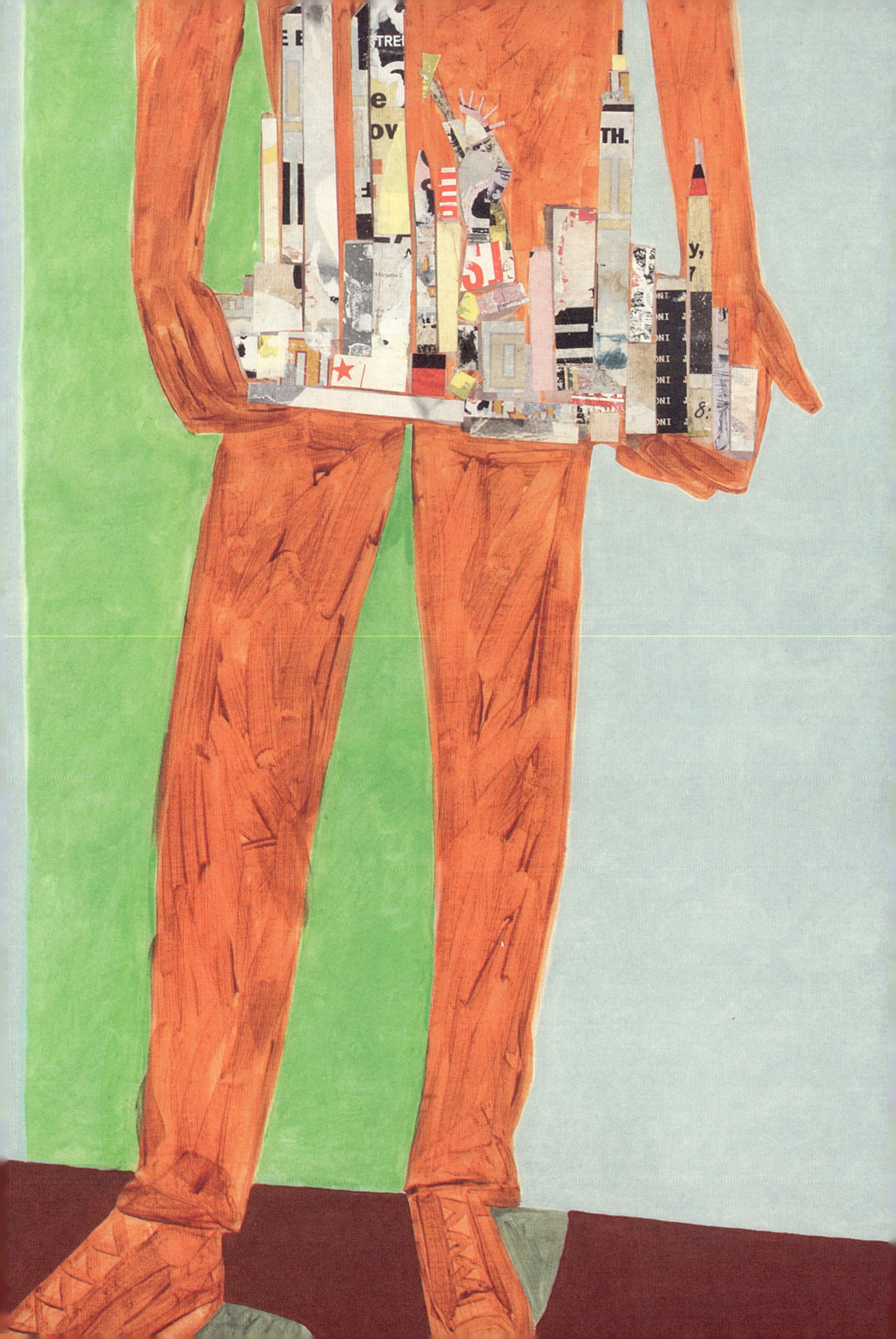

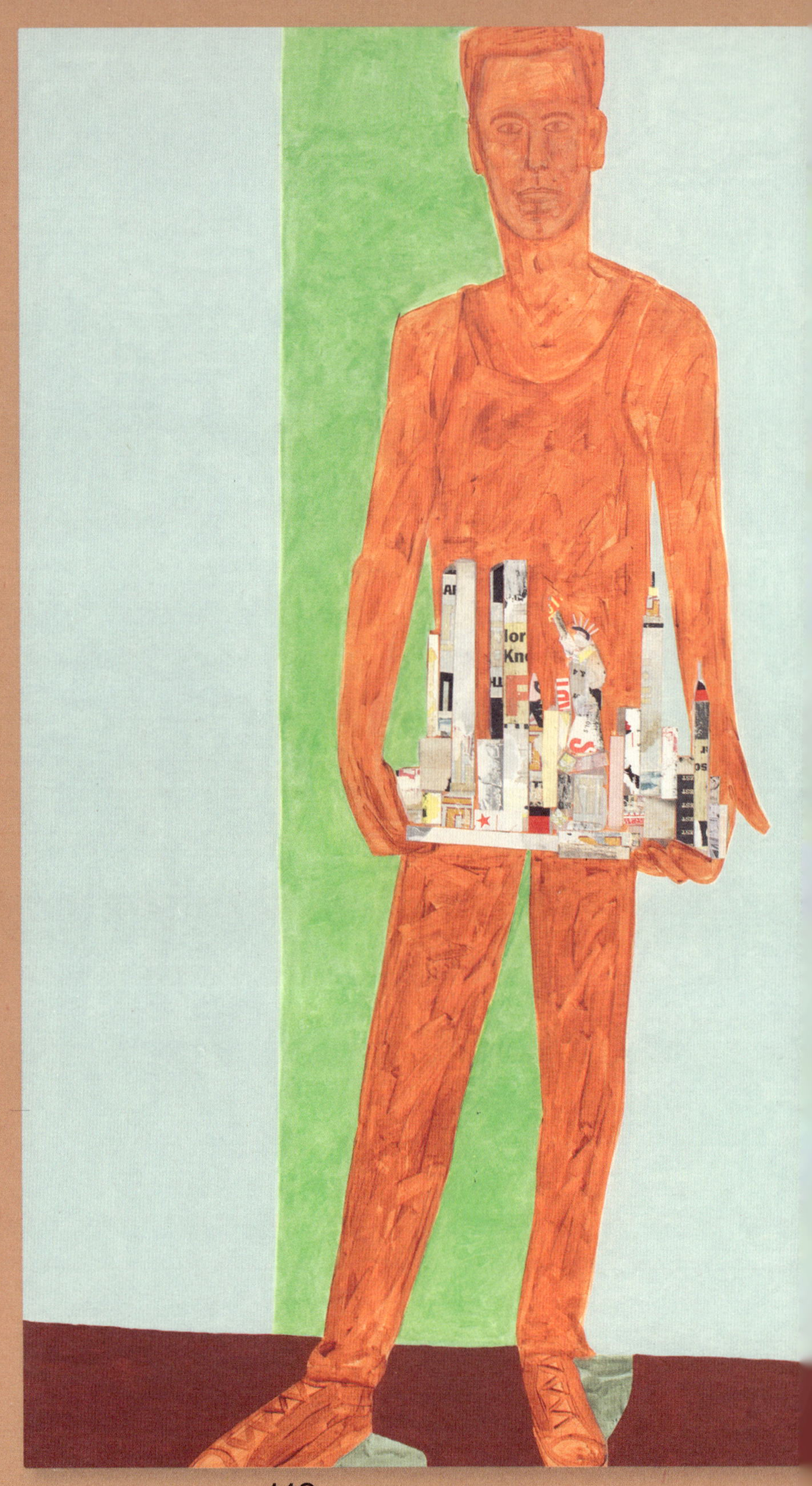

lor
Kno

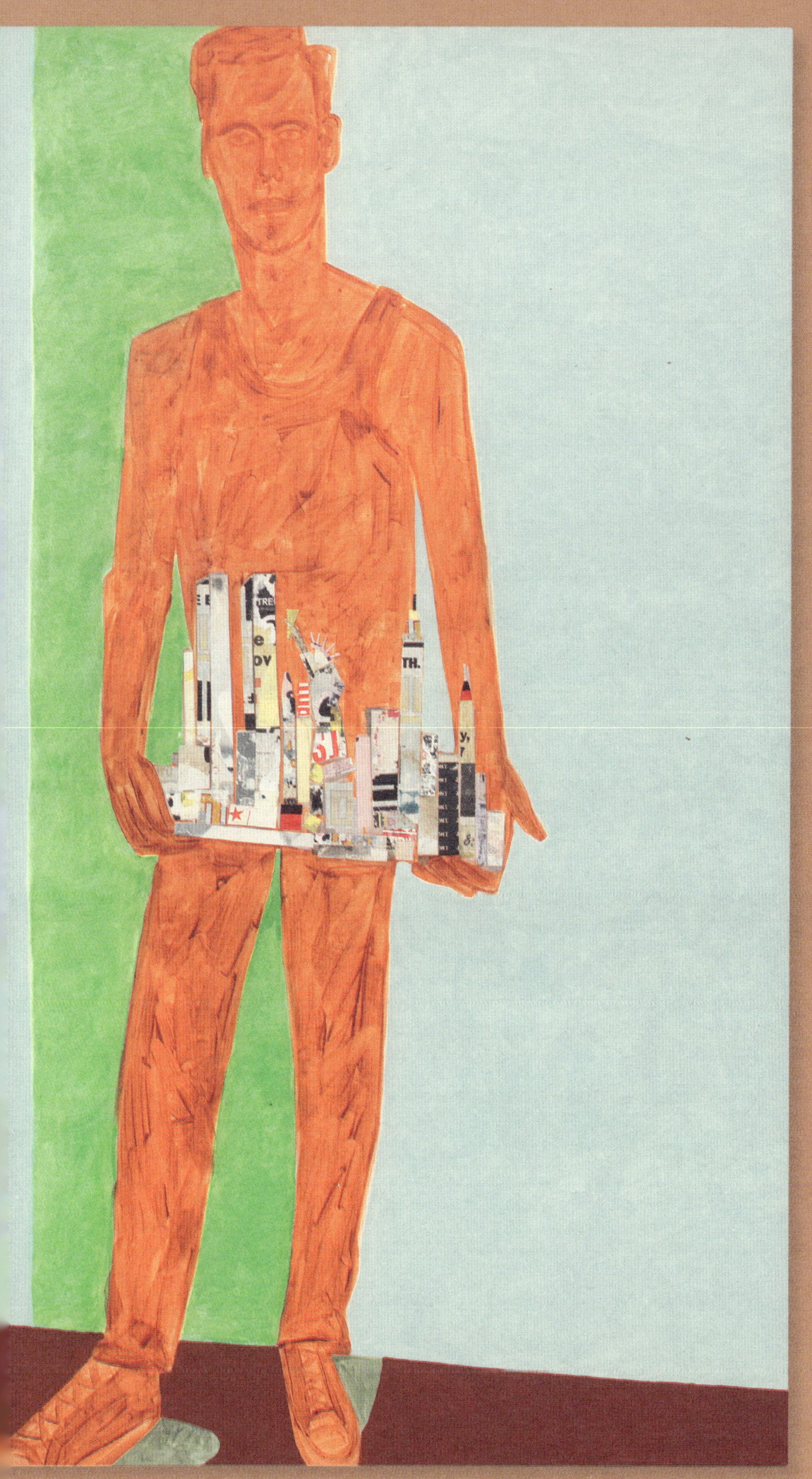

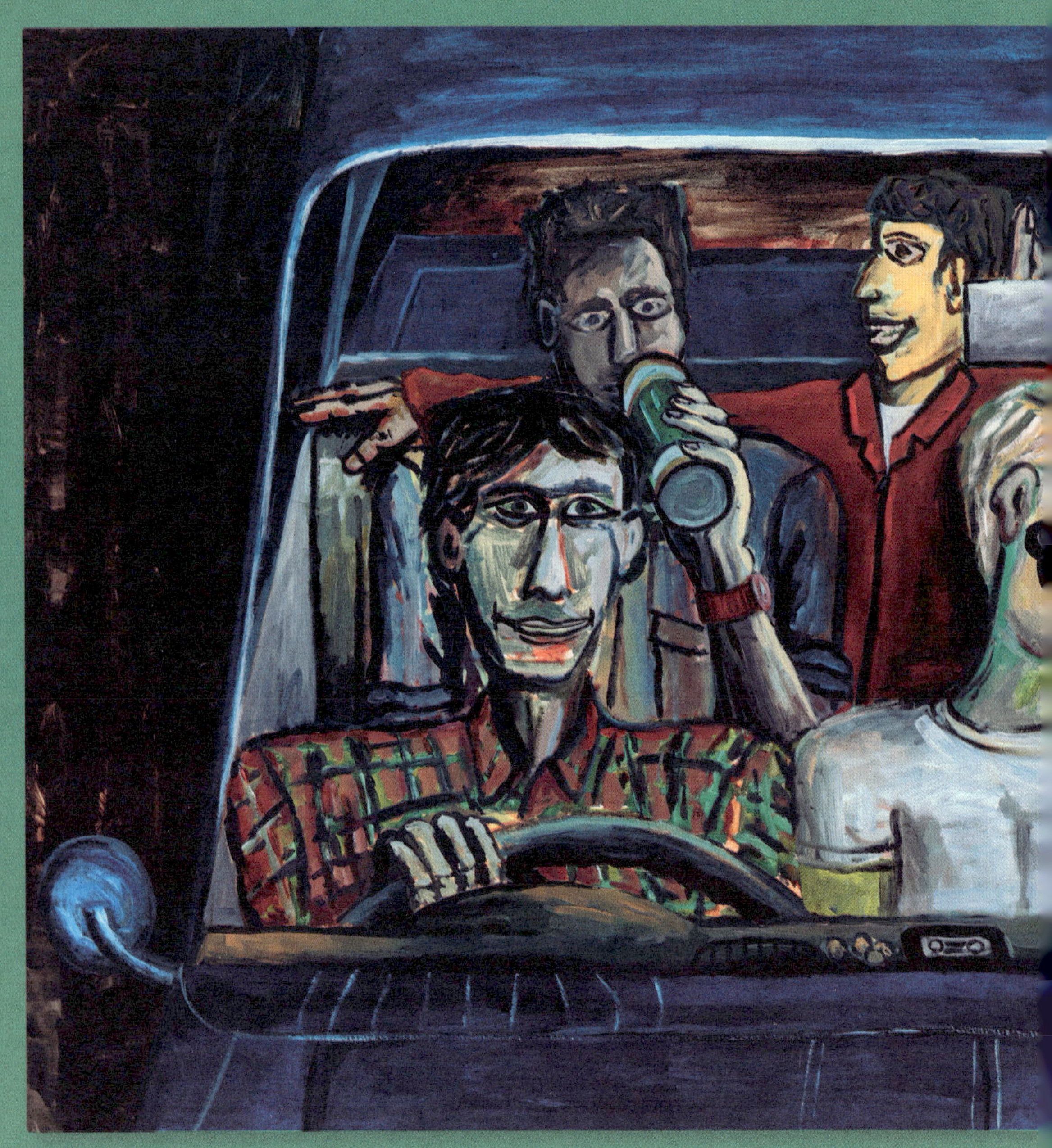

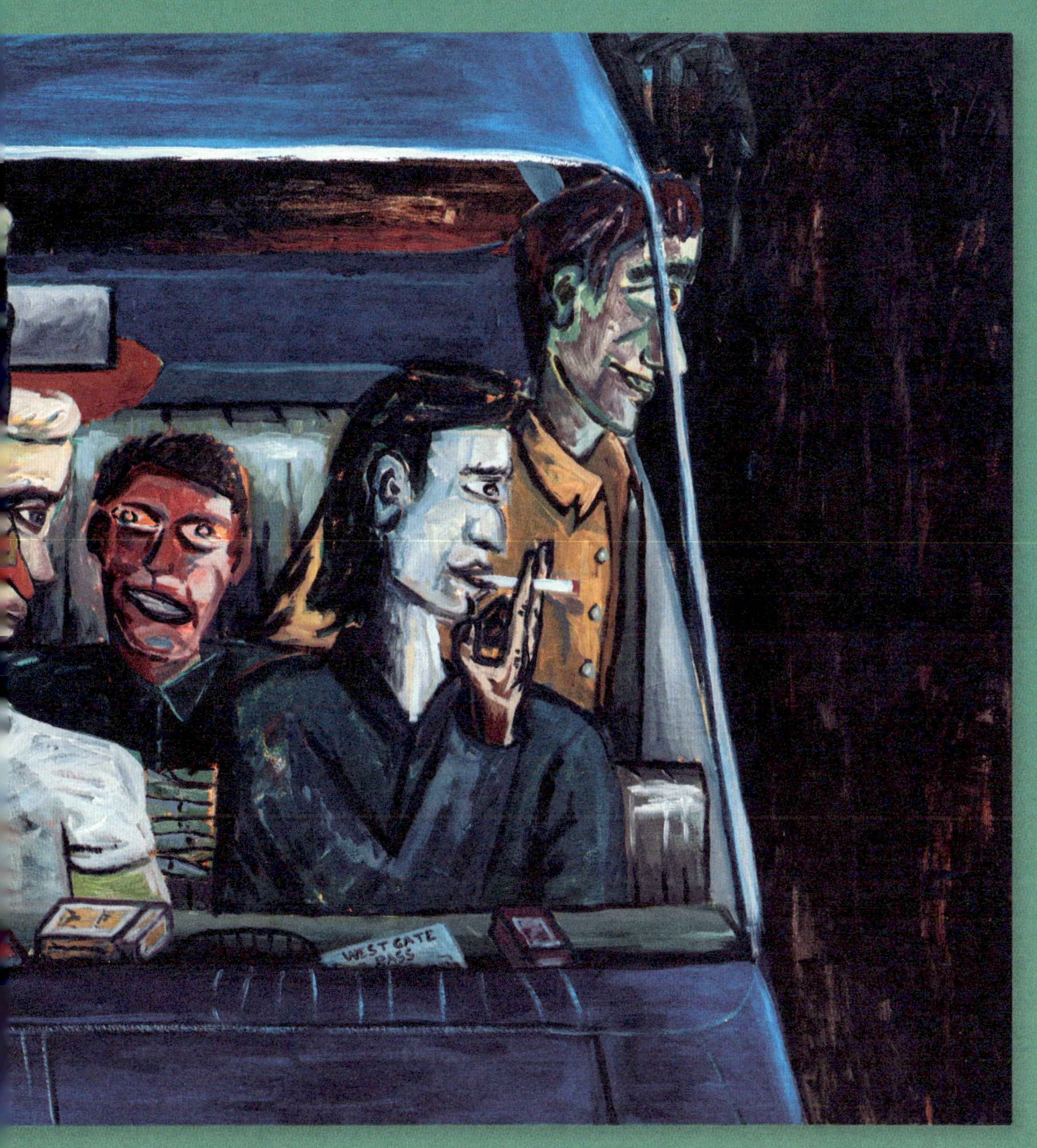
WEST GATE
PASS

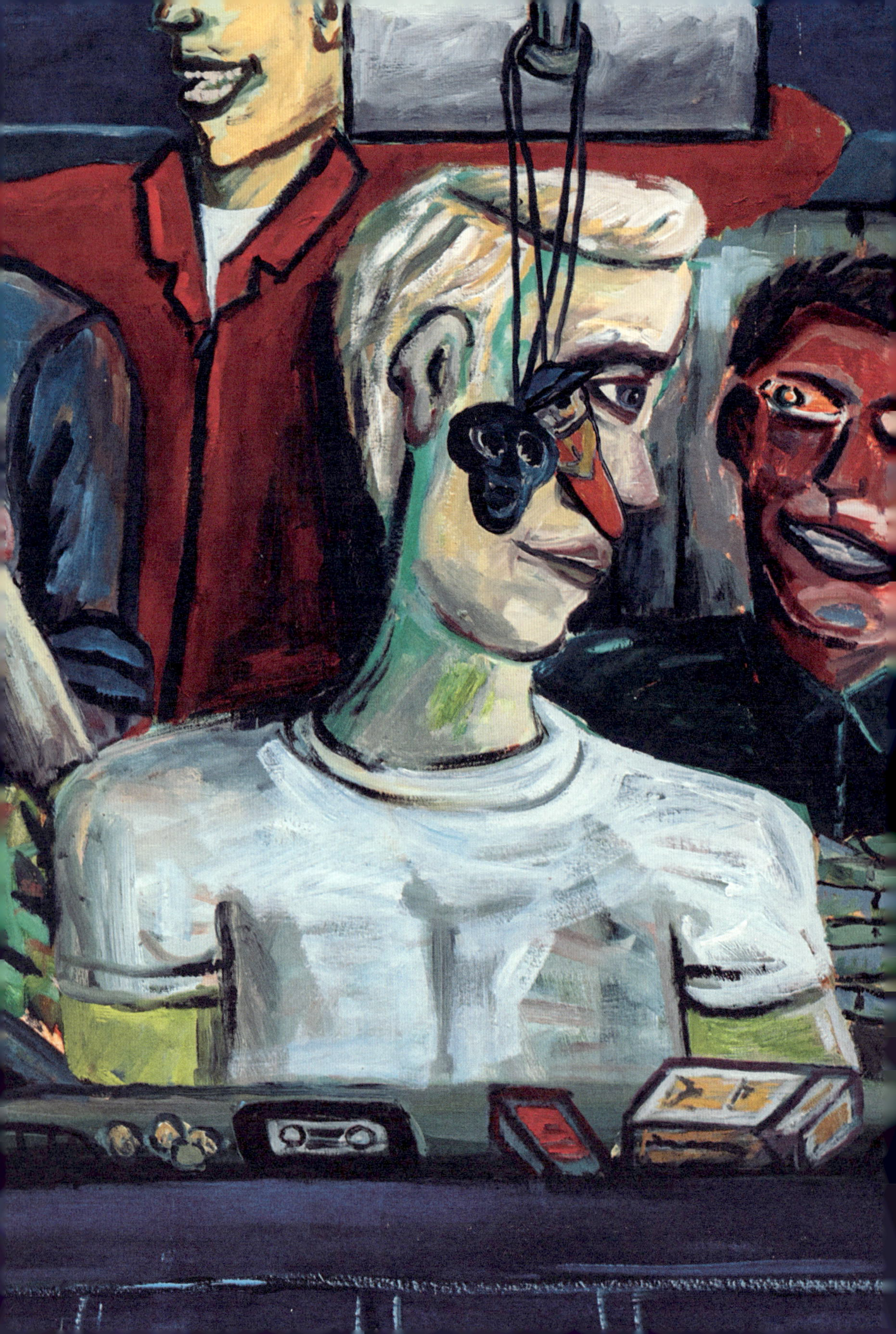

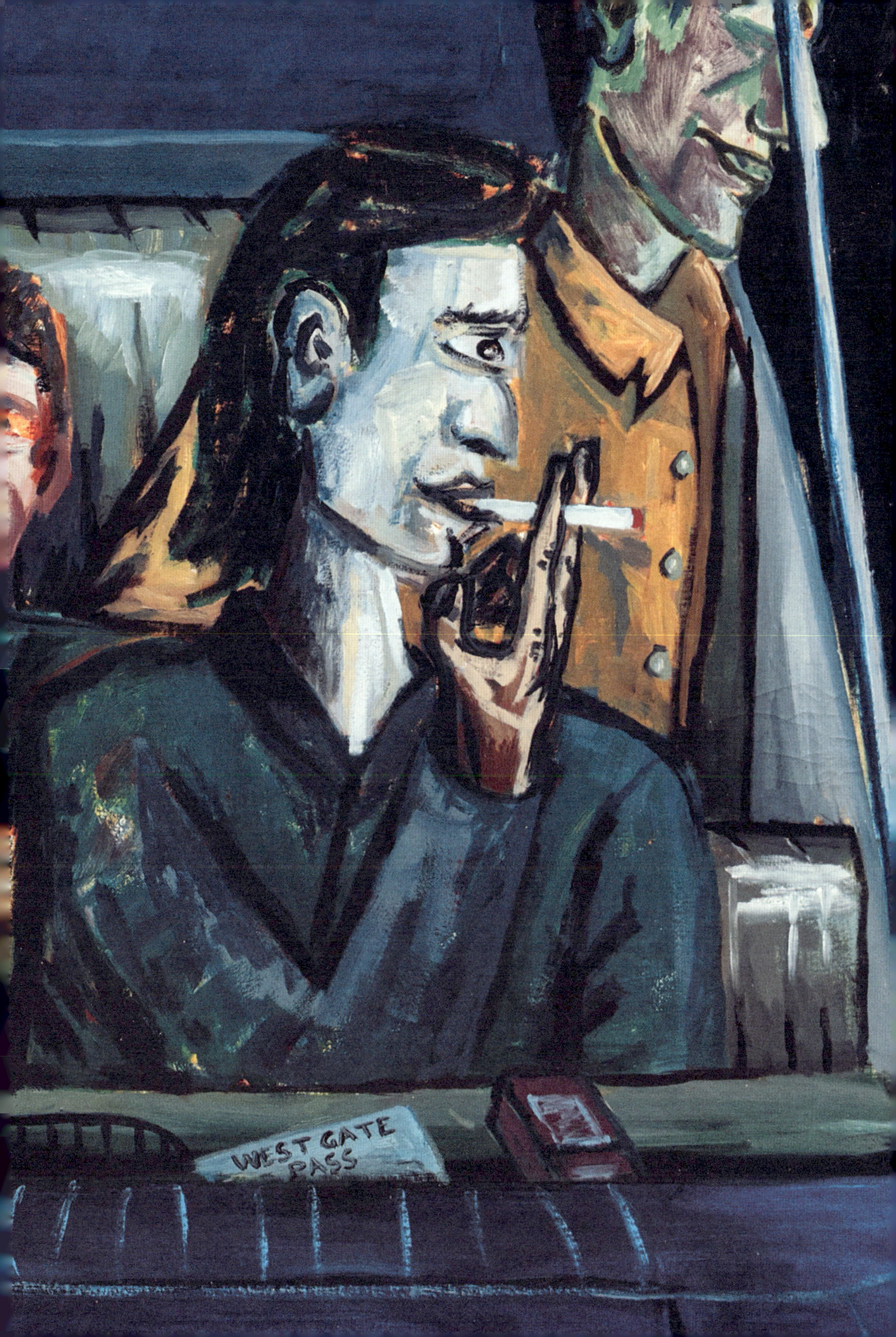
WEST GATE
PASS

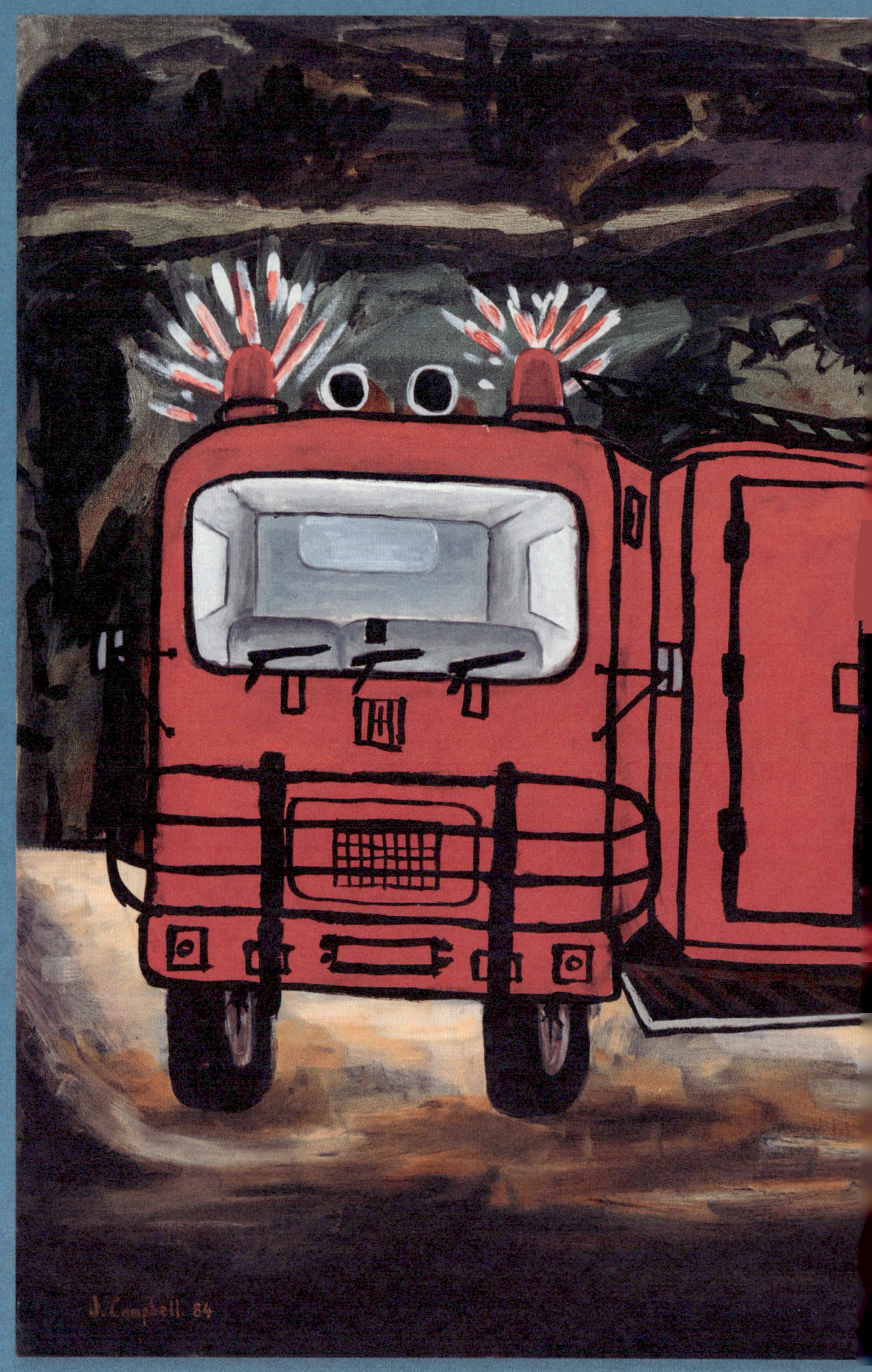

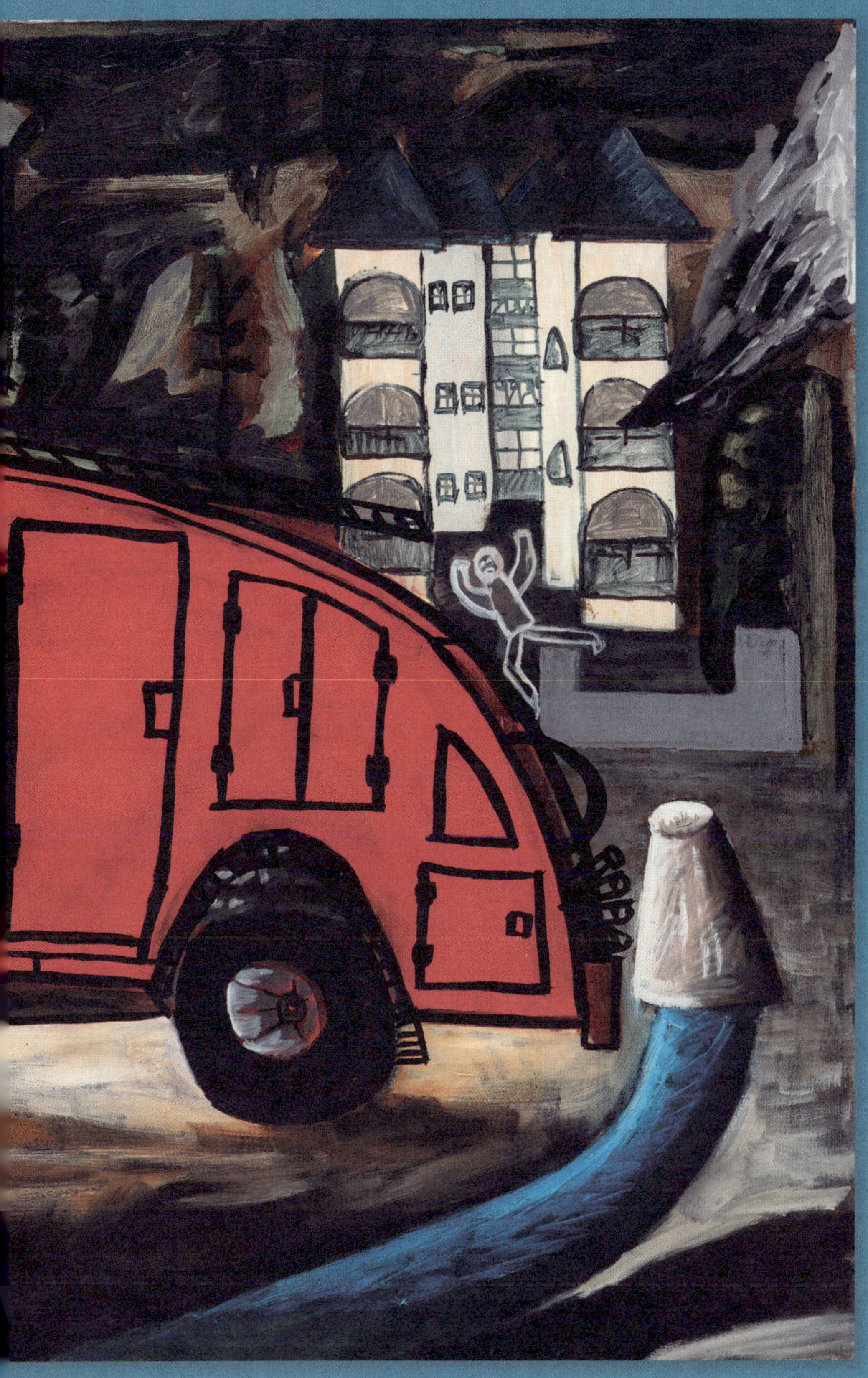

BABA

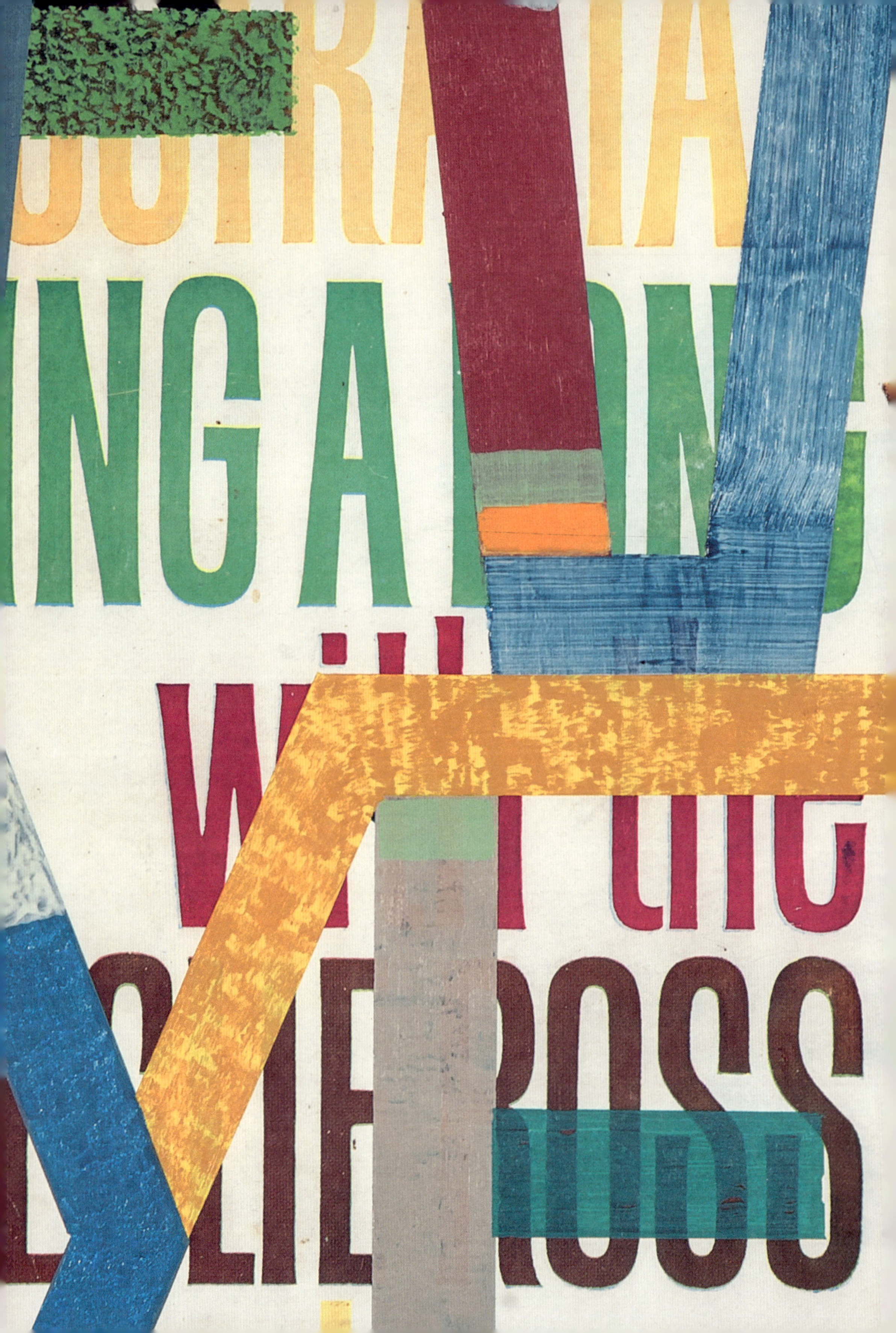

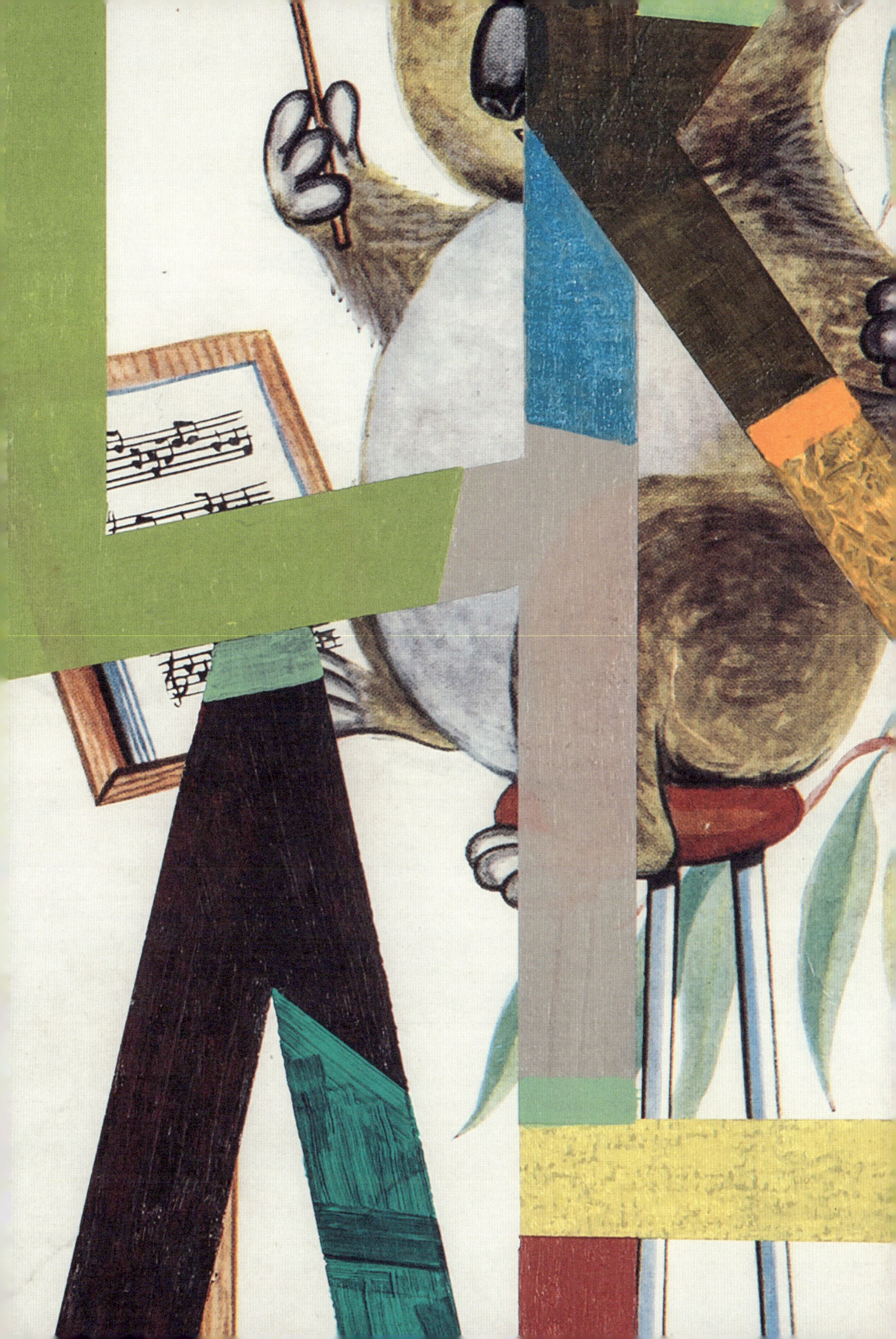

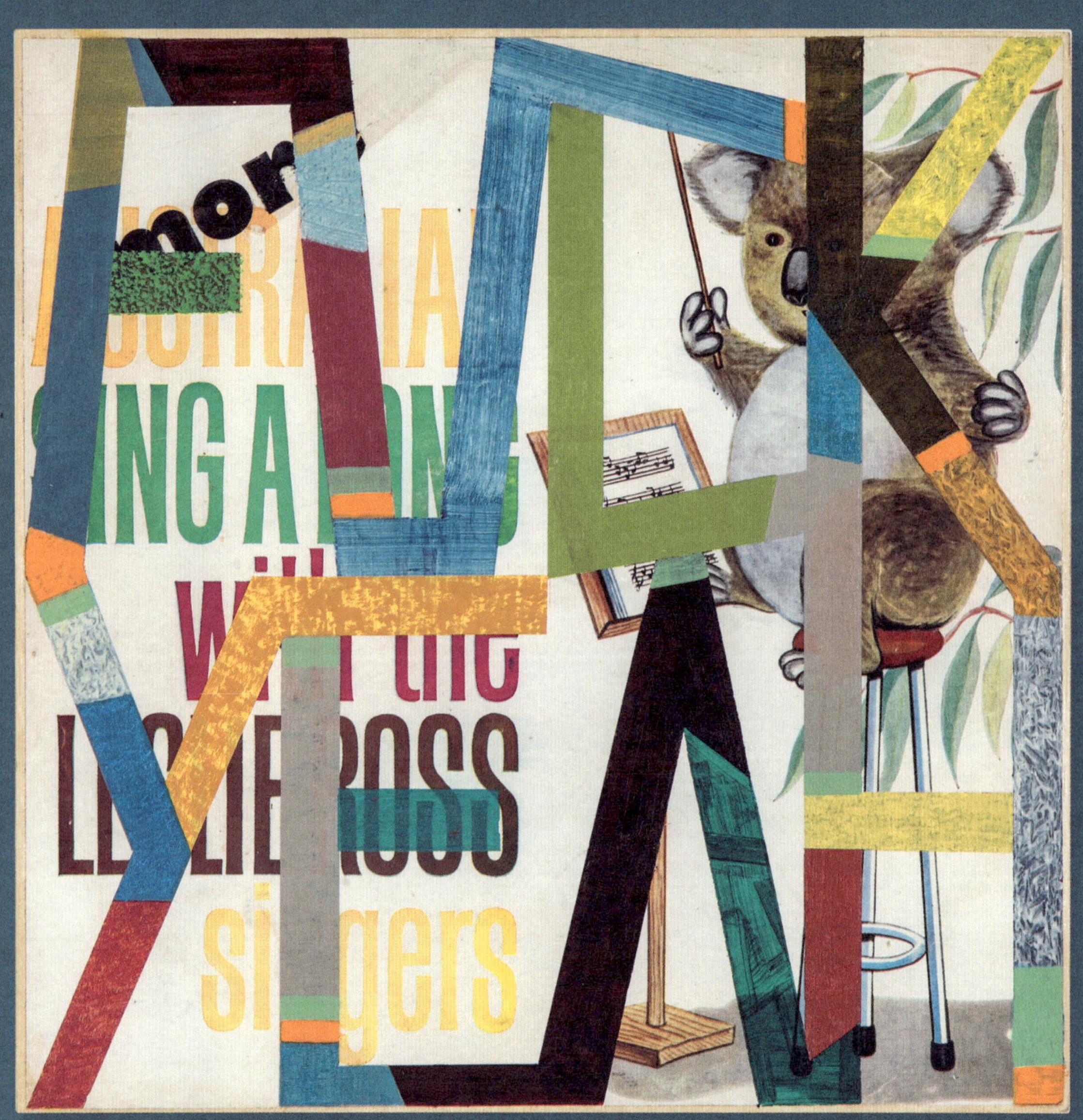
nor
AUSTRALIAN
SING ALONG
WITH THE
LESLIE ROSS
singers

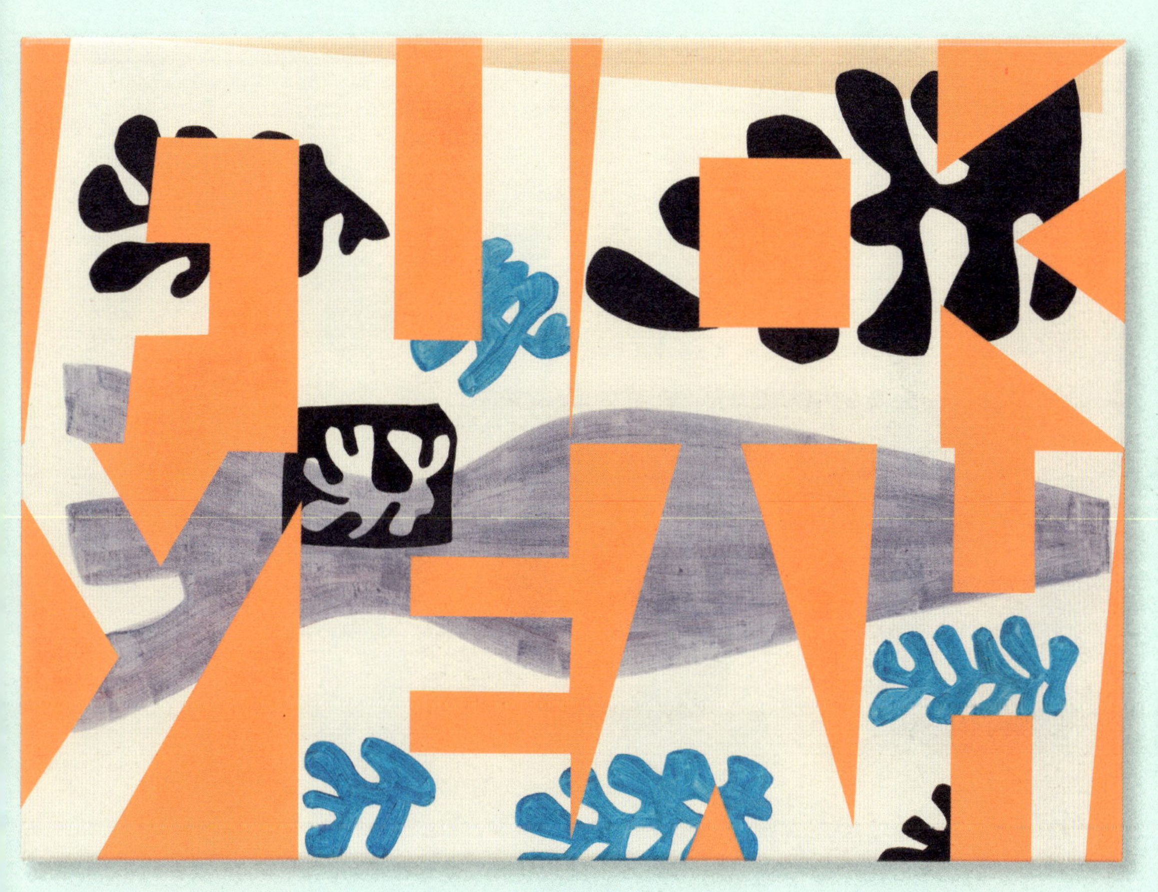

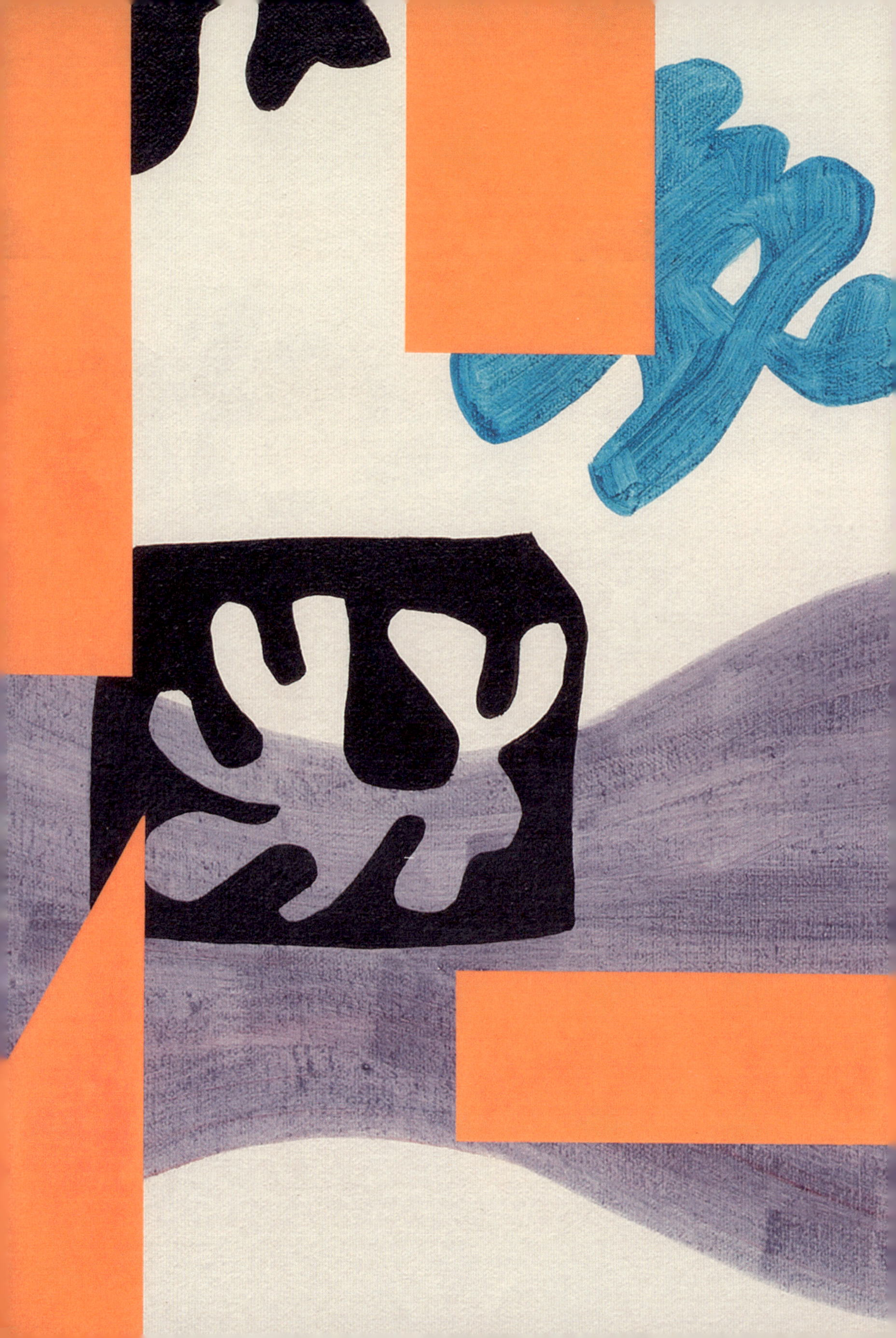

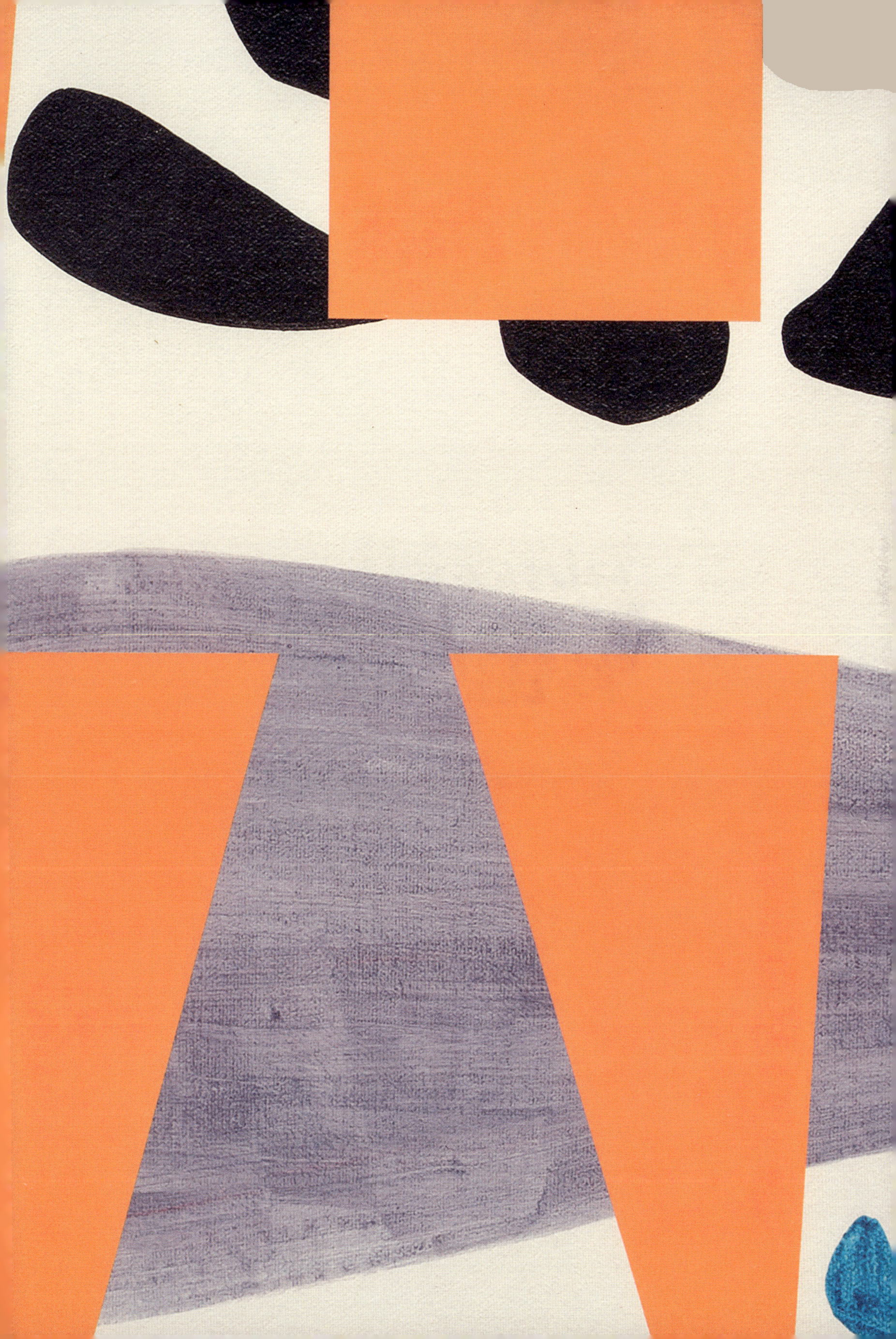

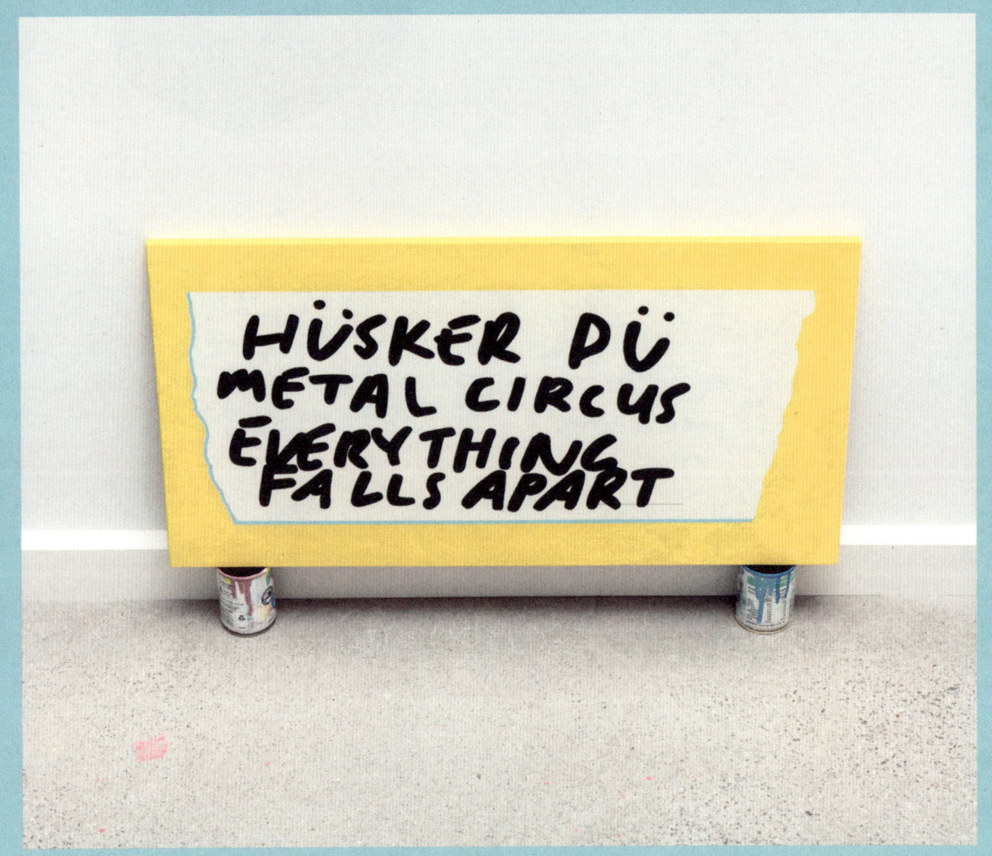

HÜSKER DÜ
METAL CIRCUS
EVERYTHING
FALLS APART

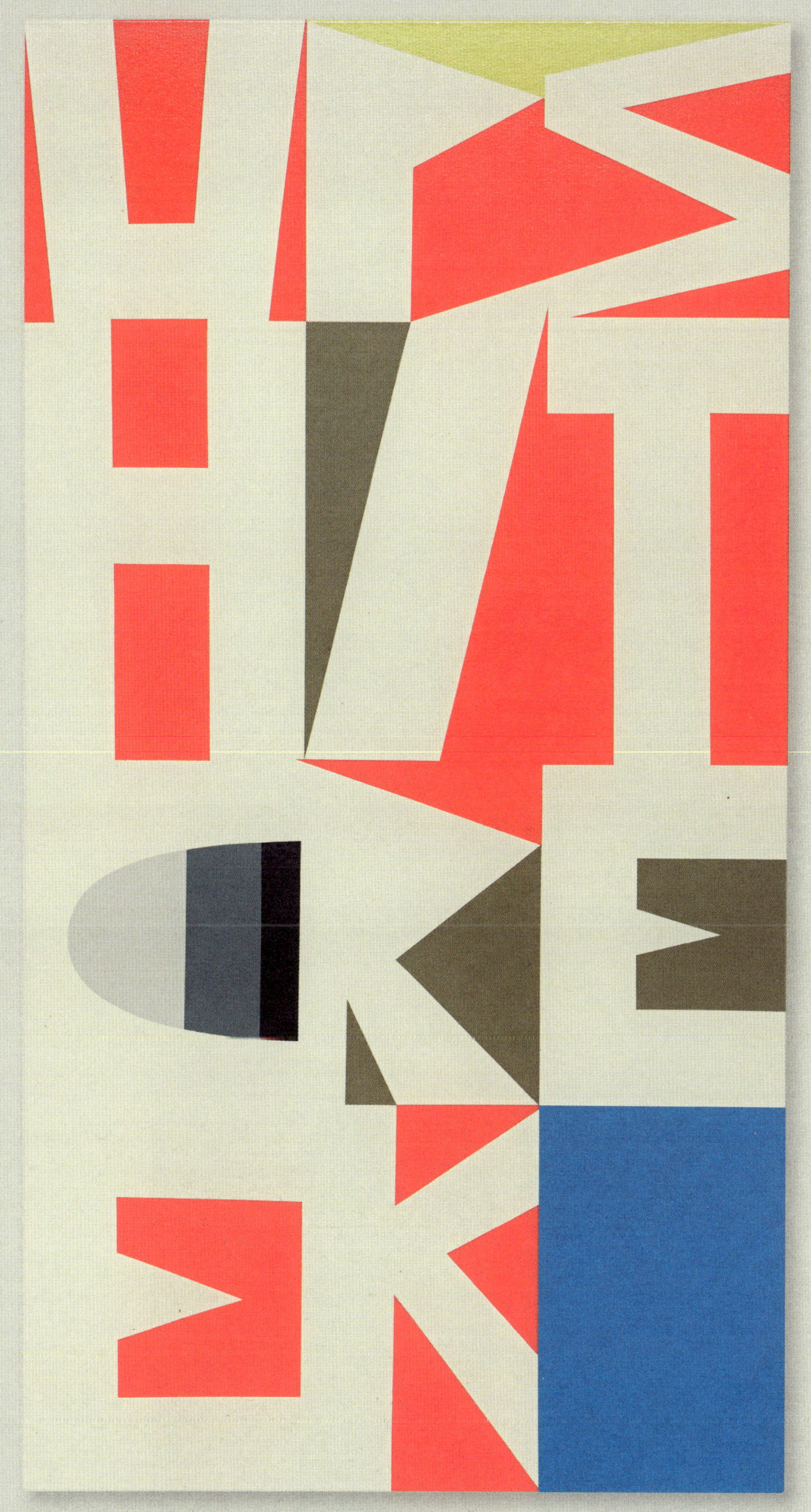

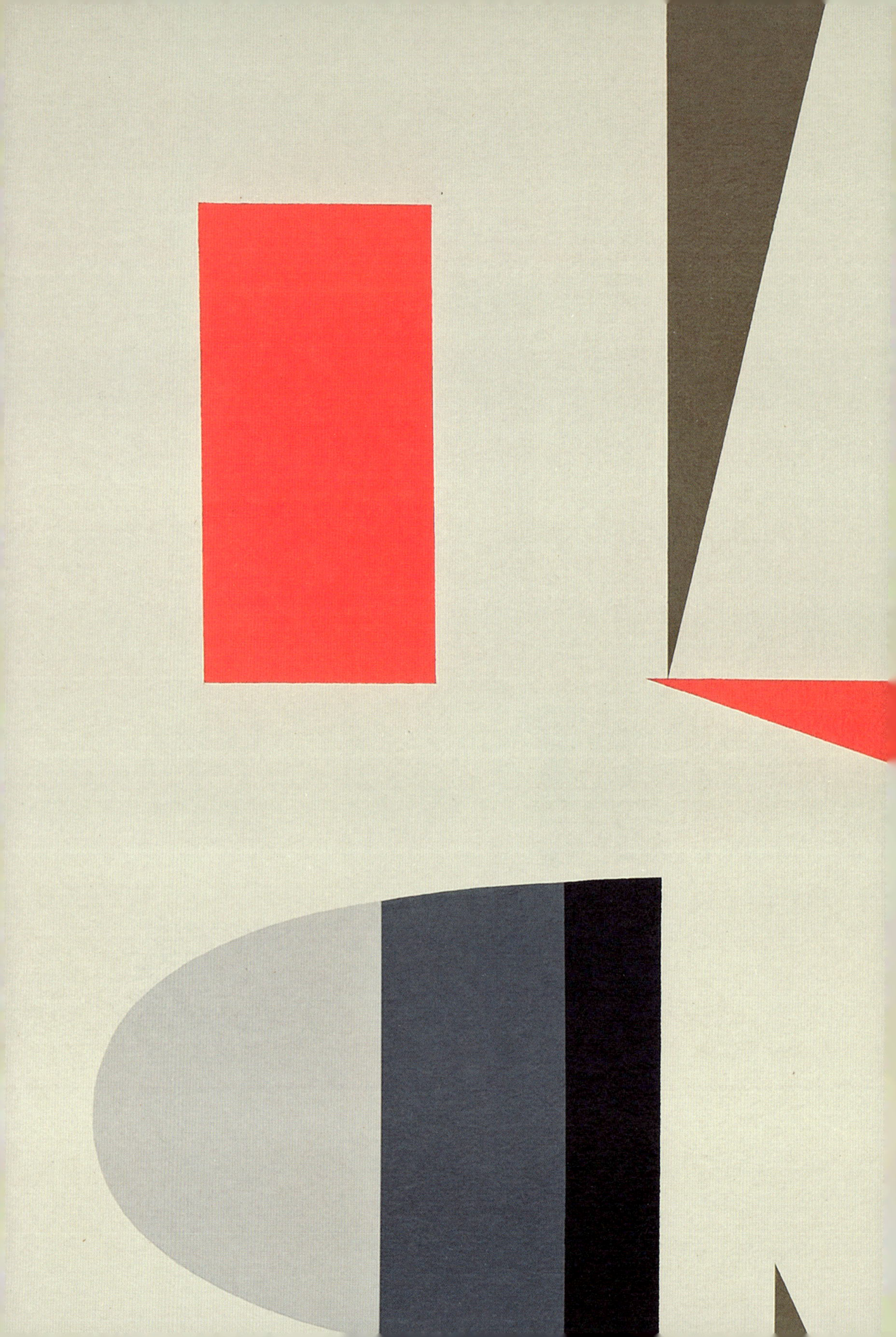

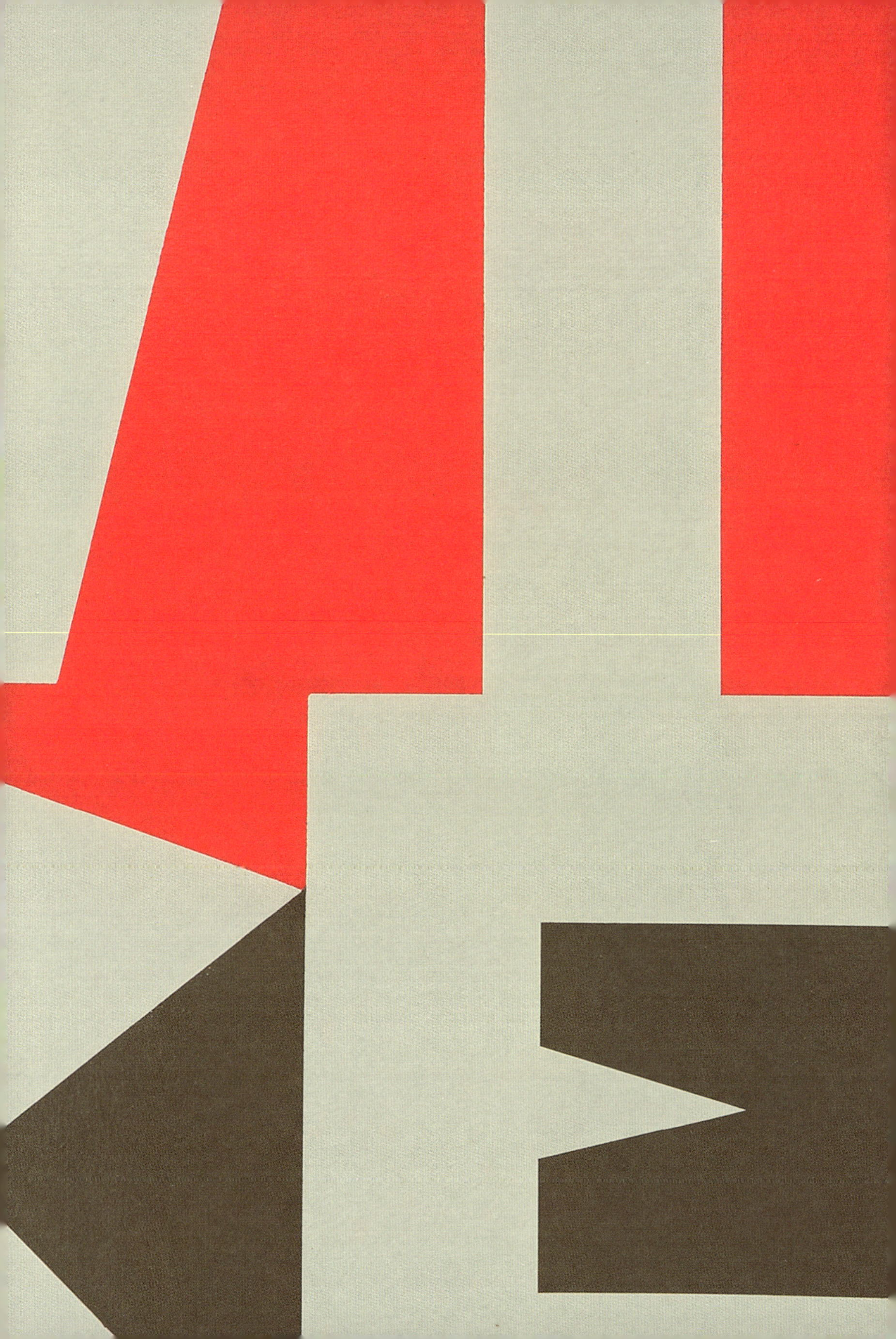

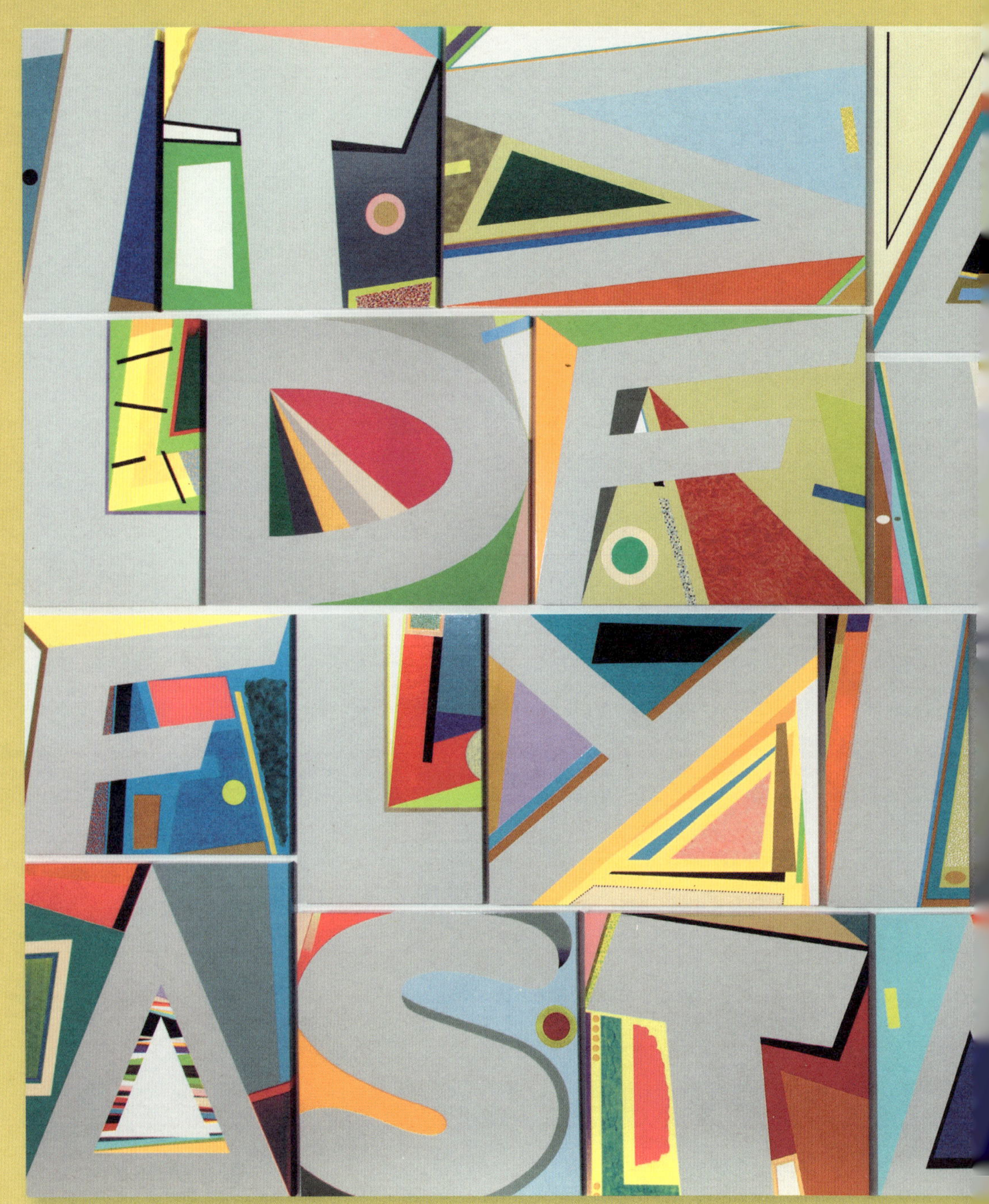

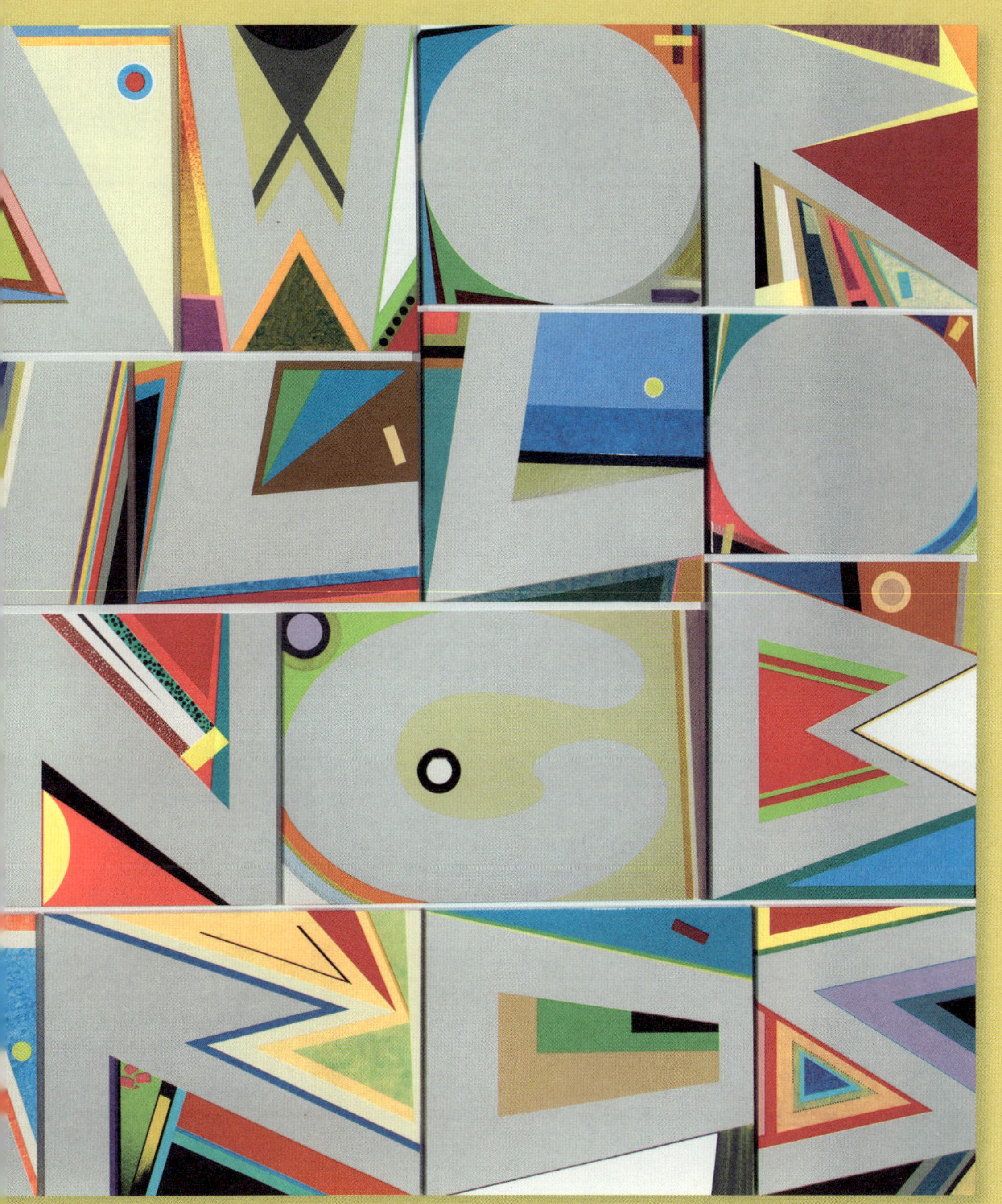

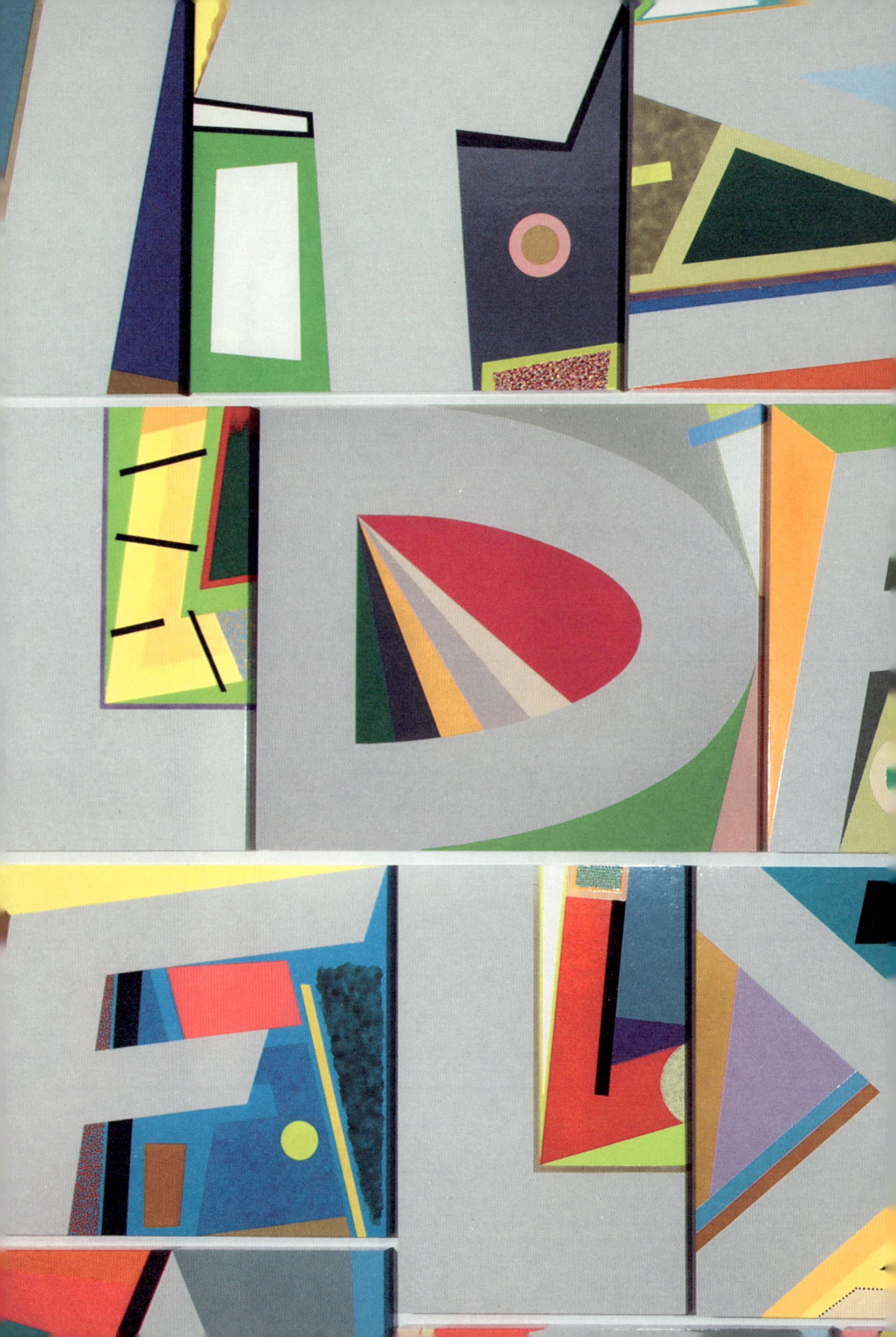

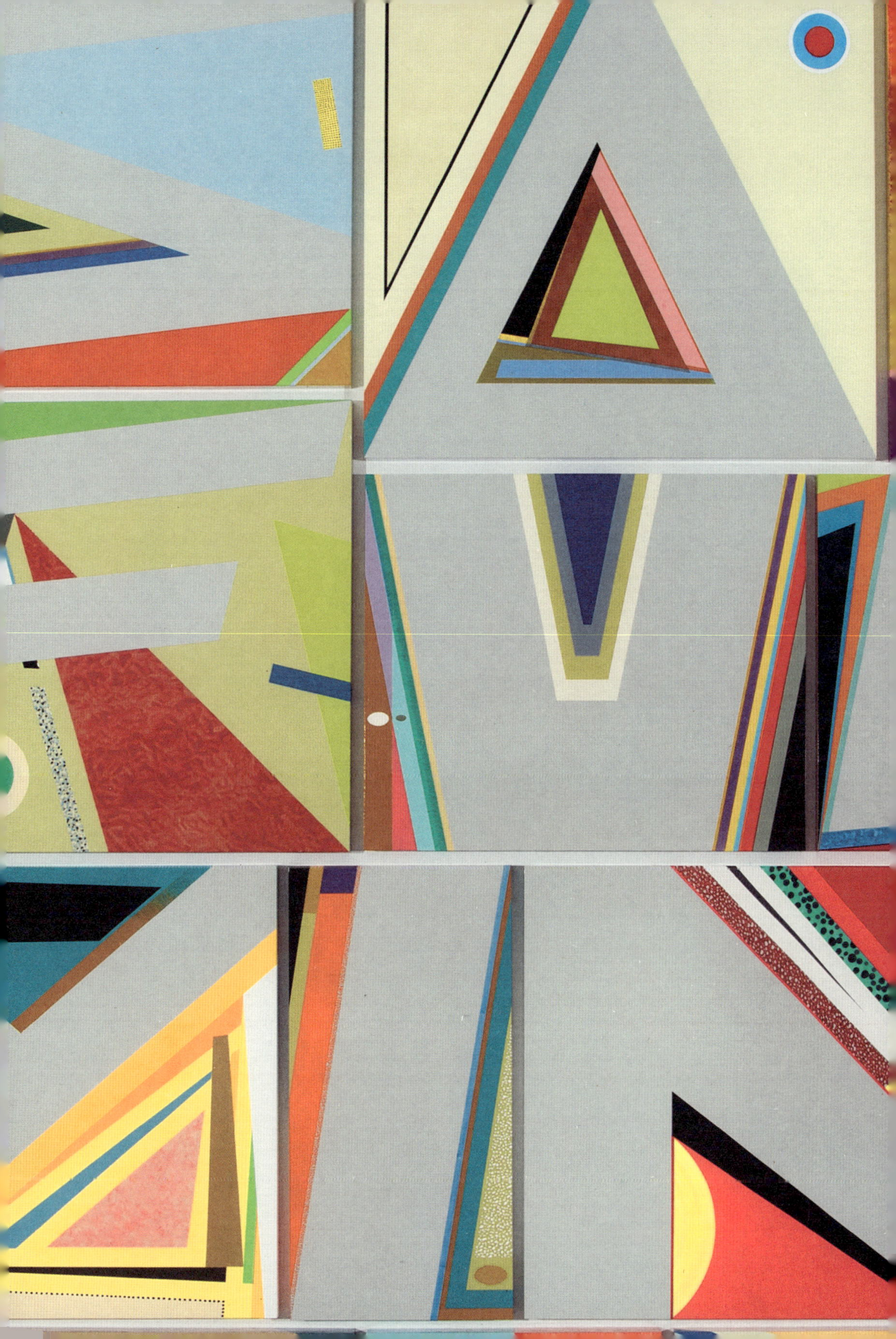

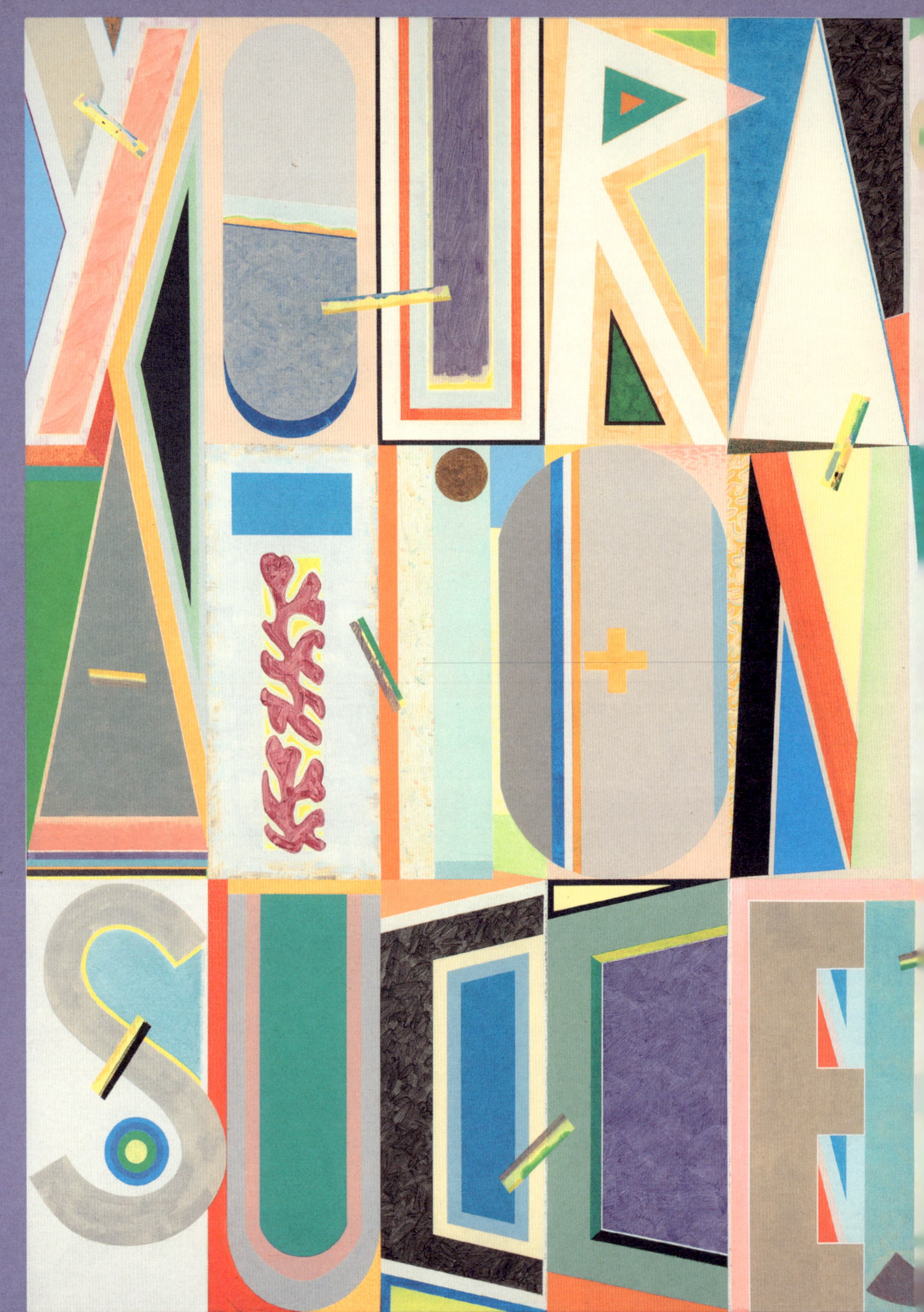

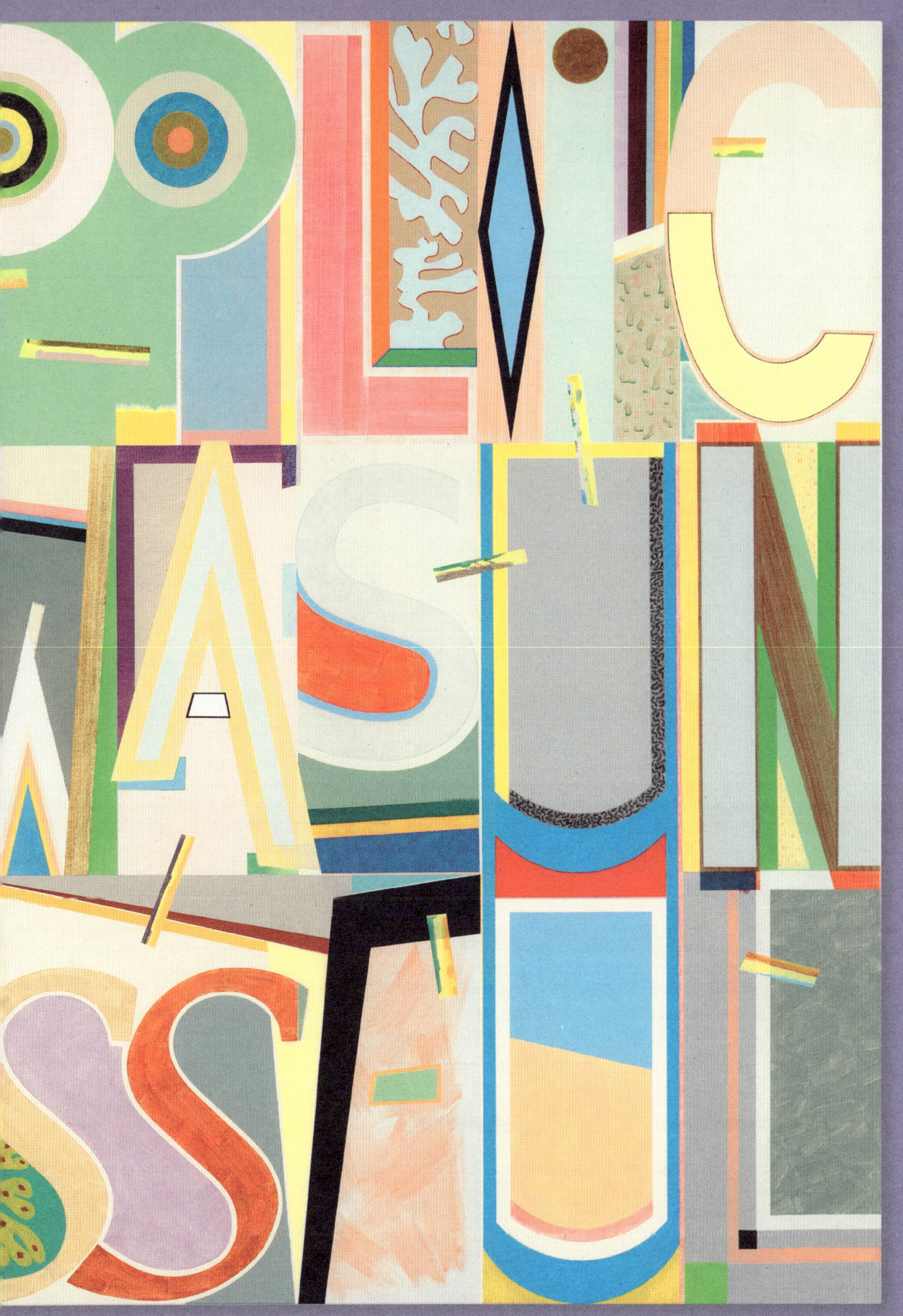

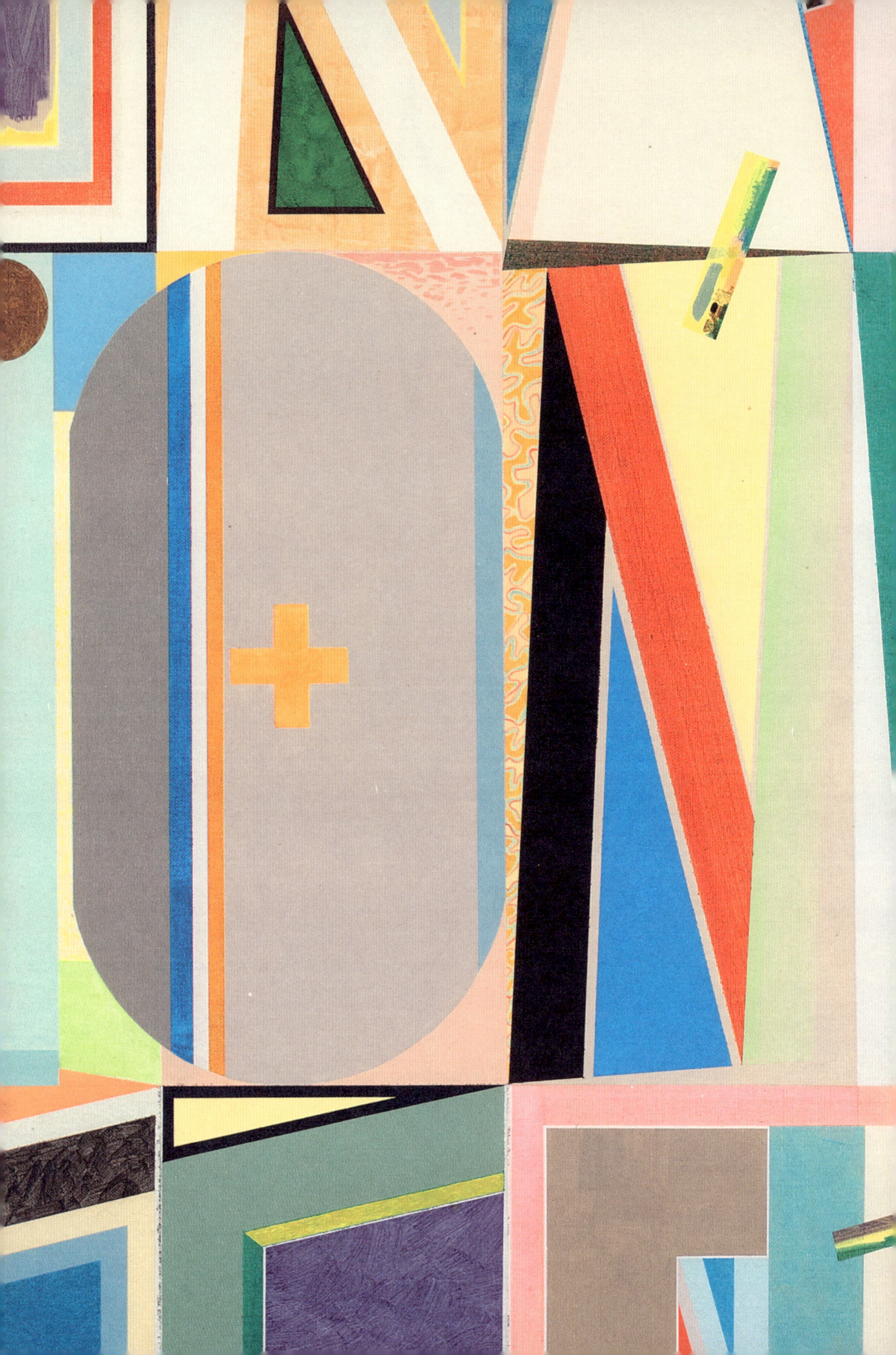

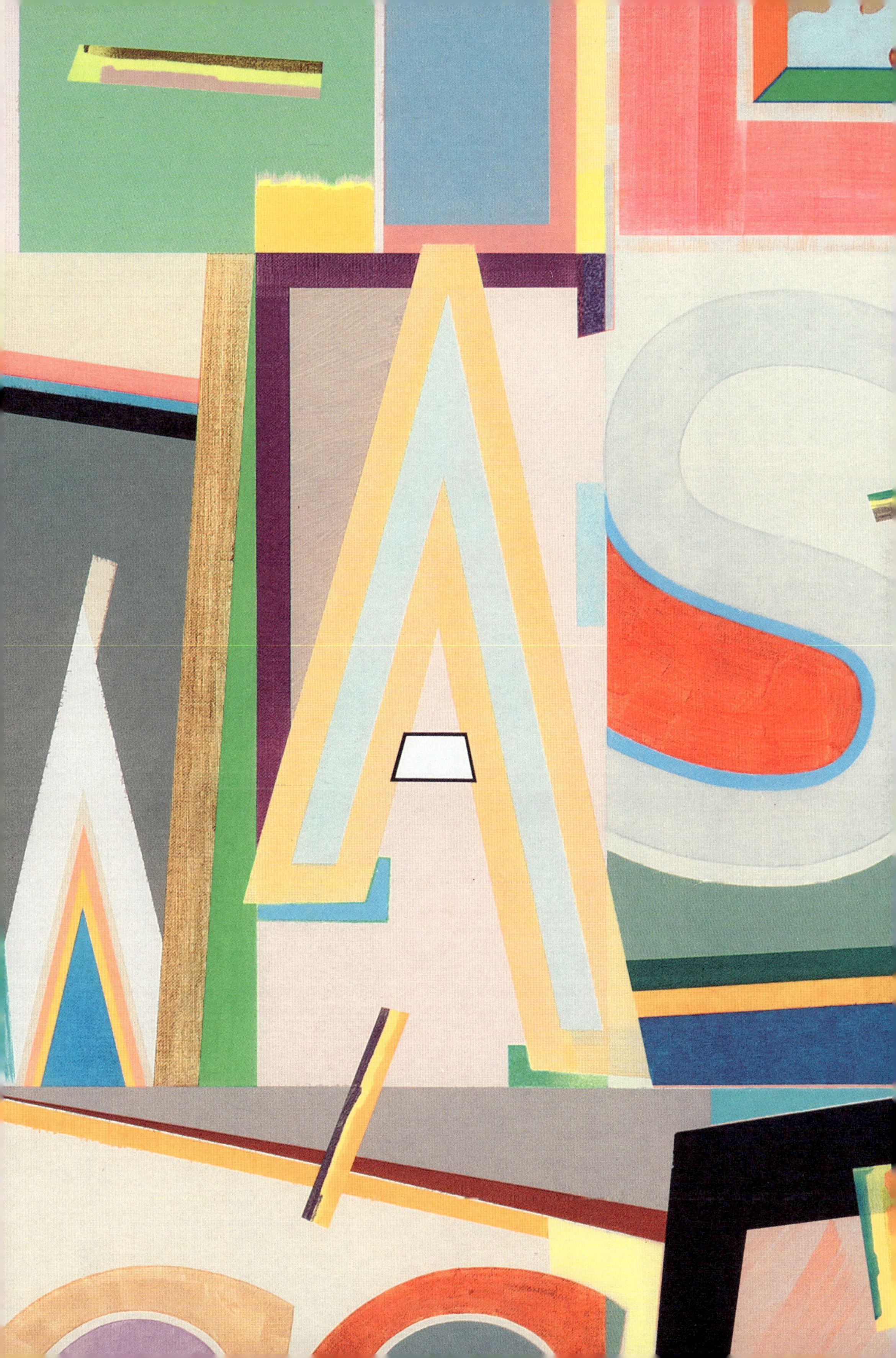

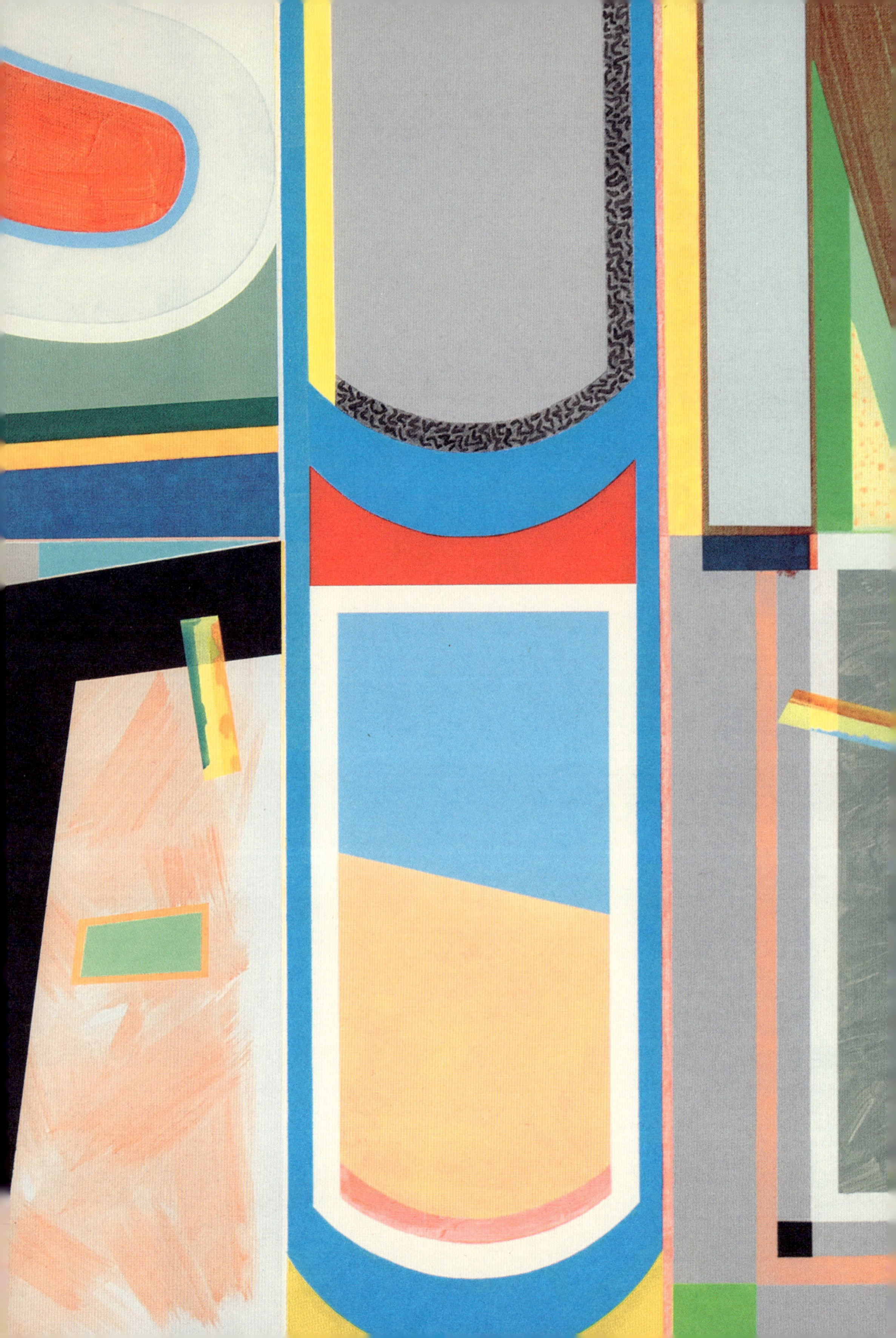

[Not illustrated]
Nadia Hernández
La Fuerza Es La Unión (Strength Comes From Union), 2015, paper on paper, perspex frame with blue mount and Tasmanian oak, 59.5 × 84.0 cm. Collection of Sasha Abram

P. 26
Nadia Hernández
Arco Iris De Colores Alegran La Lejandad (Rainbow of Colours Brighten The Distance), 2018, various textiles, grommets, thread, rope, 240.0 × 130.0 cm. Courtesy the artist and STATION

P. 18
Nadia Hernández
Bólidos Zizagueantes Atrapan La Soledad (Zigzagging Race Cars Trap Loneliness), 2018, various textiles, grommets, thread, rope, 145.0 × 88.0 cm. Courtesy the artist and STATION

P. 19
Nadia Hernández
Cae El Telón De La Noche, Un Ejército De Luces Entretejen La Ciudad (The Curtain Of The Night Falls, An Army Of Lights Interlace The City), 2018, wool, cotton, seeds, ribbon, clay, wood, metals, canvas, oil stick, felt, vintage pins, acrylic, grommets, thread, rope, 166.0 × 197.0 cm approx. Courtesy the artist and STATION

P. 41
Nadia Hernández
Consejos, cosas que son difíciles de robar, y 'Chinita' (Nuestra Señora de Chiquinquirá) / (Advice, things that are difficult to steal and 'Chinita' (Our Lady of Chiquinquirá)), 2019, oil on linen, 102.0 x 84.0 cm. Courtesy the artist and STATION

P. 69
Nadia Hernández
Una flor con amor, Diaphorina Citri, con trinos de libertad (A flower with love, Diaphorina Citri, with trills of freedom), 2019, oil on linen, 102.0 × 84.0 cm. Courtesy of the Walters family

P. 52
Nadia Hernández
Las matas en mi casa, golondrina viajera y cítricos (The plants in my house, travelling swallow and citrus), 2019, oil on linen, 102.0 × 84.0 cm. Courtesy of the Walters family

P. 50
Nadia Hernández
Por la vida: El Sol, como crece su amor, 2020, oil on linen, 61.0 × 66.0 cm. Courtesy the artist and STATION

P. 68
Nadia Hernández
Procesión, 2020, oil on linen, 61.0 × 66.0 cm. Courtesy the artist and STATION

P. 53
Nadia Hernández
El sol alumbra para todxs, el sol alumbra para todos, el, el sol, el sol, el sol el, alumbra para todxs, 2020, oil on linen, 102.0 × 84.0 cm. Courtesy the artist and STATION

P. 27
Nadia Hernández
Como el sol y toda su energía (Like the sun and all its energy), 2020, wool, cotton, linen, oil stick, acrylic, Flashe, ribbon, grommets, rope, dimensions variable. The State Art Collection, The Art Gallery of Western Australia

P. 56–57
Nadia Hernández
Entre todo, la gloria y la paz (Among everything, glory and peace), 2020, paper cut, 71.0 × 90.0 cm. Courtesy the artist and STATION

P. 32
Nadia Hernández
De mantequilla a temperatura ambiente (Of butter at room temperature), 2021, oil and acrylic on cotton, 215.0 × 100.0 cm. The State Art Collection, The Art Gallery of Western Australia

P. 70
Nadia Hernández
Varios ingredientes (Various ingredients),
2021, oil on linen, 61.0 × 46.0 cm. Courtesy
of Beci Orpin

P. 64–65
Nadia Hernández
*De pan duro, de oro puro (Of stale bread,
of pure gold)*, 2021, paper cut, 71.0 x
90.0 cm. Courtesy of Flack Studio

P. 60–61
Nadia Hernández
*De agua de azahar y mantequilla a
temperatura ambiente (Of orange
blossom water and butter at room
temperature)*, 2021, paper cut, 71.0 x
90.0 cm, Courtesy of Julie Zavaglia and
Michael Sloan. chosen by their daughter
Sofia

P. 47
Nadia Hernández
Flor, el collar de Ana y una tradición,
2022, oil on linen, 102.0 × 84.0 cm.
Courtesy of the Larholt family

P. 67
Nadia Hernández
*Pinta ... cacao, chocolate, chocolate el
perrito, el asado negro, los gusanos
colgando cuando caminamos, las matas y
la parrilla y la hamaca*, 2022, oil on linen,
198.0 × 137.0 cm. Private collection

P. 71
Nadia Hernández
*Pinta flores, pinta aguacates, pinta un
bodegón lleno de cosas que te gustan,
pinta algo que hayas cocinado con, tu
madre, pinta ...*, 2022, oil on linen, 198.0 ×
137.0 cm. Collection of River Capital

P. 46
Nadia Hernández
*Entre otras cosas ... es verdad que Rocky
se comió un ganso*, 2022, oil on linen,
198.0 × 137.0 cm. The State Art Collection,
The Art Gallery of Western Australia

P. 140–41
Jon Campbell
Firetruck, 1984, oil and enamel paint on
canvas, 91.0 × 122.0 cm. Courtesy of the
artist and Darren Knight Gallery, Sydney.
Photo: Janelle Low

P. 136–37
Jon Campbell
All the Boys, 1984, oil and enamel paint on
canvas, 106.0 × 206.0 cm. Courtesy of the
artist and Darren Knight Gallery, Sydney.
Photo: Janelle Low

P. 130
Jon Campbell
The Party, 1986, enamel and acrylic paint
on cotton duck, 209.5 × 243 cm (overall,
two parts). Courtesy of the artist and
Darren Knight Gallery, Sydney. Photo:
Janelle Low

P. 134–35
Jon Campbell
The Weight of Manhattan, 1991, acrylic
paint and collage on cotton duck, 183.0 ×
213.0 cm (overall, two parts). The State Art
Collection, The Art Gallery of Western
Australia. Photo: Simon Hewson

P. 131
Jon Campbell
Peace and Love, 1991, acrylic paint,
collage and pencil on cotton duck, 182.5 ×
60.5 cm. Courtesy of the artist and Darren
Knight Gallery, Sydney. Photo: Simon
Hewson

P. 105
Jon Campbell
Driving in '78, 2003, enamel paint and
enamel marker on paper, 59.4 × 42.0 cm.
Courtesy of the artist and Darren Knight
Gallery, Sydney. Photo: Janelle Low

P. 148
Jon Campbell
Metal Circus, everything falls apart, 2008,
enamel paint on plywood (on two paint
tins), 31.0 × 60.8 cm. Courtesy of the artist
and Darren Knight Gallery, Sydney. Photo:
Janelle Low

P. 108–09 (reverse)
Jon Campbell
it's gonna take a lotta love, 2008, bunting, cotton, handstitched reverse applique, 183.0 × 120.0 cm. Courtesy of the artist and Darren Knight Gallery, Sydney. Photo: Janelle Low

P. 110–11 (reverse)
Jon Campbell
Yeah / Mr. Football, 2009, screenprinted cotton, handstitching, 2/2, 200.0 × 120.0 cm. Courtesy of the artist and Darren Knight Gallery, Sydney. Photo: Janelle Low

P. 107
Jon Campbell
Let the Franklin flow, 2009, enamel and acrylic paint on MDF, 49.7 × 36.2 cm. Courtesy of the artist and Darren Knight Gallery, Sydney. Photo: Janelle Low

P. 115
Jon Campbell
Group Tutorial, 2013, acrylic and enamel paint on unstretched cotton duck, 98.0 × 51.0 cm. Courtesy of the artist and Darren Knight Gallery, Sydney. Photo: Janelle Low

P. 149
Jon Campbell
Up Shit Creek, 2014, enamel paint on canvas, 150.0 × 80.0 cm. Courtesy of the artist and Darren Knight Gallery, Sydney. Photo: Simon Hewson

P. 114
Jon Campbell
What are you fuckin lookin at, 2014, lithograph, 10/20, 76.0 × 56.0 cm. Courtesy of the artist and Darren Knight Gallery, Sydney. Photo: Tobias Titz

P. 145
Jon Campbell
Fuck Yeah (Matisse), 2015, enamel and acrylic paint on cotton duck, 41.0 × 56.0 cm. Courtesy of the artist and Darren Knight Gallery, Sydney. Photo: Simon Hewson

P. 144
Jon Campbell
Fuck Yeah (Australian sing along), 2018, acrylic paint on record cover on plywood, 30.0 × 30.0 cm. Courtesy of the artist and Darren Knight Gallery, Sydney. Photo: Tobias Titz

P. 119
Jon Campbell
Fuck Knuckle, 2019, acrylic paint on unstretched linen, 214.0 × 140.0 cm. Courtesy of the artist and Darren Knight Gallery, Sydney. Photo: Simon Hewson

P. 118
Jon Campbell
Undressing in Public Prohibited, 2019, acrylic paint, watercolour and pencil on unstretched cotton duck, 208.0 × 140.0 cm. Courtesy of the artist and Darren Knight Gallery, Sydney. Photo: Simon Hewson

P. 152–53
Jon Campbell
It's a world full of lying bastards, 2017/2020, enamel paint on plywood, 246.0 × 432.0 cm (28 parts). Courtesy of the artist and Darren Knight Gallery, Sydney. Photo: Tobias Titz

P. 156–57
Jon Campbell
Your application was unsuccessful, 2022, acrylic on linen, 167.5 × 243.5 cm. The State Art Collection, The Art Gallery of Western Australia. Photo: Simon Hewson

All measurements height before width
All works © the artists
Photography of Nadia Hernández's works courtesy of the artist and STATION Gallery

Nadia Hernández was born in Mérida, Venezuela, in 1987. She left Venezuela in 1997 to live in Arizona, and relocated to Brisbane, Australia, in 2004. Hernández studied design at Shillington College and completed a Bachelor of Fine Arts (with a major in Fashion) at Queensland University of Technology in 2008.

Hernández has had a number of solo exhibitions since 2013 at Mild Manners, Firstdraft, STATION and Verge Gallery in Sydney; and STATION and Blackartprojects in Melbourne. Her work has been in group shows including *Real Talk: Language & Text in Australian Art* (Brisbane City Council, Brisbane, 2017); *Speak Softly, Tread Heavily* (Peacock Gallery, Sydney, 2019); *In the fibre of her being* (Fairfield City Museum and Gallery, 2021); and *Like a Wheel That Turns: The 2022 Macfarlane Commissions* (Australian Centre for Contemporary Art, Melbourne, 2022).

Hernández was the winner of the The Churchie National Emerging Art Prize 2019, one of Australia's leading prizes for young artists, and the 2021 Grace Cossington Smith Art Award. She was a finalist in the Ravenswood Australian Women's Art Prize 2021 and the inaugural Ellen José Art Award 2022. Her work was included in the Wangaratta Contemporary Textile Award in 2019 and 2021, the John Fries Award 2019, the NSW Visual Arts Emerging Fellowship 2020, and Fisher's Ghost Art Award in 2017 and 2021. She was a recipient of the Bundanon Trust Artist in Residence Award in 2019.

In 2020, Hernández was commissioned to develop an immersive educational program and exhibition as Shepparton Art Museum's EduLAB artist. Other commissions include *Wonder* (lead artist of Sydney New Year's Eve, City of Sydney 2017); *Like The Air I Breathe (Como El Aire Que Respiro)* (Brisbane Canvas mural, Brisbane City Council, 2019); and *Fiesta Latina* (William Jolly Bridge Projection, Brisbane City Council, Brisbane, 2019).

Hernández's work is held in the collections of Artbank, the Art Gallery of Western Australia and the National Gallery of Victoria, as well as private Australian and international collections.

Hernández currently lives between Sydney, New South Wales, and Melbourne, Victoria.

Jon Campbell was born in Belfast, Northern Ireland, in 1961 and moved to Melbourne with his family in 1964. He received a Bachelor of Arts, Fine Arts, from the Royal Melbourne Institute of Technology in Melbourne in 1982, and completed a Graduate Diploma of Painting at the Victorian College of the Arts in Melbourne, in 1985.

Since he began exhibiting in the mid-1980s, Campbell has held regular solo exhibitions at Darren Knight Gallery, Sydney, and has been in many group shows including *Art, Music, Rock, Pop, Techno* (Museum of Contemporary Art, Sydney, 2001); *De Overkant / Downunder*, Den Hague Sculptuur, The Netherlands, 2007); *Melbourne Now* (National Gallery of Victoria, Melbourne, 2013–14); and *Painting. More Painting* (Australian Centre for Contemporary Art, Melbourne, 2016); *Just not Australian* (Artspace, Sydney and national tour, 2019). He presented the major installation, *Stacks On*, at the Museum of Contemporary Art Australia, Sydney in 2017–18.

In 2012, Campbell won the Basil Sellers Art Prize at the Ian Potter Museum of Art, Melbourne and in 2014 he was awarded the Australia Council, Greene Street residency in New York.

Campbell's publications include the monograph *Jon Campbell* (Lisa Radford and Jarrod Rawlins eds., Uplands Publishing, 2010); the artist books *Setlist* (The Narrows, 2009), *Lettering* (The Narrows, 2015) and *It's a World Full of Lying Bastards* (produced with Aaron Beehre, Ilam Press, University of Canterbury, 2019); and *No Planet B* (produced with Bronwyn Johnson, design by Aaron Beehre, 2021).

In 2019, Campbell designed the cover art for the 40th anniversary re-release of the first Sunnyboys album. In 2021 he completed the major work *Backyard*, a Western Roads public art commission organised by the McClelland Sculpture Park and Gallery. Campbell has also made collaborative paintings with artists Stephen Bush, Nell, Darcey Bella Arnold and Tully Moore.

In addition to performing solo, Campbell's bands include King Jerklews (1984–86), Monaros (1987), Colonial V Knees (1988–90), Gloss Enamel (1997–), ADAWO (2000), Olympic Doughnuts (2008–) and Pamela (2012–).

Campbell's work is held in many public collections including Auckland Art Gallery Toi o Tāmaki; National Gallery of Australia, Canberra; National Gallery of Victoria, Melbourne; Art Gallery of South Australia, Adelaide; Museum of Contemporary Art Australia, Sydney; National Portrait Gallery, Canberra; Monash University Museum of Art, Melbourne; Artbank, Australia; and the Australian Football League, Melbourne.

Campbell lives and works in Melbourne, Victoria.

Acknowledgements

I am grateful to Nadia Hernández and Jon Campbell for the incredibly vibrant spirit they have brought to all elements of this project. Their creative-minded professionalism has made it such a delight and a very meaningful collaborative exercise.

Huge thanks to Samantha Barrow, Laura Couttie, and Philippa Griffin from STATION Gallery in Melbourne and Darren Knight and Suzie Melhop from Darren Knight Gallery in Sydney for assisting with the logistics of the project.

Thanks to our publication writers, Lisa Radford and Diego Ramírez, for bringing new and unexpected interpretations to bear on the output of both artists. We are also grateful to the Art Gallery of Western Australia Foundation for supporting the book's production.

I would like to thank everyone in the team at AGWA who contributed to the project: Colin Walker (Director) Melanie Morgan (Registration); Todd Harrison (Exhibition Graphic Design); Dani Lye (Exhibition Design); Louella Hayes (Foundation); Rebecca Anderson and Sepsi Munalula (Events); Tanya Sticca, Sharyn Beor and Penny Tassone (Marketing); David Graves, Kate Woollet and Michael Houston (Conservation); Natalie Hewlett (Exhibitions Management), Melanie Tozawa (Records Assistant) and, of course, the terrific AGWA installation crew.

Thanks also to graphic designer Stuart Geddes for his clear vision and patient commitment to bringing the publication to fruition; and editor Kay Campbell for her sharp eye and respectful treatment of each writer's voice.

Finally, I'd like to thank the very generous lenders to this exhibition: Nadia Hernández, Jon Campbell, Sasha Abram, Flack Studio, the Larholt family, Beci Orpin, River Capital, the Walters family, Julia Zavaglia, Michael Stone (and their daughter Sofia) and other private collectors.

Robert Cook
Curator

Speech Patterns: Nadia Hernández and Jon Campbell

Published and distributed by
Mousse Publishing
Contrappunto s.r.l.
Via Pier Candido Decembrio 28,
20137, Milan–Italy

Available through:

Mousse Publishing, Milan
moussemagazine.it

DAP | Distributed Art Publishers, New York
artbook.com

Les presses du réel, Dijon
lespressesdureel.com

Antenne Books, London
antennebooks.com

First edition: 2022
Printed in Australia by Gunn & Taylor Printers
AGWA Director: Colin Walker
Curator: Robert Cook
Editor: Kay Campbell, The Comma Institute
Graphic Designer: Stuart Geddes

ISBN   978-0-6481062-6-5 (AGWA)
         978-88-6749-555-9 (Mousse Publishing)

€ 27 / $ 30 / AUD 45

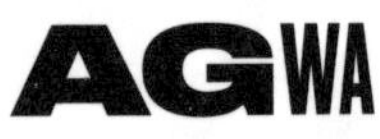

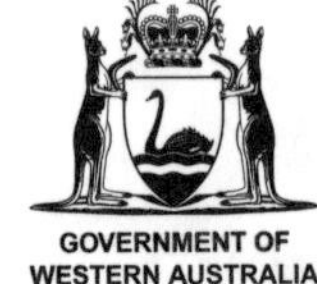

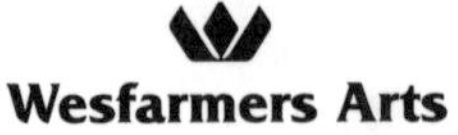